# ACTION AND REACTION IN WORLD POLITICS

*International Systems in Perspective*

# ACTION AND REACTION
## IN world politics

*International Systems in Perspective*

**RICHARD N. ROSECRANCE**   *University of California (Los Angeles)*

GREENWOOD PRESS, PUBLISHERS
WESTPORT, CONNECTICUT

**Library of Congress Cataloging in Publication Data**

Rosecrance, Richard N
    Action and reaction in world politics.

    Reprint of the ed. published by Little, Brown, Boston.
    Includes index.
    1.  International relations--History.  2.  World
politics.  3.  Concert of Europe.  I.  Title.
[JX1315.R6  1977]        327'.09        77-2329
ISBN 0-8371-9548-9

Copyright assigned to Richard N. Rosecrance, 1963

Originally published in 1963 by Little, Brown and Company,
Boston

Reprinted with the permission of Professor Richard Rosecrance.

Reprinted in 1977 by Greenwood Press,
a division of Congressional Information Service, Inc.
51 Riverside Avenue, Westport, Connecticut 06880

Library of Congress catalog card number 77-2329
ISBN 0-8371-9548-9

Printed in the United States of America

10  9  8  7  6  5  4  3  2

# FOREWORD

THERE HAS recently been a considerable increase of interest in the
theory of international relations. Works by Raymond Aron, Stanley
Hoffmann and others testify to this trend. In the past, Machiavelli,
Bodin and Hobbes offered theories of the relations among nations,
and a series of writers on the problem of reason of state, as Friedrich
Meinecke has shown, made important contributions as well. It is
true, nevertheless, that further theorizing is greatly needed to cover
not only the rather novel and complex relations between states of
such divergent nature as the United States and the U.S.S.R., but also
to extend the generalizations previously made to include the much
broader fields opened by anthropological and historical research on
earlier forms of government. A re-evaluation is necessary also because of the new perspective afforded by an increasingly dense network of international agencies of fairly permanent status, served by
a growing number of international civil servants.

Such theorizing can be approached in a variety of ways, corresponding to the alternative approaches in political theory generally.
For the theory of international relations surely has been and must
continue to be developed within the broader framework of such general theory, even if a measure of "autonomy" is conceded to this subdivision of the discipline of political science. As Aron has written:

An all-inclusive (*totale*) science of philosophy of politics would include
international relations as one of its chapters. But such a chapter would
retain its distinctness (*originalité*) since it would treat the relations between political units each of which claims the right to secure justice for
itself and to be the sole master (*maîtresse*) of the decision as to whether to
fight or not.

v

There can be no question that such readiness to have recourse to physical force distinguishes states in their behavior towards each other. Whether it is a distinctive trait when compared to such related forms as economic or psychic coercion is itself a crucial question of general political theory. Thus, unless the theory of international relations is developed within the general framework of political theory, it is apt either to rediscover and restate general political theory in a one-sided way, or to lack depth and significance. In a period when the close interaction of domestic and foreign affairs is universally acknowledged, it is surprising that such parochialisms should have made their appearance. As I wrote quite a few years ago, in discussing the relation of foreign and domestic affairs:

> . . . diplomatic history is written *as if* foreign affairs were carried on in a vacuum, following their own laws and so clearly apart from the rest of national policy as to be capable of altogether separate treatment. . . . In democratic lands the formation of national policy is a continuous process, a free-for-all in which a multitude of interests and convictions get scrambled into an unrecognizable hodgepodge of partly contradictory policies.

It would be regrettable if international relations were to develop comparably defective theory. Now more than ever the task before us would seem to be to establish the theoretical grounds for understanding the interaction of foreign and domestic policies, and to extend general theory into this field.

Professor Rosecrance, in the present work, has not set himself the task of such a projection in general theoretical terms, but the major thesis of the book is the partial dependence of international relations upon domestic politics. He explicitly undertakes to provide an empirical basis for several "models" of international relations through a typological analysis of successive configurations of the European and world state systems as they have existed from the eighteenth to the twentieth century. Such an effort at constructing what Max Weber would have called "ideal types" is both useful and rewarding, and provides an empirical matrix of other constellations now existing or in process of formation. It involves developing "systems" of international relations on an empirical basis. Such an endeavor is quite different from the abstract method of system construction employed a few years ago by Morton A. Kaplan. Kaplan tried to analyze international relations starting from "a set of primitive terms, definitions, and axioms." Rosecrance starts instead from a set of historical givens: the state of diplomatic and domestic affairs prevailing in Europe at particular historical constellations.

Professor Rosecrance would be the first to insist that typological or morphological analysis is only one of three major forms of theorizing about the relation between "independent" yet communally related political entities. Genetic theory asks how such systems come into being and pass away, while operational theory inquires into the regularities they exhibit in concrete functioning. There are undoubtedly problems in the application of systems analysis to social phenomena. Political systems are open rather than closed, dynamic rather than static. Then there is the existential problem. Is a system manifest in institutions and processes, or is it merely in the mind of the analyst? A foreword is hardly the place to develop the issues that confront systems theory today; they constitute significant problems in scientific methodology. But the point is raised to suggest that for Rosecrance systems are real; they *exist* in the world of politics. The mechanistic approach which he uses is justified in the international field where the interaction of political units may be described in terms of balance, equilibrium or pendulum motion.

Finally, a word might be added concerning the theorizing about what needs doing, and more especially therefore about the activities involved in building a "world order under law." This enterprise, if successful, would provide a universal political order, and presumably would proceed according to propositions concerning the founding of a political order. The process is little understood as yet, although the emergence of numerous new states in recent years provides an unusual opportunity for generalizing analysis. His work is a realistic one, displaying the elements of international systems that a true world polity would have to overcome or transcend as well as preserve, to use a famous Hegelian formula. The individual systems he analyzes exhibit distinct features, but they are treated in a common framework of analysis, and as his insightful work progresses, a higher systemization is realized. Historians will note structural aspects of international relations that are overlooked in traditional diplomatic treatments, and political theorists and students of international relations will be especially grateful for the sense of unity that emerges from this overview of a vast and complex reality.

CARL J. FRIEDRICH
*Harvard University*

# PREFACE

IN TERMS of both methods and conclusions this book strikes a course different from that followed in international inquiry. The author avows his belief that historical tools have been too much neglected in the formulation of theoretical approaches to the study of international relations. Contemporary history, to be sure, has found a place in some international politics texts, but that history has usually suffered from narrowness of viewpoint and lack of long-range perspective. The historical diplomacy of the past two centuries, on the other hand, has nowhere formed the basis of a theoretical survey of international relations. In part this omission must be attributed to the belief in present "uniqueness" and the failure of history to repeat itself; in part it must be laid to sheer distrust of historical methods. Political scientists have been wont to claim a novel method, both distinct from and superior to that of historical scholarship. Whether this is or is not a valid claim is not relevant here, but it may at least be said that it does a disservice to international inquiry to blur the distinction between history as a catalogue of *conclusions* and history as a catalogue of *data*. The most fastidious methodologist may disdain the former without abjuring the latter. In the writer's view history is still the greatest source of data for all the social sciences; yet it has never been more completely neglected than at present. In contrast, the study that follows relies very largely upon the standard works of political and diplomatic history as primary sources of international study.

The author also finds himself at odds with prevailing views of the respective roles of domestic and international determinants of international policy. The past concentration upon "balance of power" or "power" theories has caused a prevalent emphasis upon external determinants of international politics. Partly as a result, the nineteenth century has been regarded as a period of international orientation, domestic concerns being of little import. In fact, as the following pages seek to show, the converse is more nearly true; domestic factors largely determined the course of European relations through the entire century. If the impact of domestic factors has been somewhat neglected, the present study strives to remedy the defect: if any single thesis emerges from the following pages it is that international constellations and patterns of conflict are very often determined as the inadvertent by-product of domestic change.

It is a pleasure to record here the many intellectual debts owed by the author to friends and colleagues. The work was read wholly or in part by Professors Raymond Aron, Robert Bowie, David Cattell, Daniel Cheever, Karl Deutsch, W. Y. Elliott, Carl Friedrich, Ernst Haas, Stanley Hoffmann, Michael Lindsay, Dwaine Marvick, Robert Neumann, Charles Nixon, and Vincent Ostrom. Their criticisms, some of which were expressed at a seminar held at the Center for International Affairs, Harvard University, have been an important influence shaping the final work. Mr. Robert Lamoureux and Miss Ahuva Ben-Amram, research assistants at the University of California (Los Angeles), did significant preliminary investigations of several of the international systems included. The University of California contributed importantly to early completion of the study through various research grants and through a sabbatical grant which permitted the author to spend several months at Harvard in the closing stages of writing.

I am indebted to Harrison B. Goodman for his handsome execution of the diagrams and maps.

R.N.R.

*Santa Monica, California*

# CONTENTS

# ACTION AND REACTION IN WORLD POLITICS

*International Systems in Perspective*

# SYSTEMATIC EMPIRICAL ANALYSIS
# IN INTERNATIONAL RELATIONS

"Political scientists have a tendency to simplify in two respects, both of which are dangerous. The first simplification is that of the historical school, which would end by describing the vicissitudes of international relations without explaining them; while the second is that of the 'realist' school, which tends to hypostatize the States and their so-called national interests, to attribute to those interests a sort of patency or permanence, and to regard events as reflecting nothing but the calculation of power and the compromise necessary to achieve a balance."

—RAYMOND ARON[1]

I This book grew out of the conviction, underscored by Professor Aron in the epigraph to this chapter, that current approaches to the theoretical investigation of international relations are insufficient. This viewpoint may be best explained by a brief excursion into the broad trends of international inquiry during the past generation. Roughly speaking, there have been two fundamental approaches to the problems of international politics.[2] On the one hand

---

[1] Raymond Aron, "Conflict and War from the Viewpoint of Historical Sociology," in Stanley H. Hoffmann (ed.), *Contemporary Theory in International Relations* (Englewood Cliffs, N.J., 1960), p. 200.

[2] The works of Professors Ernst Haas, Karl Deutsch, and Robert North do not fall easily into this conspectus. See Ernst Haas, *The Uniting of Europe* (Stanford, 1959), Karl Deutsch, Sidney A. Burrell, Robert A. Kann, Maurice Lee, Jr., Martin Lichterman, Raymond E. Lindgren, Francis L. Loewenheim, and Richard W. Van Wagenen, *Political Community and the North Atlantic Area* (Princeton, 1957),

we have the approach of "general explanatory concepts": its characteristic feature is emphasis on a single explanatory concept to unite the field of international relations. At least since World War II, thanks largely to Professor Hans Morgenthau, "power" has been the most widely accepted key to an understanding of world politics, but there have been other such notions, more or less influenced by the "realist" school. "Equilibrium" and "capabilities" have also been used as central explanatory concepts in international politics. While they have not conjured up the same psychological connotations as "power," they have been equally general in their analytical ambitions. The "realists" tell us that international politics evinces a quest for power; [3] the equilibrists, that there is a universal search for and approximation to equilibrium of the social, economic, institutional, and political sort; [4] capability analysts emphasize that national actors seek to increase "capabilities" in certain ways in different situations.[5]

On the other hand there is an approach to international phenomena that may be described as "detailed empirical analysis" of individual foreign-policy decisions or diplomatic events. This is the approach of "decision-making" or of contemporary diplomatic history.[6] It focuses upon the individual case or event and explains in full detail the processes by which a given decision was made or a given diplomatic result achieved. We have had a decision-making analysis of the factors shaping the Japanese peace settlement.[7] Historians have provided us with an exhaustive analysis of the begin-

---

and Robert C. North and associates, *Report to the Ford Foundation from the Studies in International Conflict and Integration,* Stanford University, for the period September 1, 1960, to August 31, 1961.

[3] See H. J. Morgenthau, *Politics among Nations* (New York, 1960).

[4] See G. Liska, *International Equilibrium* (Cambridge, Mass., 1957).

[5] See Morton Kaplan, *System and Process in International Politics* (New York, 1957).

[6] See Richard C. Snyder, H. W. Bruck, and Burton Sapin, *Decision-Making as an Approach to the Study of International Politics* (Princeton, 1954) and Bernard C. Cohen, *The Political Process and Foreign Policy: The Making of the Japanese Peace Settlement* (Princeton, 1957). I do not wish to imply that Professor Snyder's categories are narrowly confined or bound in space or time; they are actually universalistic. But their application requires such a detailed investigation of a single case of foreign policy-making that it is the more difficult to adduce general strands or lessons for the international system as a whole.

[7] See Cohen, *op. cit.*

ning of World War I. These detailed empirical techniques have been applied and doubtless will be applied to hosts of similar situations and problems.

Both of these approaches have made important contributions to our understanding of international politics. The approach of "general explanatory concepts" has permitted a substantial unification of the field. Foreign policies of the most seemingly diverse nations could be explained in terms of a common category of power- or equilibrium-seeking. Policies of different states at different historical periods could be explained in similar terms. In short, the approach of general explanatory concepts emphasized what was common in the foreign policies of states, and therefore made a field or discipline of international politics possible. At the same time it presented a set of *desiderata* for diplomatic action. A nation's foreign policy could be criticized if it allowed substantial disequilibrium to exist in world politics; a nation could be criticized for pursuing or attempting to pursue moral factors at the expense of factors of material interest.

The contribution of "detailed empirical analysis" was quite different. The more detailed the mode of investigation, the more singular were the results derived. The decision-making approach and the dispatch-by-dispatch analysis of individual diplomatic happenings conferred particularity upon international events. If general explanatory concepts illuminated what was common in international politics, detailed empirical analysis demonstrated what was unique. And the more elaborate the case study, the less likely was it that general principles of diplomatic action could be adduced.

Thus the strengths of the two approaches were dissimilar. One explained the common features in all international events; the other explained the uniqueness of a given international event. And the strengths of these two approaches led directly to their weaknesses. For in making its own peculiar contribution each theoretical approach had to give up something. The approach of general explanatory concepts obtained its generality partly through definitional means. That is, it ensured comprehensiveness by employing concepts with broad or general reference. International affairs could be depicted as manifesting "multiple equilibrium" or a "struggle for power" precisely because "equilibrium" and "power" were protean and generic terms. If "equilibrium" may be "general and partial; unique and multiple; stable, neutral and unstable; long-term and short-term; perfect and imperfect"[8] even the League experiment could be held to manifest equilibrial tendencies, and it becomes difficult *prima facie* to conceive even hypothetically of conditions that would not manifest equilibrium of some sort. If "power is always the immediate aim"[9] of international politics (if to do something, one must have the power to do it), "power" must be a prime constituent of international action. It is difficult to conceive of examples of action in international politics which could not also be regarded as examples of power-seeking. Thus the approach of general explanatory concepts achieves its generality partly through linguistic means; a concept holds partly because it is defined to hold. And if this is true, it achieves its unification of the field at the expense of empirical content. The theoretical searchlight of general explanatory concepts encompasses an entire field, but reveals only the veneer of subject matter. Detailed empirical analysis, conversely, plunges deeply into subject matter, but produces few useful common threads of analysis. To use a somewhat exaggerated metaphor, detailed empirical analysis tends to miss the forest for overconcentration on the trees; general explanatory concepts stare so hard at the forest that they sometimes fail to discern a single tree!

This difference between the two schools affects other matters as well. The approach of explanatory concepts, by summing up international phenomena in terms of a single key notion, tends to conceive of international relations as a single system of "equilibrium" or "power." This does not mean that subsystems might not be developed subordinate to an overarching "power" or "equilibrium" system. Capability theorists have already delineated such a multi-system analysis.[10] But such attempts have been rather the exception than the rule, and the insistence upon a single organizing conception has partly discouraged such attempts, for in terms of that conception itself there is no difference between international relations conducted at one time or place and international relations conducted at another. The *ancien régime* is as fully pervaded by power or equilibrial tendencies as is the thermonuclear age. And the same holds true for the pursuit of capabilities; the conditions

8 Liska, *op. cit.*, p. 12.

9 Morgenthau, *op. cit.*, p. 27.

10 See Kaplan, *op. cit. passim.*

under which capabilities are advanced change from system to system, but the pursuit of capabilities, resources, or access to facilities is a constant.[11]

If general explanatory concepts highlight a single comprehensive international system, detailed empirical analysis tends to posit an infinite variety of international systems, each co-extensive with the event or case to be explained. Each event or diplomatic decision has to be explained *de novo*. Systems of action tend to become equivalent to individual events.

II It seems clear that there is warrant for another approach to the study of international politics. This approach would endeavor to combine in a measure the systematic features of general explanatory concepts with the empirical content of detailed empirical analysis. Of course, it could not succeed in bringing a complete unification of the field on the one hand and also explain in rich empirical detail every individual case on the other. The third approach would sacrifice some of the wealth of empirical detail to achieve comprehensiveness; it would sacrifice some of the comprehensiveness of explanatory concepts to obtain greater empirical content. In terms of the rough metaphor used previously, the approach of *systematic empirical analysis* would pay attention to the largest trees, but not to all trees; it would look at the forest, but probably fail to see all of it.

How would such an approach be carried on? If empirical depth is to be ensured, one approach to systematic empirical analysis would be founded on the essential works of diplomatic and political history. Such works could provide the raw data from which systematic characterizations of international relations could be derived. When fundamental changes occurred in diplomatic mode these characterizations would have to take specific account of them. At the same time, systematic empirical analysis should not lose itself in a welter of detail. If common threads are to be revealed, comprehensive coverage of minor diplomatic events cannot be undertaken. A satisfactory mid-course would involve the subdivision of international relations into distinctive patterns, each enduring for a limited period of time and demarcated by significant changes in diplomatic style. During a period of a given diplomatic style, international re-

11 *Ibid.*

lations would be summed up in terms of consistent habits of action; when diplomatic style was transformed, new policies and diplomatic techniques would ensue. In this sense international relations might be conceived in terms of separate "systems," each operating over a short period. These "systems" could be defined in terms of diplomatic style; when objectives or techniques of diplomacy were significantly altered, a system-change would be seen to have occurred. Such a system approach would neglect and purposely obscure internal variations within a single system of action; it would take specific account, however, of the change from system to system. It would thus seek to summarize system behavior over a time-span. As the commonality of international politics would be broken with each system-change, it might be thought that analysis would be confined to an exposition of discrete and incomparable international systems. Actually, however, individual systems would be adduced as the primary data of a second-order analysis which would be concerned with comparison and with the delineation of constituents common to the separate systems. In this manner a theoretical linkage of individual systems would be made.

It may be well to ask whether such an approach to international affairs would reveal aspects of empirical reality that are not fully uncovered by present approaches. The approach of general explanatory concepts calls attention to a single all-embracing international system; the approach of detailed empirical analysis, to an infinitude of international systems. From the point of view of the first there are no dividing points in the history of the modern state system significant enough *to be incorporated in the structure of theory;* from the point of view of the second, all dividing points are fundamental, and all must be taken into account. For the former international relations did not change *structurally* with the French Revolution; for the latter the French Revolution and the Jay Treaty marked fundamental changes of exactly equal importance. But while one may not think that the Jay Treaty and the French Revolution are of quite equal weight, the fact of change is pervasive. Indeed, one might go so far as to argue that change has been so fundamental that we can scarcely think of the system of the *ancien régime* in terms of the system that prevails today. The crucial quantities have been so altered in two hundred years that the student who approaches the eighteenth century with modern preconceptions will find it scarcely recognizable. It is not much of an exaggeration to state that eighteenth-century diplomatic style is as unlike that of the thermonuclear age as domestic society is unlike foreign affairs. An approach that takes cognizance of critical dividing points in the history of international relations may do so without falling prey to postulations of infinite variety.

In the end, of course, how far to go in incorporating empirical variety in the study of international politics is a matter of judgment. The approach of empirical systems would incorporate more variety in the structure of theory than the approach of unifying concepts; it would incorporate less variety than the approach of detailed analysis. And the primary *raison d'être* for such an approach is not that judgments of previous approaches on this count are incorrect; it is that there is room for yet another approach. There are analytical gaps to be filled. Thus, systematic empirical analysis does not seek to supersede, but to supplement.

**III** The actual bench marks of such a systematic treatment are subject to debate. In the following pages an attempt is made to characterize, on the basis of diplomatic and other historical materials, the mode of conducting international relations in nine different system-periods:

|     |           |     |           |     |           |
|-----|-----------|-----|-----------|-----|-----------|
| (1) | 1740-1789 | (4) | 1822-1848 | (7) | 1890-1918 |
| (2) | 1789-1814 | (5) | 1848-1871 | (8) | 1918-1945 |
| (3) | 1814-1822 | (6) | 1871-1890 | (9) | 1945-1960 |

These are traditional divisions of historical scholarship, and they mark important changes in international relations. In some manner or other the modes, objectives, and techniques of diplomacy changed at these crucial junctures. The *ancien régime* certainly did not conduct its diplomatic affairs as they were conducted during the French Revolution and imperium. The creation of the Concert of Europe brought a momentary halt to the frictions engendered by the revolution, but they broke out again in a new context after 1822. By 1848 the Concert could no longer contain international forces; the revolutions of that year unsettled both conservative and revolutionary factions and unleashed a new diplomacy of *Realpolitik*. When domestic stability was temporarily re-established after 1871 a refurbished Concert functioned through the alliance system. This

Concert in turn submitted to the universal quest for imperial territory at the end of the century. The challenge of World War I did
not produce a new international tranquillity; while a new Concert
was constituted in the League of Nations, a new revolutionary
ideological conflict was destined to frustrate it. When this ideological rift was overcome in the War of 1939-45, another succeeded it,
though in a very different context. Present developments raise the
question of whether we are now entering a new international system.
In each instance objectives or methods of diplomacy changed in the
shift from one system to another.

It should not be claimed that these are the only acceptable system-periods which could be listed and analyzed. The excellent
series, *The Rise of Modern Europe,* edited by Professor William L.
Langer, surveys more limited periods, and it does not always accord
with the transitional dates chosen here. As good a case could be
made for terminating a diplomatic era in 1820 or in 1830 as for the
date selected in this study, 1822. The late Professor Robert Binkley
saw the breakdown of the Concert in the Crimean War, not in the
revolutions of 1848, as it is viewed here. More important, perhaps,
the great movements of European and world relations during the
nineteenth and twentieth centuries extend beyond the confines of
any diplomatic period or system. Liberalism, revolution, nationalism, imperialism—these forces transcend traditional historical
periodization. Their influence is too pervasive to be encapsulated
by a single international system. Indeed, in the study that follows,
it is assumed that revolutionary tides such as these are at work in
many systems. It is also contended, however, that the result or outcome of these forces varied from epoch to epoch. Liberalism and
nationalism were movements to conjure with even during the period of conservative internationalism and the European Concert,
but their influence was limited in terms of the diplomatic product.

If there are grounds for including larger slices of history in the
delimitation of international system, there are also grounds for taking smaller ones. Each international system listed above and discussed below might be subdivided into two or more new systems.
Homogeneous international behavior is a chimera. Canning and
Palmerston acted quite differently in the international orbit, and
the Castlereagh of 1820 was quite unlike the Castlereagh of 1814.
In the final analysis, the choice of international systems rests on

individual judgment and accepted historical bench marks. No special validity can be attributed to the transitional dates selected.

This work as a whole rests upon a survey of secondary works in the field of diplomatic, social, and political history. It has proved impossible to encompass the monographic literature or to probe to the primary sources. With certain exceptions, the studies consulted have been in the English language. These constitute important limitations upon the results derived, and they need to be acknowledged. At the same time, an attempt has been made to survey major works of diplomatic and political history, and it is hoped that a parochial interpretation of the events in question has been avoided. Where differences of viewpoint have emerged, they have been checked against the interpretations of other scholars. If points of view could not be reconciled, the interpretation adopted here has been clearly stated as such, and alternative theories noted. The author is aware that further problems remain to be investigated, and he has tried to give appropriate recognition to this fact. In no sense does the ensuing work attempt a *comprehensive* and *sufficient* explanation of the historical record. Historical explanations are never, strictly speaking, *sufficient,* and the deficiency here is more marked than in most cases. What the author has sought to provide is an *empirical model* of historical events at a given level of abstraction. What follows is not a recital of all relevant historical facts, but a selection of facts according to certain overriding interests: what general factors have made for stability or instability in the international system? What forces have tended to disrupt the system? What factors have helped to regulate it? All events are strictly relevant to these questions, but some are more salient than others. The French Revolution is of greater importance than the Neapolitan Revolution; the Concert of Europe is more significant than a single alliance instrument. It is hoped that the distinctions adopted here between what is important and what is merely relevant will gain acceptance. If they do not, there is no court of last resort. An author includes in his model those factors he believes to be significant; if others disagree, they are free to construct alternative models, resting on other factors. All that can be claimed for what ensues is that it was formulated after an inspection of the historical record and that it attempts to deal with the problems of stability and instability in international relationships.

IV This work proceeds in three stages. In Part I an attempt is made to characterize each of the nine systems in historical terms. The discussion of each system is centered around factors making for stability and instability, *i.e.,* chaos, breakdown, and war. As mentioned above, it is certain that some of the variety of historical experience has been sacrificed in the process, and in this sense the characterizations are "heuristic" devices in that they stimulate understanding and discovery—they inform reality without directly portraying it. Models are not social facts.[12]

The second stage of the work (Part II) endeavors to systematize the historical analysis into categories in terms of which the separate systems may be specified. Each of the nine systems is then classified according to different states of the central categories. In this manner the change from one system to the next can be depicted in terms of changes in the various constituents. If Part I represents a first-order abstraction from the facts of historical reality, Part II represents a second-order abstraction. Empirical variety is further sacrificed, for the systemic categories cannot take full account of the contingency of the historical analysis.

Part III aims at a still broader view. From the systemic constituents discussed in Part II, four basic determinants are chosen for examination in Part III. These factors are deemed to be the most important determinants of the international system in that their presence or absence in different forms tended to be associated with stability or instability in international relations. If these factors are indeed important (and the reader will have to judge their significance for himself), then an inchoate diagnosis and even prognosis of the international system becomes possible. On the basis of the role of crucial variables in the past, certain statements about future possibilities may be made. If past stability or instability was associated with a given pattern of variables, the presence of a similar pattern in the future may provide clues about likely stability or instability. The third part of the study carries further the process of abstraction and is forced to neglect aspects of reality for the sake of generality.

It is important to note that the analysis as a whole does not pre-

12 See Stanley Hoffmann's criticisms on this point, *op. cit.,* especially pp. 26 and 42.

sent a developed theory of international politics in the general sense. Logical explanatory connections have not been adduced between antecedent patterns and international outcomes. Instead, "correlations" between certain factors and international instability are all that can be claimed. And even these correlations might not be seen in the same way by another investigator. At most, the ensuing pages represent an approximation to Raymond Aron's "historical sociology"; they do not constitute a unilinear theory of international relations. No secular trend can be discerned from the chronology of systems; of the nine considered, five were equilibrial; four were disequilibrial. While it is impossible to be optimistic about the future, diverse present trends hold portents of both stability and instability. Although the bases and conclusions of this study may be challenged from different points of view, it is hoped that it may contribute something to an understanding of those factors which have made for conflict in the past and thus inform the present.

V Part I is written in a very different style from Parts II and III. Part I uses the language of the historian; the latter parts that of the systems theorist. But the analytic concern is similar in both instances: the stability and instability of the international system. Because of the shift in terminology, however, it may be well briefly to anticipate here the framework and approach of Parts II and III. An international epoch, system, or subsystem is stable or unstable depending upon the balance of disruptive and regulative factors. If regulative influences are not powerful enough to contain disruption and to produce outcomes within an acceptable range, the system is unstable; if they can hold outcomes within acceptable bounds, the system is stable.

Regulative and disruptive processes presume regulative and disruptive inputs. In the historical analysis of Part I, regulative inputs are seen in formal or informal arrangements to hold international outcomes within stable bounds. The balance of power system, the Concert of Europe, the binding force of ideology—all these may play a regulative role in the international system. If the actions of states can be directly controlled at the point of origin by an international Concert of Powers, regulation may be powerful and immediate. If certain actions cannot themselves be prevented, but their consequences altered or transformed through a balance of power mechanism, regulation may be effective but less immediate. If the regulative system possesses ample resources, competition for the spoils among states will not lead to conflict until the resources are fully divided. Before that point is reached, the system contains disruption.

In Part I disruptive inputs are seen in the divisive forces of ideology and ambition, the uncertainties of domestic support, and the disparities of power-resource base. Great divergence among states as to goals, internal social structure, and tangible resource potency, will lead to disruption in the international system. Only an omnicompetent regulator would be able to contend with such wholesale disruption. From this point of view, the French Revolution was a particularly destabilizing event in international politics because it fomented disturbance in all three respects. By revolutionizing the domestic constitution of France, it posed the problem of security for successive regimes; by nationalizing the French people in the *levée en masse* it raised the spectre of unlimited diplomacy and total war; by installing new and reformist elites, it altered the objectives of France in world affairs. In all three areas, revolutionary France offered a challenge to the existence of the conservative monarchies which could not be met by the creaky balance of power system of the old regime. Regulative forces could not contain disruptive ones.

VI    The problem of stability and instability of international systems leads directly to the criteria by which one system may be distinguished from another. As we have seen previously, there is no single satisfactory means of demarcating international systems. Another investigator would doubtlessly have seen systems extending for longer or shorter periods than those depicted here. At the same time he might agree that important alterations in patterns of disturbance or regulation indicate the onset of a new international system. In the systems that follow such transformations are the dividing points of system-change. It does not follow, of course, that all transformations must be as cataclysmic as the French Revolution to introduce a new system-period. After 1822 the ideological gulf in Europe widened once again, and though it did not produce the mighty upheaval of 1789 and afterward, it did give rise to domestic revolutions in more than a few countries. The revolutions of 1848 ushered in a new system, founded not on ideological cleavage, but on internal dissension and *Realpolitik*. Though elites were not fundamentally revolutionized, their tactics were. The result was in several respects as important a transformation of the international system as that wrought by the original French Revolution. The surface diplomatic calm restored after the Franco-Prussian War concealed rumblings of nationalism, patriotism, and imperialism which were the bane of later years and which are with us today. These forces were explicitly revealed after 1890, and they culminated in two world wars. Nineteenth-century international systems have seemed halycon epochs contrasted with contemporary turbulence. Yet their placidity was delusive. As Professor William L. Langer notes: "No movement of major significance in our present world is more recent in origin than the period of 1871-1914. The great issues and divisions of modern life have their birth in the developments of these years." [13] Nineteenth-century system-change has turned out to be of vital significance for current world affairs.

More specifically, system-change may be said to occur when the internal constituents of disturbance and regulation are altered. All constituents of disturbance (goals or objectives, domestic security and stability, and resource potency) on the one hand and all constituents of regulation (institutional or informal mechanisms and the availability of goal-objects) on the other need not undergo transformation in order for system-change to occur. It is sufficient that many or most of them be altered. In the formal presentation of the nine different systems of international relations in Chapter Eleven, it will be seen that the constituents of regulation and disruption are profoundly affected in the shift from system to system. Some may argue that certain system-changes are more fundamental than others. I would not be inclined to dispute the point. Some transformations may barely exceed the threshold of system-change; others may clear the barrier with leeway to spare. In this sense the impact of the French Revolution and World War I may have been more telling than that of certain other dynamic processes or events. But change is ubiquitous, and those who view the period 1814-1914 as a stable interlude between crests of violence obscure more than

13 Lectures on Continental European History, 1871-1914, Harvard University, January 28, 1953.

they observe: the nineteenth and twentieth centuries are of a piece historically, and they convey basically similar images of instability in international politics.

In the historical analysis that follows, regulative and disruptive forces will not always clearly be labeled as such, but the forces themselves are obvious in the treatment. A concern with the Concert of Europe and the balance of power on the one hand, and with the multiform challenges to the operation of each on the other constitute the subject of Part I. Historical arguments are given to account for the respective strength of such constraining and disruptive influences, but their resultant is either stability or instability. Restraints either function or fail to function. In this sense even the historical part of this study involves an essay on stability and instability in the international system; Parts II and III do no more than make explicit strands of analysis which are the warp and woof of the historical treatment. In this light, the reader will find that the latter sections do not introduce new ideas; they merely systematize familiar ones. Disturbance and regulation are the heart of the work in all of its parts.

From this point of view the eighteenth century has a luster that has brightened with time. During the old regime conflict and containment were moderate processes, and the interactions of statesmen were held within the measured tempo of courtly etiquette. Compared to present stresses it may not be amiss for a contemporary observer to remark that the eighteenth century was an almost idyllic age in international relations. If we could recapture its simplicity, moderation and grace, present discontents would be much easier to bear.

# PART I
# historical
# analysis

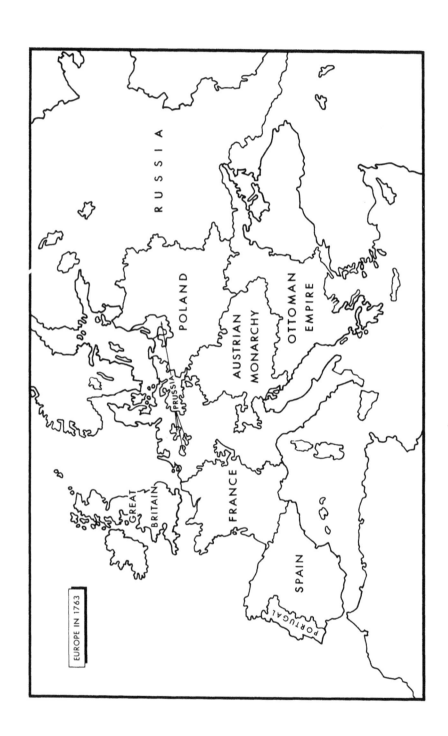

EUROPE IN 1763

RUSSIA

POLAND

PRUSSIA

AUSTRIAN
MONARCHY

OTTOMAN
EMPIRE

GREAT
BRITAIN

FRANCE

SPAIN

PORTUGAL

## chapter two

# DIPLOMACY IN THE EIGHTEENTH CENTURY

I The conditions of international relations under the *ancien régime* were far different from those of the present. Indeed, those of us reared in the twentieth century may find it difficult even to comprehend the international situation prior to the French Revolution. The term, "international," scarcely applies to the relations among states during the eighteenth century. "Nations" had yet to be invented; diplomacy referred to the relations between states governed by aristocrats and monarchs, not to the connections of nations or peoples. The absence of modern nationalism and fervent patriotism sanctioned and supported an interstate polity which was moderate by today's standards. Because the individual inhabitant did not identify himself *primarily* with government or nation, the government could not require or expect his unlimited obedience. In an era in which the channels of communications between people and government were limited or indirect, individuals could not regard the acts of the ruling elite as their own acts.

Modern nationalism could not arise in Europe until communication among members of a society had reached a high peak of intensity. In France, nationalism awaited popular establishment of direct channels of influence or control over government; by constituting for themselves a common government to act in their behalf, the French were welded into a national unit, and in so doing the process of nation-building which had been the work of centuries was completed. Popular government, or popular influence upon government, then, was the agency of a heightened communication among Frenchmen which fostered nationalism.[1] In Europe, nationalism was brought not by the principle of popular sovereignty, but as a result of the new patterns of communications ensuing from the French incursion in Europe. Nationalism in France was generated on behalf of the revolution, nationalism in Europe against it, but in both cases it depended upon the social upheavals of 1789 and after. It could not attain full stature until the winds of revolutionary doctrine had buffeted the shaky domestic structure of the old regime.

The impact of the eighteenth-century conservative domestic order upon diplomacy was far-reaching. Because the French Revolution had not happened to generate full-blown nationalism, the international policy and wars of the old regime were largely the business of aristocracies and monarchs.[2] The individual subject usually managed to avoid involvement, and he was frequently able to pursue his private enterprises wherever they took him in time of war or peace. If these projects required traveling in an enemy country and fraternizing with its citizenry, there was no disadvantage. As the war in question was fundamentally the personal affair of Louis XV or Prince Kaunitz, the man in the street was not himself concerned. Laurence Sterne, English writer and cleric, was pleased to visit France during the Seven Years' War between France and his country, to associate with French literati, and when he returned to England, to praise French life and manners before his English associates. There was no need to bear malice toward the French king; his enemy was not England but George III and Mr. Pitt.

Not only was nationalist patriotism impossible in this moderate age, a kind of European cosmospolitanism further limited parochial sentiment.[3] The subjects of the ruling princes traveled freely

---

[1] R. R. Palmer, "Frederick the Great, Guibert, Bulow: From Dynastic to National War" in Edward Mead Earle (ed.) *Makers of Modern Strategy* (Princeton, 1953), p. 50. It is worth remarking that popular influence upon government had proceeded farthest in England and that England was consequently the most national state prior to the French Revolution.

[2] Professor Leo Gershoy in *From Despotism to Revolution, 1763-1789* (New York, 1944) argues that the limitations upon wars and the pursuit of power were purely technical. See pp. 162-165.

[3] See *ibid.*, p. 235. Professor Dorn writes: "In spite of their babel of tongues, their bloody and endless quarrels, Europe still remained a vital and organic unity. The wrongs and injuries which these peoples had done one another in the past, their conquests and reconquests, groupings and regroupings, their occasional fierce

in Europe, savoring the customs of other countries and comparing them with those of their own.[4] The result of this continual intermingling of Europeans was the gradual development of a hospitality to variant ideas and institutions which transcended geographical frontiers. The age of the Enlightenment strengthened this European cosmopolitanism among the leaders of opinion.[5] The *philosophes* spoke not of men, but of man, and they assumed rational faculties had no relation to political boundaries. If certain social arrangements were archaic in one country, they might be unsuitable in others; if certain laws had utility in one state they might be commended to others.[6] In this unique age, the European was apt to find more in common with members of his own class in another country than with members of a different class in his own. Indeed, it may well be true that in several countries of Europe during the eighteenth century, the social classes were more international in their interests and outlook than they have been at any time since the French Revolution. Marxian "internationalism" may have been more applicable in 1760 than in 1890.[7]

The cosmopolitanism and moderation of this pre-nationalist age found expression in many ways. It decreed that the national origin of monarch, prince or aristocrat should not be of fundamental importance for the social cohesion of a state. As Professor Mowat says, "Peoples accepted rulers from other countries with equanimity." [8] The catalogue of foreign rulers of the *ancien régime* is impressive. A prince of Hanover became King of England; a Duke of Lorraine was made Grand Duke of Tuscany and this same Grand Duke later

---

hatreds arising from balked ambitions, had welded them into a kind of union from which even Englishmen, in spite of their insularity, have been unable to escape to this day." *Competition for Empire, 1740-1763* (New York, 1940), pp. 2-3.

4 R. B. Mowat, *The Age of Reason* (Boston, 1934), p. 24.

5 A brilliant and compact summary of the age of the Enlightenment occurs in Dorn, *op. cit.*, Chapter Five. Professor R. R. Palmer's, *The Age of the Democratic Revolution: A Political History of Europe and America, 1760-1800* (Princeton, 1959) illustrates clearly the internationalization of reformist notions during the eighteenth century.

6 Montesquieu, who pointed out the influence of climate on political organization, would constitute an exception to this generalization.

7 It did not follow from this that European social classes were homogeneous. See Gershoy, *op. cit.*, Chapter Two.

8 Mowat, *op. cit.*, p. 23.

became Emperor of Germany; the Spanish monarch was a Bourbon grandson of Louis XIV; and the greatest of Russian royalty after Peter the Great was initially a Princess of Anhalt. If peoples were content to put up with rulers of various nationalities, rulers were no less tolerant. They were happy to have subjects of varying national colorations as long as they added to the stock of state power and glory. It is perhaps worth mentioning that Austria was quite willing to take the Spanish Netherlands as recompense for her endeavors in the War of Spanish Succession despite the fact that the new territories were not Austrian ethnically, and were not contiguous to any Austrian possession.

The internationalism of peoples and rulers infected militarism as well. If the European princes were eager to acquire heterogeneous territories, they were equally disposed to employ recruits from other states in their armies.[9] "All the Continental armies of the eighteenth century contained numerous foreigners, whole regiments of them." [10] Foreign units of the French army were composed typically of Swiss Guards, and Irish units were also used when the French could recruit them. Scottish regiments were regularly found in the service of Holland. The French Army before the Revolution was half-composed of men who were not French; and the army of Frederick William I was one-third foreign. Frederick the Great's army some years later was more than half-filled with foreign mercenaries, prisoners of war and deserters from enemy armies.[11] But this was not the extent of the internationalization of warfare. The Prince de Ligne tells the story of a single warrior who was simultaneously or successively a colonel of a regiment of French infantry and of a regiment of German cavalry, chief of a Spanish expedition, captain of a Spanish ocean-going vessel, and a major general in the Spanish army. He was an "officer-general in the service of three countries whose languages he did not know, and the most brilliant vice-admiral Russia has ever had." [12] This man was recognized in

[9] Dorn, *op. cit.*, pp. 98-99.

[10] Mowat, *op. cit.*, p. 51. See also Theodore Ropp, *War in the Modern World* (Durham, N.C., 1960), pp. 36-37.

[11] It should be noted that during the Seven Years' War the proportion of native troops rose to two-thirds of the whole. See Dorn, *op. cit.*, p. 94.

[12] Prince de Ligne, *Memoires,* quoted in Mowat, *op. cit.*, p. 54.

Madrid as a nobleman of Spain and in the German states as a Prince of the German Empire. This outstanding example of the cosmopolitanism of the officer class was roughly paralleled by the internationalization of the common soldiery. As one writer noted, "The common soldier was a sort of workman of the military corporation, who toured the world and stopped wherever the trade was good — that is, where war, falling upon some fat country, could nourish its artisan." [13]

But eighteenth-century militarism was not only affected by the prevailing internationalism of the age, it was also moderated by other factors. As a result of the intellectual onslaughts of the philosophers, the chivalrous virtues of courage and honor were at a nadir, and the new virtues of national loyalty and patriotism had not yet taken their places. In the interim, the career of the soldier was scarcely a glamorous one. Even in France, which maintained the most truly national army prior to the revolution, cafés and other public places displayed signs reading: "No dogs, lackeys, prostitutes or soldiers." [14] But the inhospitable climate of opinion was not the only handicap to a fully developed militarism. Because of the exemption of the nobility from taxation, governmental revenues were limited; deficient resources meant that the professional mercenary armies employed by the monarch would be expensive. "Each soldier represented a heavy investment in time and money. Trained troops lost in action could not easily be replaced." [15] Thus, armies were valuable mechanisms which could not be hazarded in chance engagements. In this context, the threatened destruction of a prince's army was a potent reason for immediate peace, and armies were as prized as provinces.

The military machine of the old regime was additionally hindered in that certain classes of value to the state were freed from military service. Classes deemed productive, the bourgeoisie and higher peasantry were not expected to find places in the army.[16] As one writer has phrased it, the militarism of the old regime ". . . was built on an economy that did not tolerate the removal of its

13 E. Lavisse, *La Jeunesse du Grand Frederic,* quoted in *ibid.,* p. 55.
14 Palmer, *loc. cit.,* p. 50.
15 *Ibid.,* p. 51
16 See Dorn, *op. cit.,* p. 81.

useful members for military purposes. The big armies were thus composed of economically exempt classes. . . ." [17]

As a result of the inadequate rewards of status and prestige attendant on military service, the professional soldier had to be well-paid and well-nourished, or he would desert. The consequence was a dependence upon long baggage trains and an elaborate system of supply magazines, both of which imposed severe limits on military mobility. Armies had to be marched in formation to be held together; forced marches, campaigns in the forest, and night marches provided irresistible opportunities for desertion. [18] It is not surprising that Frederick the Great believed that his armies could be maintained intact only if his soldiers feared Prussian officers more than the enemy.

The limitations upon the composition and maintenance of armies affected the strategy which might be employed. Because armed forces were expensive and delicate mechanisms, large-scale pitched battles between whole armies were studiously avoided. Battles could not be fought until a battle line had been drawn and formations arranged; dispersed field attacks were rejected as presenting too strong a temptation to desertion. Battle of any sort was a considerable risk, and victory, if it entailed the decimation of the victorious force, was not to be sought. It was natural that military thinkers believed that a state might lose as much from victory as from defeat. Even when a battle gave the edge to one force, it might not be able to pursue its advantage; armies might be defeated in the confrontation of the battlefield, but it was more difficult to destroy them in full retreat. Battles, in any case, did not end wars, because they were seldom decisive. As Professor Palmer notes: ". . . the contrast between eighteenth-century and Napoleonic battles is especially clear. After Blenheim, Malplaquet, Fontenoy or Rossbach, the war dragged on for years. After Marengo, Austerlitz, Jena, Wagram or Leipzig, peace overtures began in a few months." [19] A strategy of annihilation could not be followed until after the French Revolution; the old regime had to be satisfied to wage wars of maneuver and position. The anachronistic social system of the *ancien régime*

---

[17] Hans Speier, "Militarism in the Eighteenth Century," *Social Research*, Vol. 3, No. 3 (1936), p. 336.

[18] See Dorn, *op. cit.*, p. 82.

[19] Palmer, *loc. cit.*, p. 52.

prevented the utilization of military resources which otherwise might have been tapped; wars, therefore, were limited both in terms of the standards of the age and those of a more modern era.

The prevailing moderation and internationalism of the period applied to diplomacy as well as warfare. As there was an international soldiery, there was also an international corps of diplomats and statesmen to serve Europe's crowned heads. "Nobody was excluded from employment, even from the highest official positions, on account of nationality." [20] It is often not recognized that one of the pre-eminent characteristics of "French-style" diplomacy was its European character.[21] Some European courts selected their statesmen and diplomats from certain favored foreign nations. The Danes had a penchant for Germans at the helm of state, and for twenty years a Hanoverian was the center of a Danish ruling clique. So great was his ascendancy that Frederick the Great was reputed to have coined the epigram: "Denmark has her fleet and her Bernstorff." [22] When the latter finally fell in 1770, he was succeeded by another German, a Dr. Struensee who, though he was the virtual ruler of Denmark for two years, never learned Danish. The Russians, governed by a foreign empress, sought statesmen from two foreign nationalities. The English provided their naval leadership and the Germans were found at the court. John Elphinston and Sir Samuel Greig were given high positions in the Russian Admiralty and one Peter Lacy became a Russian general. For her immediate entourage, Catherine II chose a German named Biren as her Grand Chamberlain.

The Spanish, however, surpassed all others in their appropriation of foreign talent. They were absolutely promiscuous in their choice of foreign public servants. Elizabeth Farnese brought Alberoni from Parma to become diplomatic dictator of Spain. Later another Italian, the Marquis of Squillaci, was made Minister of War and Finance. But Italians were not the only group to become entangled in the sinuosities of the Spanish court. Baron Ripperda,

20 Mowat, *op. cit.*, p. 16.
21 See Harold Nicolson, *The Evolution of Diplomatic Method* (London, 1954), Chapter Three.
22 W. F. Reddaway, "Denmark under the Bernstorffs and Struensee," in A. W. Ward, G. W. Prothero, and Stanley Leathes (eds.) *The Cambridge Modern History*, Vol. 6, The Eighteenth Century (New York, 1909), p. 740.

a Dutchman, played a brief but important role in Spanish diplomacy. He was born a Catholic in Groningen, but embraced Protestantism to qualify for the Dutch public service. When he deserted Holland to serve the Spanish monarch, first as an emissary of Alberoni and later as chief minister, he reverted to Catholicism. After his disgrace in 1726 he fled to Morocco, became a Mohammedan, and fought in a war against Spain. When Ripperda fell, his influence with Elizabeth was bequeathed to an Austrian, Konigsegg, the Habsburg ambassador. And the limits of Spanish tolerance had not yet been approached; Austrians, Italians, and Dutchmen were ably abetted by Irishmen at the Spanish court. Richard Wall was Spanish foreign minister for several years; Alexander O'Reilly was a Spanish general and Minister of War; and Sir Thomas Fitzgerald became Spanish Ambassador in London. England and France, in some ways the most conservative in their national outlooks, were not exempt from a proclivity for foreigners. George I surrounded himself with influential Hanoverians, and France gave positions of great importance to the Scotsman, John Law, and the Genevese, Jacques Necker.

The internationalization of statecraft had significant consequences. If the compulsions of nationalism could not be invoked to ensure faithful service, diplomats and intriguers could only be appeased by a liberal distribution of state funds. Between 1757 and 1769 the French subsidized Austrian officials to the extent of 82,-652,479 livres, and Kaunitz himself was ransomed to the extent of 100,000 livres. The French Abbé (later Cardinal) Dubois offered the English minister Stanhope 600,000 livres for a treaty of alliance with France. (The offer was gracefully declined, but Dubois was invited to Stanhope's house for informal conversations, and in due course a treaty was signed.) The practice of "diplomatic compensation" continued until well after the French Revolution. A Prussian diplomat in Paris summarized the situation well when he wrote in 1802: "Experience has taught everybody who is here on diplomatic business that one ought never to give anything before the deal is definitely closed, but it has also proved that the allurement of gain will often work wonders." [23] It was not only commonplace to bribe foreign emissaries, it was necessary to reward foreigners who

[23] Quoted in Hans J. Morgenthau, *Politics among Nations* (New York, 1956), p. 222.

agreed to spy or to carry on secret missions for European sovereigns. During the eighteenth century the French paid to potential spies and intriguers huge sums, generally to no practical end. In some cases systematic corruption usurped the role of traditional diplomacy. Between 1764 and 1771 Denmark, Russia, and England on the one side, and France on the other, waged an overt war of bribery for the soul and allegiance of Sweden. The first three, spending fantastic sums, seemed to have won victory when the death of Adolphus Frederick unexpectedly gave the French the upper hand.

Despite the venality of the age, money could not gain every desired goal. There were some things which the European monarchs would not stoop to do even though great issues hung in the balance. During the Seven Years' War a French agent in England proposed the destruction of the Bank of England by counterfeiting British pounds and presenting them at the Bank for payment in specie. Louis XV, however, rejected the project as ungentlemanly and claimed that it aroused his indignation and horror. When, thirty years later, the Austrian Emperor was given a similar opportunity, he gave a like reply. At another time a young Russian nobleman offered to betray his own father in order to give English state secrets to the French, but Louis and his advisers demurred. "It is, in general," the French King wrote, "too dangerous to trust a man who betrays his most sacred duties." [24]

II The conditions of social organization, diplomacy, militarism, and statesmanship in the eighteenth century led to the creation of a system of international relations which was unique in the history of statecraft and unlike any system functioning today. These conditions fulfilled almost completely the ideal precepts for a balance of power mechanism. A balance of power apparatus could not function without the existence of a state system, "that is, a group of independent 'neighboring states more or less connected with one another' and of relatively equal power";[25] it could not operate with-

---

[24] Quoted in J. W. Thompson and S. K. Padover, *Secret Diplomacy: A Record of Espionage and Double-Dealing: 1500-1815* (London, 1937), p. 162. It should of course be remarked that subornation was not limited to the old regime. Corruption and bribery continued during the nineteenth and twentieth centuries though they were no longer a major *modus operandi* of the international system.

[25] Edward Vose Gulick, *Europe's Classical Balance of Power* (Ithaca, New York, 1955), p. 4.

out a minimal homogeneity of political attitude among the participating state units and a common concern to protect the system; it
could not maintain itself without a limitation of warfare to preserve the constituent state-components. The eighteenth century met
the requirements for a balance of power mechanism in all these
ways, and the maxims of balance of power theory were obeyed as
never before or since.

Because of the lack of popular government, the subjects of prince
or aristocracy did not identify themselves with the acts of their ruling cliques — in short, the absence of popular government decreed
an absence of nationalism. King or lord could not assume popular
approval for his diplomacy or wars; hence, he could carry neither
to extremes; none of Europe's crowned heads could expect subject
populations to make great sacrifices at the altar of *raison d'état.*
The consequence of the limited diplomacy which resulted from this
condition can scarcely be overestimated. It was, fundamentally, that
the eighteenth century was destined to be a moderate, or as some
have called it, an "admirable" age in international relations.[26]

But "limited diplomacy" was not the only result of the social and
political system of the old regime. The limited revenues of the
eighteenth century states, the exemption of economically productive classes from military service, the systematic denigration of military virtues, and the internationalism of the professional soldiery
combined to produce an erudite warfare of siege and maneuver. In
practice this entailed wars of limited objectives and the drawing of
a viable distinction between soldier and civilian. The military machine of the old regime was ideally suited to the maintenance of the
state system for no great Power could hope to destroy others with
the limited resources and uncertain loyalties it commanded. A great
Power might be able to protect its own independence and perhaps
even advance it, but it could not hope to launch the kind of wholesale onslaught on the European liberties which became commonplace with the French Revolution and the Napoleonic era. As long
as limited war held sway, the balance system could not be undermined by a single Power; when the "hyperbolic war" of the twentieth century took its place, therefore, the balance machinery was destroyed.

If the archaic social and political systems of the period limited

[26] See Mowat, *op. cit.*, Chapter One.

the forms of diplomacy and warfare, they did not circumscribe the range of diplomatic choice available to European royalty. If subjects would not support unlimited *means* in interstate relations, they would not dictate the choice of *ends*. Thus, princes and nobilities enjoyed a wide range of discretion in choosing their avenues of statecraft. If one were to compare the eighteenth century with the present age, the conclusion would be that two hundred years ago political rulers were able to choose their policies in foreign relations within the range of a full circle, but the implementation of policy was severely limited by inadequate popular support. Today, on the other hand, political leaders must select their policies within the range of a short arc, but they may carry out their programs with enormous force and vigor.

But if popular limitations upon the range of policy decision did not exist in the old regime, there were other important limitations. Chief of these was the ethic of the monarch which required that he call his royal peers "brother," and which precluded an unalloyed Machiavellianism. Despite the machinations of the age, the eighteenth century did not approach the amorality of Renaissance intrigue; the interstate relations of the *ancien régime* were manifestations of "French" not "Italian style" diplomacy. As one student has noted, the princes and aristocracies of the eighteenth century, "were joined together by family ties, a common language (French), common cultural values, a common style of life, and common moral convictions about what a gentleman was and was not allowed to do in his relations with other gentleman." [27] The international gentility of the era was well-suited to the preservation and protection of the state system, for it promoted that attention to group interest on which the system rested. A balance of power mechanism could hardly have functioned in a context in which all protagonists were bent on advancing their separate interests against general European concerns.

Nor were these the only elements of eighteenth-century diplomacy which conduced to a self-adjusting balance of power apparatus. A minimum homogeneity of outlook among the great states was prerequisite to such a system, and the necessary unity of sentiment and idea was to be found *par excellence* in the old regime. The eighteenth century, unlike the centuries which preceded and

[27] Morgenthau, *op. cit.*, p. 221. See also Gershoy, *op cit.*, p. 26.

followed it, did not witness great conflicts of principle in the realm of interstate relations. If it is possible to talk of ideology in this pre-revolutionary age, one could claim with justice that a common ideology of aristocratic and monarchical conservatism, tempered by limited reform, characterized the period. The disastrous religious conflicts of previous centuries no longer disturbed the European peace, and the great social commotions surrounding liberalism, socialism, fascism, and communism had not yet arisen to disturb it once again. The philosophic and programmatic writings of the Enlightenment had not yet generated the conflicts of 1792 and afterward. There were, therefore, no perverse ideological issues to disrupt the free play of a balance mechanism. The balancing system of Europe required states to ally or oppose each other according to the presumed distribution of power: if ideological bonds or animosities had arisen, states could no longer have charted their courses on power considerations alone; states would have refused to balance against their ideological *confrères* or to align themselves with ideological opponents, regardless of the configuration of power. The absence of divisive intellectual issues then, permitted a European balancing of considerable scope.

The freedom from ideological grievances sanctioned a phenomenal competition for power and empire both within Europe and outside it.[28] The eighteenth century was the age of Franco-British struggles in America, the Caribbean, in Canada and India; it was the time of the enormous Russian territorial expansion at the expense of Sweden, the Ottoman Empire, and Poland; it was the century of Frederick the Great's rape of Silesia and the three partitions of Poland which removed that historic state from the European map, except for a brief interlude, for more than one hundred years. But the pursuit of power and glory was restrained not only by the conservative domestic constitution of Europe's aristocratic states, but also by the balance of power system.[29]

The balance mechanism itself reinforced the internationalism of the century. The equilibrating system presumed the unlimited mobility of each participating state and as the locus of power was constantly in flux, each state would combine alternately with several

---

[28] Professor Dorn goes so far as to assert: ". . . warfare became a function, if not an actual necessity, of the structure of European society." (*Op. cit.*, p. 5.)

[29] See *ibid.*, pp. 2-3.

others. In the process of the *"renversement des alliances"* a state would ultimately sense the presence of a European system of which it was but a single part, and this consciousness would force recognition in turn of the useful role played by other constituent units. In this manner, the perception of a European system led directly to a sentiment of fundamental unity.

This minimal consciousness of unity among the European sovereigns was reflected in a tolerance of the Great Powers for one another which permitted each to maintain its basic character. "Intervention" of one Power in another's domestic affairs did not become commonplace until after the French Revolution; nor was it ever an essential principle of eighteenth-century diplomacy.[30] It was, in fact, at odds with the moderate tenor of the age. Intervention only became necessary when some Powers ceased to give serious concern to the maintenance of the system. When France breached the limits of eighteenth-century toleration in overturning the domestic constitutions of conservative states during the Revolutionary and Napoleonic periods, the conservative states, in turn, proclaimed the right of "intervention" to forestall the use of revolutionary force. "Intervention" then, was more nearly a reflection of the breakdown of the balance of power system, than it was an intrinsic principle of it.

In the pre-revolutionary period, Frederick II was perhaps the most Machiavellian of the eighteenth-century monarchs (and, fittingly, the writer of *Anti-Machiavel*); yet, even he did not use the interventionist tactics of Bonapartism. When he launched his unprovoked aggression on Silesia, he did not contemplate the destruction or domestic overturn of the Habsburg monarchy; rather, he sought Silesia as his price for defending the "Pragmatic Sanction" and Maria Theresa. Thus, one should not attempt to read the old regime through Polish glasses. The partitions of Poland were not hallmarks of European relations because Poland was not a constituent member of the European system, and, as Professor Mowat tells us, ". . . Poland was the frontier-country."[31] "Europe" stopped at the Vistula.

The balance of power system of the eighteenth century, however, could not be molded into an effective European Concert. There was no conference of Powers meeting periodically to decide questions of

30 Cf. Gulick, *op. cit.*, pp. 62-65.
31 Mowat, *op. cit.*, p. 21.

war, peace, and the distribution of power. But this omission revealed the halcyon character of the age: a Concert of Europe could
be created only after a period of revolutionary cataclysm and war
had spurred men to organize peace and a rudimentry machinery of
international government. Though the wars of the *ancien régime*
were taxing and violent for those directly involved and often disastrous for the public purse, they were not sufficiently catastrophic to
call forth the concerted effort of Europe to prevent their recurrence. Even such a desperate and bloody struggle as the Seven
Years' War was mild in comparison to the revolutionary convulsions of a half century later. The absence of a regular Concert, then,
was an indirect tribute to the relative moderation of the century of
the old regime.

Despite periods of warfare, the eighteenth century was a generally stable period in international relations. The balance of power
mechanism did not prevent military contests, but it did prevent
them from getting out of hand. The limited ambitions of European
autocrats and cabinets resulted in limited diplomacy and militarism. The outcomes of international politics did not exceed the
bounds of convention and precept. There were no permanently dissatisfied major participants in the European state system: a more
or less placid stability was the order of the day.

The objectives and techniques of diplomacy were both strictly
limited. Prince and monarch had modest ambitions in the international environment, and they had restricted means at their disposal.
They did not aim, nor could they expect to overturn the internal
constitution of other states. The cosmopolitan internationalism of
statecraft and war prevented drastic outcomes in world politics. Europe held itself at bay.

# chapter three
# THE REVOLUTION AND ITS AFTERMATH

It is difficult to overestimate the impact of the French Revolution and the ensuing Napoleonic Empire upon the structure of European diplomatic relations. If, before the Revolution, the diplomacy of European states was largely guided by kings and aristocratic elites, after it, diplomacy was increasingly influenced by the imperious force of the nationalized peoples. The sudden irruption of nationalism into the relative harmony of European relations transformed the international environment. Fundamentally, the impact of the developing age of nationalism ushered in by the Revolution was to destroy the placid moderation characteristic of diplomacy during the old regime. In every sphere limitation was no longer a fact of life. As a result of the Revolution, wars no longer were limited in scope, the *levée en masse* replacing the employment of mercenary troops; diplomacy was no longer regulated by international loyalty to a European cosmopolitanism or by the genial practice of corruption and bribery; it was governed by a perfervid devotion to the *Patrie*. The international soldiery, corps of diplomats, and public servants of the eighteenth century were replaced during the nineteenth century by national armies, national foreign offices and a national bureaucracy. Indeed, it does not do violence to the course of international relations during the nineteenth century to view it as the progressive embodiment of nationalist forces engendered by the Revolution and Empire.

But the effect of the revolutionary years upon interstate relations was not limited to the production of nationalism. As a result of the social and political reforms inaugurated in France after 1789 the

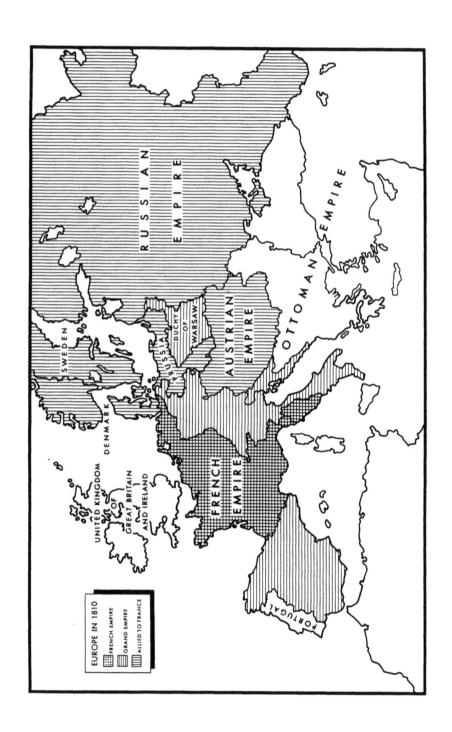

RUSSIAN EMPIRE

OTTOMAN EMPIRE

SWEDEN

DUCHY OF WARSAW

PRUSSIA

AUSTRIAN EMPIRE

DENMARK

UNITED KINGDOM OF GREAT BRITAIN AND IRELAND

FRENCH EMPIRE

PORTUGAL

EUROPE IN 1810

FRENCH EMPIRE
GRAND EMPIRE
ALLIED TO FRANCE

aristocratic consensus of the *ancien régime* was shattered, and a growing rift appeared between those groups eager to advance the principles of the Revolution and those seeking to retard them. At some point in the century the cleavage of ideas which divided internal political life would find expression in the foreign policies of states and nations. If the ideas of equality before the law, economic liberalism, and a modicum of representative government were principles around which political groups within a nation rallied, whole nations eventually would embrace them; the consequence would be a conflict between liberal and conservative Powers in the international arena. States desirous of implementing and extending the innovations of the Revolution could hardly find a community of interests with those whose very existence depended upon checking the Revolution and stamping out its principles.

But if the French Revolution and the Napoleonic Era were potent sources of conflict among states over nationalism and social reform, they also gave rise to certain unifying forces. The European Concert of Powers had not existed in the eighteenth century because wars did not attain the degree of violence necessary to urge statesmen and monarchs to attempt to regulate the international conflict through institutional procedures.[1] The beneficent influence of the twenty-five year revolutionary period was its creation of a new sentiment against war. After 1814 and for the first time in history a conscious attempt was made at rudimentary international government, and the European Concert meeting several times after the Congress of Vienna to deal with threats to the European order was the expression of this novel effort.

I  In France the Revolution carried to final completion the gradual construction of a French nationality, and it crowned nationality with nationalism. The process was consummated in several ways. The Revolution occurred first in France because as de Tocqueville pointed out, France was the most advanced nation on the European continent.[2] Discontent with the old order was the product of the intellectual ferment of a developed civilization; because of the changes already inaugurated in French society, further change be-

1 See Crane Brinton, *A Decade of Revolution: 1789-1799* (New York, 1934), p. 85.
2 See Alexis de Tocqueville, *The Old Regime and the French Revolution*, translated by Stuart Gilbert (New York, 1955), Part III, Chapter 8.

came possible. The reforms of the Revolution, therefore, were not received with the apathy or outright hostility which greeted the centralizing and rationalizing measures of the Enlightened Despots in other European countries. The social and economic changes of the revolutionary period were approved, with certain exceptions, by the affected populations. The elimination of vestiges of feudal tenure was deemed apposite by the peasantry; the establishment of equality before the law was demanded by the bourgeoisie; and despite the Civil Constitution of the Clergy, a modest secularization of the social order was accepted by a nation which had long borne the heavy weight of ecclesiastical oppression. On the whole, the transformations of the Revolution were acknowledged by the populace, and these transformations unified public sentiment because they gave the separate fractions of society a stake in the maintenance of the revolutionary reforms.[3] As they became conscious that the new regimes were responsible for the gains achieved, it was natural for Frenchmen to support their new rulers more vigorously than they had their late monarch and the court nobility. Because government was responsible for manifest social improvement, they rallied to its cause.

The reforms achieved, however, were not the only cause of a new and more intimate relationship between governors and governed. Because the successive political reformations permitted greater public participation in and influence on government than before, the citizen was given a stake in the political order that was direct and immediate. No longer could it be claimed that the edicts of government were instruments of a ruling elite, untrammeled by public sentiment; the acts of government came to be viewed as acts of the citizenry, and the revolutionary French constitution of 1793 was ratified by a large popular majority. As popular will linked itself with the actions of its political representatives, tremendous support for the government ensued, as a consequence, the government came to be regarded as the head of a national society of Frenchmen, not, as in the case of the *ancien régime,* as ruler of a mere "geographical expression." In this sense, as many writers have seen, modern nationalism was inconceivable without the development of the doctrine of popular sovereignty.

[3] See R. R. Palmer, *The Age of the Democratic Revolution* (Princeton, 1959), particularly Chapter 15.

But if the recognition of a common governing head helped to make a nation of the French, nationalism also made representative government possible. A people cannot govern itself unless its boundaries are delimited, unless it has learned to think of itself as a body distinct from foreign nations. While government by one man is potentially world-wide in scope, government by a *people* requires a consciousness of both nationality and foreignness. As Lord Acton has written: "To have a collective will, unity is necessary, and independence is requisite in order to assert it. . . . A nation inspired by the democratic idea cannot with consistency allow a part of itself to belong to a foreign State, or the whole to be divided into several native states." [4] Hence, if nationalism was in part the result of popular government, it was also in part its cause. In either case the precise chronology is unimportant; what is important is that nationalism and popular sovereignty were mutually reinforcing.

As nationalism developed within France, it underwent a profound metamorphosis. In April, 1792 when France declared war upon Austria it was in terms of self-defense. "The National Assembly proclaims that the French nation, faithful to the principles consecrated by its constitution, 'not to undertake any war with a view to conquest nor ever to employ its forces against the liberty of any people,' only takes up arms for the maintenance of its own liberty and independence; that the war which it is forced to prosecute is not a war of nation against nation, but the just defense of a free people against the unjust aggression of a king; that the French nation never confuses its brethren with its real enemies; that it will neglect nothing which may reduce the course of war, spare and preserve property, and cause all the unhappiness inseparable from war to fall alone upon those who have conspired against its liberty; that it adopts in advance all foreigners who, abjuring the cause of its enemies, shall range themselves under its banners and consecrate their efforts to the defense of liberty, and it will promote by all means in its power their settlement in France. . . ." [5]

A scant eight months later the new National Convention took a different tone; humanitarian nationalism was transformed into Jaco-

---

[4] John Emerich Edward Dalberg Acton, "Nationality," in *Essays on Freedom and Power*, Gertrude Himmelfarb (ed.) (New York, 1955), p. 158.

[5] Cited in Carlton J. H. Hayes, *The Historical Evolution of Modern Nationalism* (New York, 1950), pp. 39-40.

bin nationalism, coalescent nationalism into expansive nationalism.
The new nationalism emerged in an odd amalgam of circumstance.
In the interim Louis XVI had been deposed and a republic organized; the nation had been under acute military stress until the "can-
nonade of Valmy" dissolved the Prussian offensive; the "September
Massacres" had provided a foretaste of the "reign of terror." And
yet, the propaganda decrees of November and December, 1792,
which gave expression to a new nationalism, were carried in an atmosphere of enthusiasm, unity, and triumph. After the Prussians
bumbled at Valmy, revolutionary armies conquered Savoy and Nice,
occupied Mainz and Frankfurt, and overran the Austrian Netherlands. Because of the divisions within France, an even more cohesive
nationalism was necessary; because of external triumphs a heightened nationalism was possible. Revolutionary conditions have a cu-
riously ambivalent impact upon nationalism. On the one hand they
must quicken the flow of common experiences and thus telescope
into a few years nation-building processes which would otherwise
take centuries.[6] On the other hand, as one student remarks, "Revolution implies . . . the speaking of a previously unheard of language,
. . . the emergence of another kind of logic, operations with other
proofs. . . . Each major revolution has used another style of argument, a way of thinking which pre-revolutionary men simply could
not conceive nor understand." [7] In one of its impacts then, a revolution speeds up and facilitates general communication; at the same
time it destroys and inhibits social and intellectual interchange.
When the division between the mobilized revolutionary population
and the underlying population becomes too great, nationalism must
weaken; when there is no revolutionary mobilization, the *ancien
régime* may consolidate itself. The revolution made the best of both
situations in the fall of 1792: French victories abroad facilitated general communication at home; and the political and intellectual
divisions within France were not so great as to forbid the creation of
new unifying symbols. Expansive nationalism provided the new
rallying cry; and the devotion to the *Patrie* supplanted at least in
part the traditional appeal of revealed religion. In December, 1792

6 Karl W. Deutsch, *Nationalism and Social Communication* (Cambridge, Massachusetts, 1953), p. 93.
7 Eugen Rosenstock-Huessy, *Die Europaeischen Revolution* (Jena, 1931), pp. 23-24,
cited in *ibid.*, p. 234, n. 10.

the National Convention reformulated French war aims: "The French nation declares that it will treat as enemies every people who, refusing liberty and equality or renouncing them, may wish to maintain, recall, or treat with the prince and the privileged classes; on the other hand, it engages not to subscribe to any treaty and not to lay down its arms until the sovereignty and independence of the people whose authority the troops of the Republic shall have entered shall be established, and until the people shall have adopted the principles of equality and founded a free and democratic government." [8] As one historian has noted: "In practice, this meant the overthrow of the established authorities, the abolition of the feudal regime, the sequestration of feudal and ecclesiastical property and the compulsory acceptance of the French *assignats*. In prospect, it meant the stirring up of rebellion in all the monarchies of the continent." [9] The French would force the rest of Europe to be free.

The circumstances in which expansive nationalism was first generated in France were similar to those surrounding the Reign of Terror. Historians have sometimes argued that the Reign of Terror was necessitated by the military peril to France, or that it was a preliminary manifestation of the struggle of the working classes against the bourgeoisie. But, in the first case, the Terror was inaugurated in an improving military situation. In September the Austrian advance was repulsed at Hondschoote, and two months later the Austrians were forced back toward Mainz; there was no need of a "terror" to ensure a victory already in progress. In the second case, the Robespierrists were not forerunners of proletarianism: they were lower middle class in character and scarcely thought in economic terms.[10] On the eve of the Terror "the situation . . . was hardly worse than the situation in the summer of 1792 had been: in a military way, things were far better than just before Valmy; internal dissension was a bit more open, but hardly greater; economic conditions, and especially the condition of the poor, if slightly worse in the cities than in 1788-89, were far better than they were to be later under the comparatively lax and unrevolutionary government of the Directory." [11] The new outburst of nationalism and patriotism associated

---

8 Cited in Hayes, *op. cit.*, p. 40.
9 Leo Gershoy, *The French Revolution: 1789-1799* (New York, 1932), pp. 48-49.
10 Brinton, *op. cit.*, p. 137.
11 *Ibid.*, p. 119-120.

with the Republic of Virtue and the military triumphs of the spring of 1794, then, cannot be explained solely in terms of the existence of internal and external enemies: a society which is attacked without and sundered within may as easily fall apart as become united. The greatest periods of danger to the new republic never coincided with the excesses of nationalism. It is worth recalling that expansive nationalism was abjured by the Committee of Public Safety when the crisis of the spring of 1793 was at its height. The propaganda decrees of the previous year were renounced and the Committee declared that "France would not interfere in any way with the government of other states." [12] Danton himself negotiated with the European Powers for an armistice, and action which later earned him the epithet, "traitor," not "patriot." Expansive nationalism could reclaim its hold on France only when new victories rallied the people and distracted attention from their divisions.

II As French nationalism moved from coalescent to expansive phases, it was bound to exert an important influence upon Europe. In Europe nationalism was not to be roused by the same process as in France; while French nationalism was linked with the development of the doctrine of popular sovereignty, nationalism in Europe was a reaction to French hegemony. It has often been assumed that the revolutionary incursion of one group into an area controlled or inhabited by another must lead to the development of nationalist feeling in the latter. This may be true where the second group already manifests the essential traits of nationality, for in this case the intrusion of another people is viewed as a "foreign" intrusion, and it must reinforce nativist sentiment. If a nationality is only imperfectly formed, however, a "foreign" intrusion may eventually succeed in pacification and in the assimilation of the aggrandized group. In Europe, on the eve of December 1792, it was difficult to know just what impact the French Revolution and the Napoleonic Empire would have. If it was possible that the French military intervention would provoke nationalism directed against the French, it was also possible that France would be able to assimilate new territories to the French nation. As the revolts in the culturally and economically backward Vendée had been put down, as Alsatians, Bretons, and Provençals had been assimilated, there remained the

12 Cited in Gershoy, *op. cit.*, p. 54.

possibility that other European areas could become and remain French. Certainly, there seemed a good chance that the border countries of France could be successfully amalgamated to the French Republic and Empire. In Belgium, Mainz, Savoy, and Nice the procedure involved four steps: French occupation took place; Jacobin Clubs were organized among French officials and willing local inhabitants; the clubs petitioned for annexation by France; and the Convention then formally incorporated the new area in the French Republic. The reforms of the revolution, both economic and administrative, were applied to the newly acquired region, and with the exception of periods in which the French were forced to retreat, the border countries remained a part of France until the overthrow of Napoleon. Despite rather highhanded treatment by the French, the border countries were docile under French rule, and did not revolt even in the waning days of the Empire. In the main, the social and legal reforms introduced by the French were retained after 1815.

In contrast to the grudging acquiescence accorded French reforms and rule in the border countries is the reception of the revolution in England. In general terms, the more advanced a people, the more readily it accepted French institutions and innovations, and the less likely it was, therefore, to develop strong nationalist sentiments against France. It was not accidental that the most profound nationalist revolt occurred in Spain while national movements animated Austria and Germany; nor was it surprising that the advanced border states patiently endured French domination without rebellion. Applied to England, this mode of reasoning would seem to suggest a ready enthusiasm for French reforms and for the Revolution; it might even lead one to predict a liberal alliance between France and England to advance the principles of the revolution. This *entente* was actually to occur later, but the impact of the Revolution was in a precisely opposite direction. The friends of the revolution, Paine, Priestley, and others, were exiled or execrated, and parliamentary reform was postponed for forty years. The reason for the hostile attitude toward the revolution was not that England was more backward than she seemed; it was that England was more nationalist than she seemed.[13] As popular sovereignty had been the engine of nationalism in France, the modicum of representative government in England had evoked national sentiments of considerable

13 See Boyd C. Shafer, *Nationalism: Myth and Reality* (New York, 1955), p. 137.

proportions. As Professor Trevelyan tells us: "In England alone was it possible to appeal successfully to the national spirit in war time, because in England alone, before the French Revolution, did the Government normally make appeal to public opinion." [14] At least from the times of the "Great Commoner" governments depended in part on the vagaries of public sentiment. There was a link between Government and governed in England which, however tenuous, was stronger yet than that which bound any other European people prior to the revolution.

Even English liberties were national in character. The issues between English patriots and Stuart kings in the seventeenth century revolved around the "rights of Englishmen" and the "privileges of Parliament" and were specifically related to the English historical and constitutional tradition; the issues between the *ancien régime* and the Revolution in contrast were universal in scope. It is slight wonder then that the French shibboleths of 1789, claiming universal significance, came into conflict with historic and national English principles. In Western Europe, where advanced social principles were not buttressed by nationalism, societies yielded to the even more advanced principles of the Revolution; in England, where advanced social principles were guarded by nationalism, French revolutionism could only provoke reaction.

The English reaction to the revolution proceeded in two stages. The initial response to the events of 1789 was not unfavorable, but when the great patriot Edmund Burke rallied the nation with his *Reflections on the French Revolution,* a nationalist anti-Jacobin tide set in. Burke was at pains to note the national character of English liberties: he saw these rights as an *"entailed inheritance* derived to us from our forefathers, and to be transmitted to our posterity, as an estate specially belonging to the people of this kingdom, without any reference whatever to any other more general or prior right." [15] Burke's nationalist rejection of the French Revolution gave vent to passions almost as unbridled as those evoked by the French patriotic support of it. Dissenters, exponents of parliamentary reform and republicans were subjected to every indignity; with the execution of Louis XVI and the coming of war in 1793 the anti-Jacobin movement

[14] George Macaulay Trevelyan, *British History in the Nineteenth Century and After (1782-1919)* (London, 1948), p. 73.
[15] Cited in Shafer, *op. cit.,* pp. 136-37.

reached a new intensity, and the Government itself embarked on a systematic persecution of unpopular opinions. The Tory reaction which ensued prevented any measure of reform for the entire period of the struggle with France.

The reception of the Revolution and Empire in Austria was similar to that in England, but for entirely different reasons. How much less successful would foreign conquerors be in striving to reorganize Austria, a polyglot empire which could not be reformed by its own rulers? Joseph II had labored to impose upon Austrian domains the very reforms destined to be accomplished in France with the Revolution; but his edicts made enemies among the nobility, aroused the bureaucracy, alienated the clergy, and even failed to gain the wholehearted support of the peasantry. Social, economic, and intellectual conditions in the Austrian lands had simply not advanced far enough to permit systematic reform. In the absence of a growing and articulate middle class the Habsburg realms endured their moderate thralldom, appeased by a benign climate and a plentiful food supply.

The campaigns and coalitions of the period placed France and Austria in almost permanent opposition. Each gain won by Napoleonic armies in the Netherlands, Savoy, Italy, the Illyrian provinces, and Poland was directly or indirectly at the expense of the Habsburgs. By 1808 even the Austrian populace was fired with desire and ambition to prevent another French victory at the expense of the Emperor: the incursions of the French had been justified and actuated by principles wholly alien to the inhabitants of Austria, and had been borne by a policy of intervention that was becoming insupportable. Accordingly, when all Austrian men between eighteen and forty-five who could carry arms were called to the defense of the fatherland, the Emperor's subjects reacted enthusiastically. New manifestos and literary appeals caused patriotic demonstrations in Vienna, the Spanish revolt was hailed as a praiseworthy example, and the French were decried as arch-enemies of German liberty. Before Austerlitz Habsburg subjects had not warmly supported war: before Wagram they were alive with patriotic and military sentiments. The War of 1809 was the first Austrian war to be fought "in the name of national identity and by an army based on conscription";[16] indeed, it might be said that the War of 1809 was the only struggle in which nationalism militated in favor of the unity of Habs-

16 Henry A. Kissinger, *A World Restored* (Boston, 1957), p. 18.

burg possessions, for ever afterward nationalism would be a factor auguring for the disintegration of the Austrian Empire. In any case the appeal to nationalism did not produce the desired victory over Napoleonic armies, and the peace that followed Wagram was the most far-reaching of the four French humblings of Austria.

In England, one of the most advanced, and in Austria, one of the most backward of European states, the revolution was greeted with hostility. Austria did not understand the revolution and could not sympathize with it; England understood it perfectly, but viewed it as an assault upon English nationalism. Spain's situation was different from both. Like Austria, Spain neither sympathized with nor understood the revolution: unlike Austria, Spain had to endure direct French rule. The generation of nationalist revolt was related to two conditions—the hatred of French government and the enforced application of that government. While England and Austria fulfilled the first condition, Spain fulfilled both. This is not to say, of course, that French internal reforms were carried out in Spain as they were in Italy and the Germanies because the degree of pacification achieved in Spain was never complete enough to allow the measure of French reorganization which occurred elsewhere. But Spain suffered under a French military rule far more drastic than the three months' French occupation of Austria. "Of all the western European peoples the Spaniards were the least disposed . . . to welcome the revolutionary program of reforms." [17] The landowners and the clergy were antipathetic to the French, and no middle class existed on which a structure of French reforms might be built. When Napoleon deposed the Bourbons and sent a French army into Spain, Spanish resistance flared. The raw French recruits were defeated by a combination of Spanish, Portuguese and English armies during the summer of 1808 and it was not until November that Napoleon was prepared to send 200,000 French regulars to recapture Madrid. But even after French successes and new Napoleonic proclamations, Spanish resistance did not cease and when organized opposition became impossible, guerilla war continued. That the Peninsular War was one of the most persistently unsuccessful French military operations during the Napoleonic Em-

[17] Geoffrey Bruun, *Europe and the French Imperium: 1799-1814* (New York, 1938), p. 161.

pire, is a partial tribute to the strength and ardor of a burgeoning Spanish nationalism.

In the Germanies, Napoleonic reforms were instituted with a vigor that was only exceeded in North Italy, in the border states, and within France itself. The Confederation of the Rhine had not only to endure French militarism, but social and economic transformation as well. In Belgium and the Rhineland, as in France, the manorial system disappeared without compensation; in the states adherent to the Rhine Confederation the peasants were required to pay indemnities to their former lords. Equality before the law was established, church and state divided, and religious toleration proclaimed. The guilds restricting productive enterprise were either abolished or reduced to impotency, and an entirely new administrative system created. "In general, in all countries of the Grand Empire, some of the main principles of the French Revolution were introduced under Napoleon, with the notable exception that there was no self-government through elected legislative bodies." [18] Where the ground had been prepared for the revolutionary innovations, opposition was slow to materialize; in South Germany particularly, the French had a profound and beneficent impact. Yet as French exactions multiplied in number and scope, the Germans became more reluctant to make the sacrifices necessary to maintain the revolutionary regime. In the end the ferment in the Germanies produced sentiment in favor of a war of liberation. The climax of this war, the battle of Leipzig, has been aptly called the "Battle of the Nations" because it signalized the first awareness of German nationalism.

The pattern of nationalism in Europe in reaction to the French expansion was largely determined by the antecedent character of social communication. Where pre-existing attitudes and communications patterns were entirely out of harmony with the revolutionary and enlightened ideas first engendered in France, French rule and reformation could not be accepted passively. In Spain, Austria, and to a lesser extent in the Germanies, peoples were not ready for the French reforms; they could not understand them or welcome the administrative upheavals which they involved; where anti-French nationalism reached its peak there was the greatest lack

18 R. R. Palmer, *A History of the Modern World* (New York, 1951), p. 404.

of comprehension of the new revolutionary language; hence, there was the greatest division between French and subject peoples. By contrast where social economic and intellectual conditions most completely approximated those in France, nationalism directed against the Republic or Empire did not emerge (except in England). Thus, the French did not automatically produce nationalism in each area they touched; and if the Vendée could assimilate itself to the revolution, so also could other regions of Europe. One historian writes that "national sentiments are stronger obstacles than provincial loyalties, and Europeans as a people had no sense of a common political bond." [19] But this conclusion assumes that national sentiments were already fully formed. In the Continental Europe of the revolutionary era, nationality was still incompletely developed, and the acceptance of French rule and regulation depended not upon national sentiments but cultural, political, and economic advancement. Where French reforms were appropriate, they were embraced and a process of assimilation with France began. That this assimilation did not succeed can be ascribed more to the military defeats of France than to any natural development of nationalism.

England, of course, was a special case. In social, economic, and intellectual terms the revolution was not out of harmony with English development. But in contrast to the continental countries, England already possessed the essential traits of nationality which would proscribe the revolution and denounce as "traitors" those who sympathized with its cause. In England a distinct and exclusive insular pattern of communication had developed which, though similar in content with that of the French, could never be amalgamated with it.

III   The development of nationalism in France and its communication to Europe vastly altered the conditions of international life. As nationalism became a pervasive fact of European diplomacy, it progressively undermined the moderation and cosmopolitanism of the previous age. It had two major impacts: the limited warfare of the eighteenth century was destroyed by a new militarism; the limited diplomacy of the old regime was replaced with a diplomacy of interventionism. While the benign balance of

[19] Bruun, *op. cit.*, p. 138.

power mechanism of the previous century had not sanctioned crusading intervention, the new system assumed that states could not
be protected without it. Nor were the tactics of intervention employed only by revolutionary forces: they were used by the tra-
ditionalists as well.

The conditions of militarism were revolutionized by the development of nationalism and patriotism. The *levée en masse,* or the
organization of social life for military purposes, was perhaps the
greatest innovation of the new means of warfare. No longer was it
true that only certain classes could be asked to serve in the armies:
no longer did militarism rest upon the limited revenue of prince
or monarch: no longer were the incentives of war punitive or
pecuniary. With the adoption of social equality, classes no longer
were supposed to exist and hence, there could be no rationale for
limiting military service to certain unproductive classes—consequently all were asked to serve. The existence of mass armies made
the elaborate calculation of risks less imperative. Armies were no
longer expensive and delicate mechanisms which could not be replaced: they could usually be supplanted by new levies on the home
front. The provisioning of the revolutionary forces was not restricted by the governmental coffers, for with the creation of a
nation in arms, the people themselves could be expected to contribute their money, their labor, or their lives for the national
cause.

But most important of all, the new nationalism provided an incentive for war which significantly changed the nature of strategy.[20]
The assumption of the *ancien régime* had been that soldiers had to
be well-paid or well-nourished or they would desert, but nationalism altered all that by providing payment in terms of patriotic sacrifice. The ordeals that might be required of an army fighting for

---

[20] "It was the French Revolution which opened the way. While the revolutionary
armies could not indulge in intricate maneuvers, they were free from conventional
limitations; they could endure privations and fight wherever it seemed advan-
tageous; they could attack regardless of cost in men because they could call upon
the total resources of the nation. This change in social conditions made possible
a highly mobile strategy. The divisional system developed; supply was largely
provided by requisition. In the battles themselves the individual could be relied
upon; deliberate fire, individually aimed, replaced or supplemented the rolling
volleys; *tirailleur's* tactics were adopted in order to prepare for the mass attack."
Hans Rothfels, "Clausewitz," in Edward Mead Earle (ed.) *Makers of Modern
Strategy* (Princeton, 1943), p. 97.

its *patrie* were of a different order from those that might be asked of an army fighting for pay. Since it was no longer necessary to take careful precautions against desertion, mass attacks and dispersed field or forest maneuvers could be and were often undertaken. The tactic of forced marches, an anathema under the old regime, was a prime means of concentrating French forces against the continental antagonists and thereby gaining many startling victories. Because of the national incentive unwieldy baggage trains and a complex system of supply magazines were not required at each juncture. Soldiers were willing to go hungry and to do without the elaborate paraphernalia of civilized life as long as they were fighting for their nation. Requisitioning replaced the dependence upon rigid supply lines, and the result made for a vast improvement in military mobility. As Napoleon found after his campaign in Russia, the major limitations of the new military system were not manpower or provisions, but military materiel. Now that the engine of democracy was pressing onward, it proved easier to replace the slaughtered recruits with new ones than it was to find new muskets, powder, and artillery pieces. After the development of nationalism the conditions of warfare depended more upon industrialism than upon political form.

Nationalism not only revolutionized the conditions of warfare, it also made draconic innovations in diplomacy. The signal character of the diplomacy of the *ancien régime* had been its refusal to countenance the destruction of the domestic constitution of another state. The three partitions of Poland remained exceptions to this broad rule, justified in terms of Poland's exclusion from the general European system and the exigencies of a revolutionary period. It is not surprising that there was such a general abstinence from interference with the internal constitution of states. In the absence of nationalism, intervention, demanding new sacrifices of the population, could have been no more endured by the invader than by the invaded. Even more important, in the international framework of the age, domestic subversion of another ruler would have seemed a breach of etiquette, a violation of the moderate canons of the era.

With the generation of nationalism, however, intervention became a principle of diplomacy. As Lord Brougham wrote in 1803: "Whenever a sudden and great change takes place in the internal structure of a State, dangerous in a high degree to all neighbours, they have a right to attempt, by hostile interference, the restoration of an order of things safe to themselves; or, at least, to counterbalance by active aggression, the new force suddenly acquired." [21] Paradoxically perhaps, the adherents of the old regime had to adopt revolutionary methods and to reform their policies after the model of Napoleon in order to survive. It was nationalism which first brought violations of the domestic order of Europe: the revolutionary armies of the Republic and the Napoleonic Empire not only assaulted the conservatives' armies, but their domestic constitutions as well. In response the leagued monarchs and aristocracies had to use interventionist methods against France despite their anti-nationalist attitudes. They had to intervene against France, in spite of their conservative character. Thus, even though the principles of the revolution and the nationalism which accompanied them could never be fully embraced by the defenders of the old regime, the conservatives had to use the methods to which they gave rise. From this point of view the theory of intervention and the principles of legitimacy were just as revolutionary as the theory of nationalism and the principles of the rights of man. When nationalism arose in France, it forced the continental monarchs to employ methods that were quite different from the traditional policies they had pursued during the eighteenth century.

IV The changes in inter-state relations produced by the Revolution and Empire, however, were not all to be explained by nationalism and its consequences. The Revolution injected into Europe new social, political, and economic principles that were to have profound effects upon international relations. Throughout the Continent and in England during the century before the Revolution, an aristocratic ethos had prevailed. And an important reason for the moderation of the diplomacy of the old regime had been the tacit agreement upon certain conservative social principles. When the ideas of social equality, minimum political rights, and economic liberalism emerged to challenge the aristocratic consensus, new frictions would inevitably follow. As long as the conflict over social principles was confined to the internal political realm, as it

21 Cited in Edward Vose Gulick, *Europe's Classical Balance of Power* (Ithaca, New York, 1955), p. 63.

had been during the eighteenth century, international relations would not be affected. But with the Revolution, France undertook to advance reforms in other states. In consequence, France, temporarily at least, could no longer be a member of the European system because she had broken the rules on which that system was founded. It was not surprising that Europe undertook to intervene against the Revolution even before it was apparent that there was any threat to the balance of power. France had become and would fundamentally remain a new political force in Europe. More important to the long-term future was the fact that France had implanted the seeds of social liberalism that would seek to make other Powers revolutionary as well. Where France moved, she brought the new regime with her, and the result was enclaves of liberal thought dotting the Continent. As we have already seen, the conditions for the acceptance of reform were most propitious where there had been social, economic and cultural advancement. In the low countries, the Rhineland, Switzerland, and northern Italy, the Revolution had its greatest impact: in the Confederation of the Rhine, Poland, and central Italy, the Revolution was less acceptable: in Prussia a moderate reformation occurred on the French example: in Spain and Austria, the revolution had least impact. During the Napoleonic era then, nationalism and liberalism were almost reciprocal quantities. Nationalism signalized cultural lag and a lack of comprehension for French reform, while liberalism suggested a preliminary enthusiasm for the French which waned as the economic and military exactions grew excessive.

Despite the separation of liberalism and nationalism during the revolutionary era, however, the two forces became linked after 1815. Nationalist movements did not become liberal, but liberal movements became national. In many instances, liberal movements could not be successful without a degree of national consolidation, and liberal reform in more than one country could not be obtained without overthrowing an existing regime which was also a foreign regime. As Lord Acton wrote: "At first, in 1813, the people rose against their conquerors, in defence of their legitimate rulers. They refused to be governed by usurpers. In the period between 1825 and 1831, they resolved that they would not be misgoverned by strangers. . . . No dispossessed princes led the Greeks, the Belgians, or the Poles. The Turks, the Dutch, and the Russians were attacked, not as usurpers, but as oppressors, — because they misgoverned, not because they were of a different race." [22] But not only was it true that liberal reform could often be secured only by jettisoning a foreign master. When liberal principles were adopted, the result would benefit nationalism as it had in France, and to the extent that liberalism was related to the doctrine of popular sovereignty, its application would lead to nationalism. In any case, as the causes of liberalism and nationalism advanced in increasing alliance with each other, the challenge to the old order could not be disregarded. The principles of the old regime were both anti-liberal and anti-national; the dynastic principles of the eighteenth century paid no heed to the national or linguistic character of a region. As new states adopted liberal or national principles, then, an almost inevitable conflict with the conservative monarchs ensued. Thus the French Revolution and Empire introduced into European relations conflicts of ideas, the like of which had not been seen since the religious wars of the seventeenth century. The new ideology contending with the old would eventually come to disrupt the free play of a balance of power mechanism. As we have seen, the balancing system enjoined states to combine or oppose each other on the basis of the distribution of power; when ideological issues arose, states could no longer decide their policies on power considerations alone; states might refuse to join their ideological opponents, or to align against their ideological allies despite dictates of the balance of power. A fundamental impact of the Revolution was to inject into the relative harmony of eighteenth-century relations, a conflict of ideas which was to affect, perhaps even determine European alignments until the middle of the nineteenth century.

V Despite the ultimate divisive impact of the revolution in terms of the ideological conflict and nationalism, the immediate result of the period of revolutionary hegemony was greater unity and the creation of a European Concert of Powers. If one can generalize from World Wars I and II and the Napoleonic struggles, it would seem that each great period of cataclysm and war gives rise to two antithetical forces: on the one hand it creates new conflicts which may cause future war; on the other, it impels statesmen and nations to try harder to avoid war, and thus to negate future war.

22 Acton, *op. cit.*, p. 155.

Each period of conflict develops tendencies which seek to repeat it and those which seek to abolish it. Thus, if the Napoleonic era fostered nationalism and an ideological antagonism, it also stimulated European statesmen to new efforts to avoid war. Certainly, in the minds of men of the mold of Castlereagh and Metternich, the twenty-year period of war and social conflict was not an adventure that one should lightly seek to reproduce in another decade. The revolutionary and Napoleonic contests had been far bloodier than any of the limited competitions of the eighteenth century, and they gave rise to an effort to regulate a conflict which could not have taken place during the old regime.

The irony of history was that this effort took place under adverse conditions. A European Concert of Powers meeting periodically to deal with threats to the peace and to the domestic order would have succeeded admirably in the eighteenth century when fundamental unity prevailed. There would have been no need to exalt a "principle of legitimacy" as governing maxim of statesmen and monarchs for the old regime was "legitimate." Just as it was not necessary to defend royal prerogatives with the theory of divine right until they came under attack, it was not necessary to erect the moderate conservative ethos into a principle of legitimacy, until revolutionary forces were undermining it. Legitimacy was not and could never be a policy *of* the *ancien régime:* it was a policy designed *to restore* the old regime. And in the same manner the policies pursued by the coalition against Napoleon in 1812-1815 were not the policies of a previously operating balance of power system; they were attempts to reinstate that system and secure it from revolutionary force. Because of this, the precepts of 1812-1815 were more fundamental, and perhaps more anxious, than the self-confident maxims of the old regime. Never before had a statesman striven to "legitimize" a coalition as carefully as Metternich in the waning days of the French Empire; the Austrian diplomat's insistence upon "acceptance," a felicitous conjunction of principle and possibility, indicated a concern with the system which the eighteenth century had not manifested.

But of course no matter how long Metternich, Castlereagh, and Talleyrand labored on behalf of a restoration of the old world, it never could really be restored. Napoleon could never be brought to accept a legitimate order, and all of Metternich's attempts to induce the French Emperor to moderation were in vain even at the very end. But even the elimination of Napoleon from the scene did not result in the permanent triumph of legitimacy, functioning through a European concert. Agreement upon the possible and the just could be attained among the Great Powers only so long as each had an important stake in the maintenance of agreement. Legitimacy functioned admirably so long as the Napoleonic presence served to remind the leagued monarchs of their principles but it became increasingly innocuous as the lessons of revolutionary war were forgotten. Nations tend to make the greatest effort to moderate or obliterate international conflicts at the close of a period of great strife. As peace ensues and the remembrance of war is obscured by the intervention of events, nations are no longer inspired by the effort and sacrifice necessary to keep the peace, and within a decade after 1815 the common concern for peace and cooperative agreement had largely vanished.

Even more important for the future of the Concert was the development of radical social principles, liberalism and nationalism, in opposition to legitimacy, conservatism and the dynastic order. The European Concert could operate only on the basis of ideological agreement: all major nations had to accept the principles on which the Concert would act or it could not act. As liberalism and nationalism burrowed into the European structure and nations came to act in defense of revolutionary principles, the Concert could rule no longer. This was the more true because of the extreme antagonism of conservative and radical principles. If "legitimacy" had symbolized agreement in the international sphere alone, it might have been made compatible with various social principles in the domestic order. But as "legitimacy" in the international realm forbade revolutionary change, "legitimacy" in the domestic realm was directed to the maintenance of the legitimate monarchs against insurrectionary upheaval. As the members of the Concert, working under the thrall of Metternich, tried to protect the international *status quo*, the principles of the Concert as applied within a state dictated a domestic *status quo* ensured against revolution.

Of course, it was in every way logical to extend the operations of the Concert to the domestic sphere. The Revolution in France had proved that domestic insurrection, unless checked, very quickly poses a threat to other states. The theorists of Vienna, seeking the root of the problem, equated peace with domestic tranquillity and sought to apply their remedy in the domestic sphere. In doing so, of course, they substituted an entirely new kind of international system, and they paid effective if mute tribute to the revolutionary example. If the principles of the revolution would subvert within, international force would be applied within; if revolutionary maxims sanctioned a crusading intervention in the domestic affairs of other states, legitimate maxims justified an equally crusading intervention to repress the revolution. In this manner, the revolution remade diplomacy in its own image, and the conservative monarchs, forced to defend themselves, adopted some of its central tactics. But to give official sanction to domestic intervention on behalf of international conservatism was to stimulate, not to repress, the new social forces. A conservatism of the *ancien régime* might have been endured because it left domestic affairs to the local inhabitants, but a conservatism of the Holy Alliance could only arouse the anger of liberals. Those states who were in principle inclined toward liberal and national principles would be more likely to embrace them fully in an atmosphere of international reaction, than in an atmosphere of international moderation. Paradoxically then, it was the great effort expended on restoring the old international system which virtually guaranteed its early demise.

VI    The system of international relations which prevailed between 1792 and 1814 was quite different from the eighteenth-century system. The eighteenth century had witnessed the perfection of the balance of power mechanism, and because conflicts were moderate and slow to reach an issue, the balance system was adequate to deal with them. The balance apparatus responded only to overt changes in the equilibrium of forces, and it did not form itself until power relations were in process of alteration. The rusty ponderousness of the balance system, however, could not be tolerated after 1792. The monarchs and aristocracies of the turn of the century were not dealing with an antagonist whose moderate diplomacy and limited warfare might be constrained by the old balance techniques. France, whether in the guise of Republic or Empire, was a revolutionary force on the European Continent, and it could not be handled by traditional means. The Concert of Europe, a logical expression of the developments of the revolutionary era, was designed to operate more quickly and more effectively than the old balance mechanism. An international conference could be called at the first domestic threat, even before that threat spilled over into the international realm, and it could use interventionist tactics of conservative internationalism to combat the interventionist tactics of liberalism and nationalism. Fundamentally, the struggles against the Republic and Napoleon and the assumptions of the European Concert reflected a vast cleavage of symbols in the international and domestic order. As long as nations are agreed upon the symbols which are to be advanced, a certain moderation in the conditions of international politics is possible: when, however, new symbols emerge to challenge pre-existing ones, the result is revolutionary force opposed to traditional force, and the revolutionary force must transform the nature of the traditional force, if the latter is not to suffer an untimely death. Thus, the revolutionary era did not, as many writers have thought, manifest the operation of a balance of power system. It reflected, rather, the attempt to restore a balance system which had been undermined; and it sought to re-establish a symbolic unity that had been shattered. As long as that unity was not repaired, a balance apparatus, implying fundamental agreement, could hardly function.

In the result, the international system of the revolution and imperium was a fundamentally unstable structure. The disruptive challenges of the revolutionaries and of Napoleon could not be contained or blunted by the balance of power device. The conservatives, until the very end, were helpless before Napoleon's onslaughts. The consequences of the system were distasteful or repugnant to most if not all of its participating members. International outcomes could not be held within acceptable bounds.

There could be no doubt that a new international system had emerged. The objectives and techniques of foreign policy had been completely revolutionized. The aims of the Napoleonic empire were the domination of Europe; the methods were national war, the *levée en masse,* and unlimited diplomacy. The old proscriptions on domestic intervention were cavalierly overthrown. After the French Revolution international politics were conducted in a manner very different from that of the old regime.

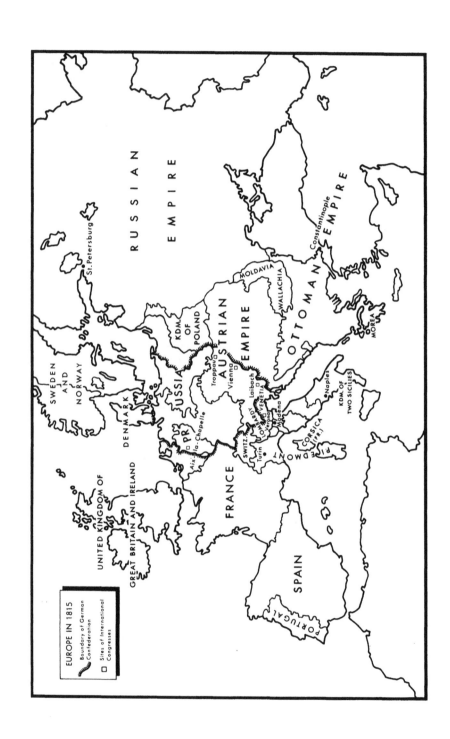

EUROPE IN 1815

Boundary of German Confederation

Sites of International Congresses

SWEDEN AND NORWAY

St. Petersburg

RUSSIAN EMPIRE

DENMARK

UNITED KINGDOM OF GREAT BRITAIN AND IRELAND

PRUSSIA

Aix-la-Chapelle

KDM. OF POLAND

AUSTRIAN EMPIRE

Troppau

Vienna

Laibach

SWITZ.

LOMBARDY-VENETIA

Turin

Verona

Modena

PIEDMONT

CORSICA (FR.)

MOLDAVIA

WALLACHIA

OTTOMAN EMPIRE

Constantinople

MOREA

Naples

KDM. OF TWO SICILIES

FRANCE

SPAIN

PORTUGAL

## chapter four

# AN INTERNATIONAL INSTITUTION

The year 1814 represents an important division in the history of modern international relations and diplomacy. It marks the ending of an era of war and revolutionary upheaval; it marks the beginning of a century which saw no general European war. It would be to argue *post hoc ergo propter hoc* to attribute the halcyon character of the age to the Concert of Europe which was constituted in the Quadruple Alliance of November 20, 1815. It would be superficial to overlook the significance of the precedent thus established. International institutions do not, in and of themselves, preserve international peace and tranquillity; they do often manifest an inchoate force which tends in that direction. In addition, they have an elemental persistence which makes nations and peoples pay attention to them even after their greatest usefulness is at an end.

The Concert of Europe was created at a uniquely favorable time. The ravages of war and revolution demanded a new effort for peace and domestic stability. The repression of revolutionary liberalism and the triumph of militant conservatism made for a temporarily united view of political and international realities. A common conservatism facilitated the achievement of agreement in the councils of the European Concert. Even the philosophic fashions of the age railed at the doctrinaire rationalism of the Enlightenment and fostered a new attention to traditionalism and romanticism. The perfection of man would not be attained by the application of reason to social processes; it would be found immanent in regular historical development. In 1760 the past was not a standard to be observed in the future: in 1814 it was a prime *desideratum*. Even the peoples themselves were ready for a period of stability and order. The French endured the restoration of the Bourbons for a fifteen-year period. The English put up with the mismanagement of the old Tories for a similar time. The revolutionary impulse, it seemed, had been at least temporarily quelled.

This did not mean a relapse into the methods and policies of the old order. The conservatives could not dispatch their opponents by the moderate techniques of the old regime. Domestically they adopted the system of police surveillance used by Bonaparte, internationally they sanctioned intervention and war for conservative purposes. Eschewing the old system of balance of power, they created a new Concert of Europe capable of dealing with threats to the peace and the domestic order before the international balance had been upset. Instead of returning to calculations of pure material power, they relied upon a new ideological harmony of self-conscious conservatism to assure the peace.[1] The old theory was that the real danger to the European order stemmed solely from a revision of the relationships of material interest; the new theory watched besides for any breach in the solidarity of social ideas. Liberalism would be opposed even before it had led to a change in the material position of the Great Powers. Material power was only the necessary, not the sufficient, criterion of diplomatic action.

The new international institution which issued from these considerations had a fundamental impact upon the structure of international relations. National and state interests now had to be formulated in accordance with institutional formulae. Methods of action had now to include the international conference. Whatever a state did, it had to be prepared, ultimately, to face a conference and to defend its actions before an international assemblage. Policies calculated in terms of historic interest had to be reconsidered in the light of institutional precepts. In short, though institutions are at their inception the result of antecedent forces, they soon come to have a measure of independent impact upon the course of events.

[1] This is not to say that power factors were discounted. The early discussions at Vienna had to come to grips with the problems of British maritime supremacy and with Russian territorial ambitions. See J. H. Pirenne, *La Sainte Alliance* Vol. I *Les Traités de Paix, 1814-1815* (Neuchâtel, 1946), Part II, particularly Chapters Six, Seven and Eight.

Who could understand the diplomacy of the interwar or of the post-World War II period without reference to the League of Nations or to the United Nations? In similar fashion the diplomacy of the period following the Napoleonic wars cannot be grasped without a consideration of the role of the Concert of Europe. And perhaps surprisingly, the Concert continued to meet to ratify the facts of international existence after it had ceased to have an important influence on them. The stamp of multilateral approval which it provided was still deemed necessary.

I An observer recalling Pitt's proposals for Parliamentary Reform and the extent of English liberties prior to the French Revolution could easily conclude that the impetus for liberal change would be resumed after 1815. One could believe that it was the war with France, demanding conservative cohesion and firm opposition to revolutionary liberalism, which alone postponed reform. Yet, after 1815 the progress toward liberalism in England was not immediately resumed; indeed, the first years after the war were noteworthy for their black reaction. If the middle classes had not been pressed from the left, this probably would not have been the case,[2] and movement in a more liberal direction might have begun at once. As it was, the "lower orders" of society could no longer support the burdens which the long regime of war and the dislocation resulting from its end placed upon them. The sudden restriction of the market for war and war-related industries, the return of half a million men from the fields of battle, the precipitous decline in the prices of agricultural commodities which had been artificially supported by the Continental System, and the general introduction of labor-saving machinery contributed to the increasing misery of the toiling classes. The inequitable and regressive structure of taxation and the bad harvest of 1816 compounded the impoverishment of the workingman.[3] These failings of the social and economic order may not have produced a genuine revolutionary ferment, but they did incline the English toiler toward more radical action—as it was, the Luddites sought to destroy machinery, and

[2] See H. W. V. Temperley, "Great Britain (1815-1832)" in A. W. Ward, G. W. Prothero, and Stanley Leathes (eds.) *The Cambridge Modern History*, Vol. 10, *The Restoration* (Cambridge, 1934), p. 573.

[3] *Ibid.*, pp. 575-576.

bread riots were frequent. In November, 1816 a mob at Spa Fields rioted, stormed a gunsmith's shop, and killed its proprietor. The combination of events frightened the middle classes, the bulwarks of reform sentiment, into alliance with the old aristocracy. Soon afterward, Parliament prohibited all public meetings and suspended the writ of habeas corpus. When the economy wavered again in 1819, a new wave of unemployment occurred, followed by a resurgence of radical agitation. A vast meeting at St. Peter's Fields was dispersed by a squadron of cavalry, and in the ensuing mêlée eleven people were killed and several hundred injured. The so-called "Peterloo Massacre" led to the passage of the Six Acts, "the most repressive laws Great Britain had known for generations." [4] It was not until after Castlereagh's suicide in 1822, that the British Government was to move once again toward reform.

The conservative reaction in Great Britain made limited cooperation with the continental allies possible, and it postponed the ultimate political impact of the French Revolution. Britain could work, at least to a restricted degree, with the other conservative states as long as British conservatism held sway, although she would find it impossible to maintain constant cooperation with the continent when political reform was the order of the day. Castlereagh understood continental problems and continental statesmen perhaps better than any previous English Foreign Secretary, and the intimacy of insular Britain and Continental Europe was perhaps more complete than at any previous time.

In France, the restored Bourbon regime of Louis XVIII tried to avoid the extremes of reaction but most often succumbed to the attacks of the ultra-royalists. The Constitutional Charter of 1814 was vague and inconsistent on the important questions of effective representative government and ministerial responsibility. Could the king govern by himself, or was predominant authority vested in the legislature? The French people themselves seemed remarkably indifferent to these questions; they were lukewarm toward their Bourbon monarch and equally passive to the Emperor during the 100 days' interlude.[5] After Waterloo and the exile of Napoleon, a royalist reaction seized the country and a chamber *"plus royaliste que le roi"* presided over a kind of white terror. The Allied

4 Frederick B. Artz, *Reaction and Revolution, 1814-1832* (New York, 1934), p. 125.
5 *Ibid.*, p. 129.

Powers were so afraid that the Ultras would provoke a new revolution that they persuaded Louis to dissolve the *Chambre Introuvable* in September, 1816.

The events of the following six years seemed to show that there was no majority in France for a moderate constitutional monarchy. Between 1816 and 1820 the king managed to maneuver an unsteady course between the Scylla of reaction and the Charybdis of liberalism, but extremism of both sorts was a growing force. Left and Right sometimes linked to challenge the Center, and the Center itself saw its adherents joining Right or Left. Benjamin Constant, who originally supported the monarchy, moved increasingly toward the Left. The Ultras sought increasing popular support by demanding an extension of the suffrage. The Royalists of 1816 realized even before Louis Napoleon and Bismarck that the enfranchisement of the peasants was an effective reactionary device. After the assassination of the Duc de Berri, the reaction resumed in earnest. Richelieu carried through a new press law which decreed a general, if temporary censorship, and he supervised the passage of an electoral act which in effect gave the highest fractions of society a double vote. "This Law of the Double Vote greatly increased the power of the government to influence elections and assured the political domination of the landed aristocracy." [6] The decade of conservative pre-eminence after 1820 meant that the only avenue of reform was through revolution.

The success of the exponents of the *ancien régime* guaranteed political cooperation with the conservative victors of 1815. The royalists in France even desired a continuance of the Allied occupation as an insurance against the Left. In these circumstances France, potentially the most radical Power on the continent, could cooperate with the arch-conservative states. In the years immediately following the end of the Napoleonic wars, both France and England were won for reaction and this victory permitted a brief period of highly successful diplomatic activity for the European Concert. Ideological *confrères* could establish a degree of intimacy unattainable among states of varying political complexions.

Political solidarity was not the only factor which smoothed the work of the Concert. The aftermath of disastrous war often witnesses a new effort at collective action designed to forestall future

6 *Ibid.,* p. 224.

war. The years between 1814 and 1822 constituted such a period. The very recentness of war enjoined a new consultation upon European Powers. Entirely aside from political and ideological factors, the European Concert began its period of decline when the remembrance of war began to blur. The European states were willing to make sacrifices to maintain the peace only so long as they retained a vivid recollection of war. For eight years this image was held in the mind's eye; thereafter it rapidly faded.

II The Congress of Aix-la-Chapelle met in 1818 without the historic tasks of the Concert having been defined. Britain, as an insular Power, could afford to take the most facile interpretation of the causes of the revolutionary wars.[7] Despite the Continental System, Britain had perhaps suffered less than the continental antagonists of Napoleon, she was aware that European affairs affected her at best indirectly. She could therefore tolerate a quasi-isolationism which would have been an expensive luxury for Austria or Prussia. A continental despot had to transform the European balance and build a navy before the British Isles were threatened; the continental expansion of a European state, however, could only take place at the expense of one of the established Powers. In matters of continental hegemony the British interest was always secondary, the European primary. Hence, the British Cabinet could assume after 1815 that the Vienna Settlement and the Quadruple Alliance were designed primarily, even exclusively, to deter a new threat from France.[8] The Central Powers, on the other hand, were convinced that it was not France alone, but the revolution which they should oppose. The British were concentrating on France, the past foe, while the continentals were preparing for revolution, the threat of the future. The assumption that France would constitute the only danger for the European peace was convenient for the English. If France was the only potential miscreant, a pacification of France would secure the peace for years to come. After revolutionary tendencies had been extirpated in France, the British could return to their quondam unconcern about affairs of the continent.

There was another reason for different international assumptions prior to the Congress. British conservatism functioned in the con-

---

[7] See Henry A. Kissinger, *A World Restored* (Boston, 1957), p. 215.
[8] See Harold Nicolson, *The Congress of Vienna* (New York, 1946), p. 260.

text of constitutional monarchy and representative government. British institutions, though both corrupt and archaic, were amenable to liberal reform. Representative government having been established in principle, the change from conservative to liberal political principles merely awaited a change in the basis of representation. Unlike France, where the *ancien régime* had to be revolutionized, Britain and her institutions merely had to be reformed. A political and social change was necessary in the first case, a technical alteration in the electoral machinery would suffice in the second. Though the British were adamant conservatives in the period between 1814 and 1822, therefore, they never had to fear the type of social revolution which haunted the European apostles of the old regime. While constitutionalism and representative government were bugbears in central Europe, they were traditional and congenial in Great Britain. British institutions were implicitly and incipiently liberal though the conservatives had traditionally controlled them. European institutions were implicitly conservative and would be destroyed by a liberal regime. Again, the English could adopt a superficial approach to the problem of war. Because of their insularity they could focus their attention on France; because of the insulation against revolution they could ignore revolutionary currents elsewhere. Castlereagh was much more sympathetic to the problems of the continental monarchies, but he was hamstrung by the attitude of Cabinet and people. As one writer had phrased it, ". . . the Congress of Aix-la-Chapelle not only brought to a focus the difference among the Allies regarding the interpretation of the international order, but also the incompatibility of Castlereagh's intentions with what he could legitimize domestically." [9] The British, through their Foreign Secretary, had authored the system of regular conferences enshrined in Article VI of the Quadruple Alliance, but they were the first to go back upon it. Even Castlereagh could not bring himself to look upon the Concert of Europe as a means of suppressing social revolution; he looked upon it only as a method of political consultation. [10]

Aix-la-Chapelle effectively disposed of the major causes of future war so far as the British were concerned because it dealt with the problem of France. On October 2, 1818 it was agreed to withdraw

[9] Kissinger, *op. cit.,* p. 221.
[10] Nicolson, *op. cit.,* p. 224.

the allied force of occupation from France and on October 12th the four Powers renewed the quadripartite alliance and secretly pledged themselves not to allow France to become a member of it. Nevertheless, to appease French feelings, it was decided to permit France to participate in the regular conferences of the Concert of Europe, sanctioned under Article VI. Thus, the Congress of Aix-la-Chapelle, by making a final disposition of French issues remaining from the late wars, gave the English less reason to participate in the affairs of the Concert thereafter. If France was the cause of war and France had been reformed, to what profit the Quadruple Alliance? It was foreordained that when Tsar Alexander proposed an *Alliance Solidaire,* guaranteeing both territorial integrity and internal institutions of the Vienna Settlement, the British would demur.[11] The British Cabinet was agreed on the principle of nonintervention in continental affairs, and the Tsar's draft treaty demanded wholesale intervention. Castlereagh argued that the mere existence of domestic revolution could not justify intervention to repress it; in each case the Powers would have to consider whether the danger was so great that intervention was required.

In this sense the British were returning to an amended balance of power system while the continental states were espousing a streamlined Concert. The British wanted the balance system with political consultation under the conference mechanism. They believed there was no need to act until an overriding danger had arisen. Political consultation would merely afford an occasional investigation of threats to the peace and their significance; the Concert would not act until the balance had been upset. The continental concern, on the other hand, was precautionary.[12] The European monarchs looked on the Concert as an inchoate international government, designed to act at the first alteration of domestic institutions. They would act while the structure of material power was unchanged: the British would wait until it had been transformed. The differences of the two views reflected the real balance of security in each case. Though England was virtually impregnable,

11 See Pirenne, *op. cit.,* Vol. 2, *La Rivalité Anglo-Russe et le Compromis Autrichien, 1815-1818* (Neuchâtel, 1949), pp. 366-368.

12 Nicolson, *op. cit.,* p. 262.

domestically and externally, the continental states were in grave danger on both heads.

III The revolutions of 1820 in Spain and Naples which presented the new Concert of Europe with its first direct challenge could hardly have been predicted from the events of the Napoleonic generation. *Prima facie,* it seemed that revolutions would occur first in those areas where liberal principles had been most completely accepted. This pointed to revolutionary ferment in France and its border states, and conditions of internal peace and stability in Spain, southern Italy, and Russia. In fact, of course, revolutionary tides were the product of two factors: the presence of liberal myths and the context of unyielding reaction. Where moderate liberal sentiments confronted a moderate conservative regime, there might be no revolution; where moderate liberal sentiments were faced by a total return to the *ancien régime,* revolution remained a possibility. Spain and Naples could not be explained on the first count, but the second had a measure of application. This is not to say that liberal ideas were popularly accepted in either country; since in both cases the revolution was the work of a very small fraction of the population.

There was another factor which helps to explain the developments in southern Europe — the predominance of military influence in both revolutions.[13] In Spain, Ferdinand VII was resolved on a course of adamant reaction and political corruption. Commerce and industry lay in ruins, the Treasury was bankrupt, and the army and navy went unpaid and starving. The King had the audacity to issue an ordinance which forbade the military to complain when it did not get its pay.[14] The officers of the army had come into contact with liberal ideas during the war of independence with France, and the military was the only fraction of society with the power and discipline necessary to carry through a successful revolution. In Naples, Ferdinand IV had virtually made himself an Austrian vassal, while applying in internal affairs the

---

13 See Raphael Altamira, "Spain (1815-45)" in *The Cambridge Modern History,* Vol. 10, p. 210, and Carlo Segré, "Italy," *ibid.,* p. 112. Also, H. G. Schenk, *The Aftermath of the Napoleonic Wars* (New York, 1947), pp. 151-52.

14 Schenk, *op. cit.,* p. 141.

twin principles of despotism and subornation. Only secret societies could conspire to overthrow the oppressive regime, all legal avenues of reform having been closed. The Carbonari, the most influential and extensive of these clandestine groups, was composed in part of landowners and the prosperous middle class, "but the majority of its members were soldiers who hoped for advancement, provincials, lawyers in search of employment, and finally, those who, by reason of their political views or of the positions which they had occupied during the French *régime*, were opposed to or mistrusted the Government of the Restoration." [15] The pre-eminent role of military men in both the Neapolitan and Spanish revolutions is in part explained by the concrete grievances caused by a depressed economy and unemployment for the returned soldier. It must be partly attributed, however, to the impact of armies with a broadened popular participation upon a hierarchical social structure.[16] Mass participation in warfare tends to introduce an equalitarian element in an important fraction of society which may lead to equalitarian movements elsewhere. In this sense, the military participation ratio in a society may have a direct impact on the degree of social stratification.[17]

In any event, the revolutions in Spain in January and in Naples in July, 1820 were primarily military in character and did not reflect an irresistible tide of popular sentiment. Indeed, the Spanish word *pronunciamiento* (insurrection) describes the outbreaks of 1820 more aptly than the English "revolution." There was no comprehensive overturn of the established order engineered and sustained by the general population. The risings of 1820 succeeded more as a result of the ineptitude and procrastination of the central authorities than as the results of their own strength. When the new regimes were faced with the opposition of a determined foe, they collapsed. There is no greater contrast than that between the heroic resistance of the Spanish people to the French invader in 1808 and its mild submission to French armies in 1823.[18] The French were resisted when they sought to instill a revolutionary

[15] Segré, *loc. cit.*, pp. 111-12.
[16] See Schenk, *op. cit.*, pp. 143-44, 153, and Stanislaw Andrzejewski, *Military Organization and Society* (London, 1954), pp. 63-64, 106 and Chapter 2, *passim*.
[17] Andrzejewski, *op. cit.*, p. 73.
[18] See Altamira, *loc. cit.*, p. 228.

liberalism, whereas they were supported when their purpose was to restore a conservative regime.

The challenge of these two upheavals to the Concert of Europe could not be overlooked, but they were bound to elicit different responses from different states. Castlereagh's attitude was as preordained as that of the continental monarchies. The British would not intervene in Spain to suppress the revolution, nor did the Foreign Secretary approve the idea of an early conference to consider the matter. The alliance was made against France. "It never was . . . intended as an union for the government of the world or for the superintendence of the internal affairs of other States." [19] Spain held no threat to the peace of Europe — militarily, she was the least dangerous Power in Europe. As to "the principle of one State interfering by force in the internal affairs of another in order to enforce obedience to the governing authority. . . . No country having a representative system of Government could act upon it, and the sooner such doctrine shall be distinctly abjured as forming in any degree the basis of our Alliance the better. . . ." [20]

The continental autocrats, on the other hand, worried by the very existence of an unquelled revolution in their midst, supported intervention. The French wanted another conference, the Russians declared for intervention even before the revolution in Madrid had been consummated, and Metternich was deeply shocked at the turn of events. When the Neapolitan revolution occurred, jeopardizing the Austrian position in all Italy, it was clear that Austria would have to act, alone or in concert. Castlereagh would countenance a separate Austrian intervention to put down the revolt in Naples, but he was averse to any joint action there. Metternich tried to hold the Concert together by preventing it from meeting; if it convened in conference, the British would be absent because they would not enter into consultations whose object was the undermining of the principle of nonintervention. Metternich tried to square the circle by seeking to persuade the Tsar that allied unanimity was so complete that a conference was not necessary to demonstrate it, and at the same time implicitly accepted Castle-

---

[19] Cited in C. K. Webster, *The Foreign Policy of Castlereagh, 1815-1822* (London, 1925), p. 238.
[20] Cited in *ibid.*, pp. 239-40.

reagh's assumption that the division in the Concert was so complete that a meeting could not repair it. Despite all his efforts, in the end Metternich yielded to the Tsar in preference to Castlereagh. A five-power conference was called at Troppau for October to consider the situation in Spain and Naples.[21] Castlereagh could not sanction plenary British participation, though by sending an observer, a formal rupture with the Continent was postponed.

Though Castlereagh was loath to proceed to a final break with the continent, it was clear that the results of Troppau would be hardly to his taste. Metternich had striven vainly to write a formula which would enshrine the British doctrines of nonintervention, but the result reflected Russian programs and designs. The protocol said nothing about the desirability of nonintervention but inveighed against "the evil with which the body social is menaced." [22] It went on to declare that States which had undergone revolutionary change ceased to be part of the European Alliance, that the Allied Powers would refuse to recognize any such change, and that "when States where such changes have been made, cause by their proximity other countries to fear immediate danger, and when the Allied Powers can exercise effective and beneficial action towards them, they will employ, in order to bring them back to the bosom of the Alliance, first friendly representations, secondly measures of coercion, if the employment of such coercion is indispensable." [23] The only concession to the English attitude was the stipulation that "friendly representations" would be the first method employed. The British and the French ambassadors at the conference refused to consider signing the protocol. The British declined because of non-intervention, and the French did likewise because they still harbored certain liberal sentiments. The regime of Louis XVIII was in its most moderate phase, and even before the conference opened the French had declared that they would not countenance any unilateral Austrian intervention in Italy — indeed, they obliquely hinted that separate Austrian action might oblige the French, against their will, to ally with the constitutional cause in Italy. The

---

[21] A military revolution after the Spanish model had occurred in Portugal in the interim, but it was assumed that this nation remained in the exclusive preserve of British action.

[22] Cited in Webster, *op. cit.*, p. 295.

[23] Cited in *ibid.*, p. 295.

French were now aware that intervention by the Holy Alliance had not been a wholly beneficent phenomenon between 1815 and 1818; they were not willing to see this precedent acted upon elsewhere. The French, like the English, had sent only an observer to Troppau, and they were no more enamoured of the *Protocol preliminaire*. When the Concert proposed to act upon the protocol in respect of Naples, an Anglo-French abstention seemed automatic.[24]

The conference reconvened at Laibach in January, 1821 to hear the pleas of Ferdinand IV and to authorize an Austrian expedition to remove the limitations upon royal power. Stewart, the British observer, was all outraged innocence when he found that the Allies were about to sign a new declaration which emphasized European solidarity against the revolution and omitted to mention the British reservation. In the end, however, Metternich's triumph was complete. Ferdinand's liberties were restored by the prospective Austrian intervention, and Metternich had obtained the blessings of all major Powers but England to his enterprise. Even the British were more opposed to the mode of the decision than its content. Castlereagh circulated a memorandum in opposition to the Troppau protocol in January, but he did not deny Austria's right to intervene. Indeed, the British minister expressed his government's "strong disapprobation of the mode and circumstances under which [the Neapolitan] Revolution was understood to have been effected," [25] but went on to state that while the British would not intervene themselves, "Austria and the Italian Powers, might feel themselves differently circumstanced." [26] Castlereagh proceeded to instruct his representative that the different ways in which the Allied Powers had viewed the questions at hand should not be allowed to "produce some abatement in the cordiality of their union, which, upon all points really embraced by treaty, you will always regard and declare to subsist in full harmony and vigour." [27] While the British

---

24 As it happened, the French Ambassador at the Congress of Laibach was much more reactionary, and though his views were not entirely approved of by the French Government, they could not be disavowed for fear of outcries from the Right. At Laibach the French agreed with the three Eastern courts and the British had to go their separate way.

25 Cited in Webster, *op. cit.*, pp. 321-22.

26 Cited in *ibid.*, p. 322.

27 Cited in *ibid.*, pp. 323-24.

were at one with the Allies in the results of Austrian pacification
of Italy; they were at odds over the means employed to secure it.

IV  While deliberations were still continuing at Laibach, Pied-
       mont was convulsed by a new revolutionary outbreak, per-
haps the first genuinely nationalist insurrection. Piedmont had
been incorporated into the Greater France set up by Napoleon
during the Empire, and had readily adapted to French Rule.[28]
The efficiency of the French military and bureaucracy appealed
to elements of the Italian soldiery, and it was the military garrisons at Allesandria and Turin which took the lead in the revolt.
The insurrection was not directed primarily at Victor Emanuel;
the demand was for the Spanish Constitution of 1812 and for
war against the Austrian oppressors. And the rallying cry at the
beginning of the revolution was "Long live the King." [29] Piedmontese leadership was not decried, and was asked to support a
war on Austria which would permit a heightened liberalism. Since
liberal reform could not be accomplished without nationalist reform, any liberal cause had also to espouse a national revolution
against the Habsburgs. Victor Emanuel could not bring himself to
support the insurrection and break his promises to Austria, but
at the same time he could not take up arms against his country-
men. His alternative was abdication in favor of his brother, Carlo
Felice, and this course was adopted.

Carlo Felice was at Modena, and he temporarily entrusted the
Regency to Carlo Alberto, son of Victor Emanuel. The Prince was
aware that he should await the decrees of the new King, but,
pending command of the new sovereign, he allowed the revolutionaries to proclaim the Spanish Constitution. The exultation of the
populace was unrestrained but short-lived, for in five days the new
monarch sent decrees from Modena annulling the new constitution
and directing Carlo Alberto to leave Turin. Rather than side with
the insurgents against the King, the Prince acceded. At Novara
loyal and insurrectionary armies clashed; the former, aided by the
Austrian troops, won complete victory, and the reaction had triumphed in Italy. The French and British now had second thoughts

28 See Geoffrey Bruun, *Europe and the French Imperium, 1799-1814* (New York,
1938), p. 112.
29 Segré, *loc. cit.*, p. 116.

about the desirability of oppressive regimes, and, after witnessing the stern measures of the new monarch, declared informally to Victor Emanuel that they would be glad to see him resume the Piedmontese throne. This was, of course, out of the question, but the proposition itself is effective testimony to the two Powers' incipiently liberal sentiments.

The Congress of Laibach ended on a note of compromise. Britain was still party to the treaty structure and would not desert her allies despite the disagreements over the treatment of Italy. Metternich, recognizing that Britain could not completely endorse his Concert-mandated intervention in Naples and Piedmont, at the same time strove to keep open his British connection. Despite all the Tsar's promptings nothing had been done about Spain in deference to the British protest, nor was France disposed to intervene. While Metternich had used 100,000 Russian troops as a reserve behind Austrian action in Italy, he had restrained Alexander's urge to intervene in Spain. Metternich maintained the link between the Eastern and Western ends of the alliance.

V A new threat to the unity of the Concert emerged as the Congress of Laibach was drawing to a close. In March, Prince Alexander Ypsilanti staged an uprising against Turkish rule in the Danubian provinces. The Greeks hardly could have expected massive popular support in this area for they were in effect the feudatories of a hated Turkish regime.[30] But they did hope that an insurrection in Wallachia and Moldavia would draw the Russians in against the Turks. In this belief, they were misled, and Metternich played the theme of solidarity against the revolution once again, and Alexander temporized. In June, the Turks crushed the abortive revolt in the duchies. As it happened, however, the uprising in the Danubian principalities was merely a prelude to a much more pervasive revolutionary movement in Morea. The Greeks, though they had never endured French rule, had been much influenced by French ideas and propagandized by French agents during the Napoleonic wars. The ideas of liberty and nationality seemed to have particular application against the alien Turkish rule and its infidel

[30] See W. Alison Phillips, "Greece and the Balkan Peninsula," in *The Cambridge Modern History*, Vol. 10, p. 180, Kissinger, *op. cit.*, p. 290, and Webster, *op. cit.*, p. 353.

religious doctrines. Turkish rule was perhaps the most unen-
lightened in Europe, and the infusion of revolutionary ideas created
an explosive situation. The revolt in Morea, perhaps the first truly
popular revolution since 1815, sought political and religious reform by way of national reform. By the end of 1821 "the whole
Vilayet of the Morea had passed from the obedience of the Sultan,
and the insurrection had spread beyond the Isthmus of Corinth,
throughout continental Greece, and over the mountain passes
into Thessaly and Macedonia." [31] In reply, the Turks slaughtered
the Greek community in Constantinople, and the Greek Patriarch
was hanged at the entrance of his cathedral. This was an affront
that Alexander could not overlook. "The issue . . . resolved itself
into a contest whether the maxims of a legitimizing principle could
defeat the claims of national interest." [32]

The Greek question raised the contradictions of the Tsar's mind
and demanded a final resolution. Alexander's attitudes were a
refractory amalgam of enlightened despotism, religious mysticism,
and revolutionary liberalism. His romantic and mystical sentiments
could be turned to support the revolution, and they could be deflected into rank conservatism. The Tsar's agents in different countries had worked for reform as well as reaction. His policy in
Naples and Piedmont at first seemed to be: "Quell the revolt so
that reform can take place under conditions of stability and internal peace." Implicitly, the Tsar sought to take away with one
hand what he was granting to Metternich with the other. At
Troppau, to be sure, the Russian enigma had accepted a protocol
enshrining conservatism and unanimity against the revolution,
but those paper sentiments remained to be tested. Greece was their
ordeal by fire.

Unexpectedly, Metternich found a new ally to help keep the
Tsar on the conservative path. Castlereagh rejoined the alliance
with a burst of enthusiasm when Greece raised the Eastern Question anew. Britain could afford to be indifferent to Italy, where no
vital interests were at stake, but she could not stand by and see
control of the Eastern Mediterranean fall into the hands of the
Russian Emperor. A Russian threat to the Near East would ultimately jeopardize India. Thus, Castlereagh's "empirical" policy

[31] Phillips, *loc. cit.*, p. 180.
[32] Kissinger, *op. cit.*, p. 292.

permitted him to take a position which could never have been allowed on "theoretical" grounds. Resistance to Russian pressure on Turkey did not follow from an abstract devotion to the *status quo* and monarchial conservatism; it followed from the challenge to a concrete British interest. What Castlereagh had to persuade the Tsar to do was what he himself would not have considered— the sacrifice of an "empirical" interest at the altar of "abstract principle." Thus, though the only British interest in maintaining the integrity of the Porte was a practical one, Castlereagh's expostulations to the Tsar had to be couched in theoretical terms. The Greek revolution was a "branch of that organized spirit of insurrection which is systematically propagating itself throughout Europe, and which explodes wherever the hand of the governing Power from whatever cause is enfeebled." [33] While Britain did not hesitate to pursue its interests, Castlereagh asked the Tsar "to afford posterity a proud manifestation of your Imperial Majesty's principles . . . by exercising toward this . . . semi-barbarous state that degree of magnanimity which a religious . . . respect for the system which your Imperial Majesty has so powerfully contributed to raise in Europe could alone dictate under such provocations." [34] The Russian Emperor was being asked to support the very "system" and "principles" which six months previously Castlereagh had sought to undermine. Castlereagh was implicitly invoking the *Protocol préliminaire* which had been the cause of the British demurral at Troppau.

The pressure on the Tsar increased when Castlereagh and Metternich agreed to meet for separate talks in Hanover. It was agreed at these discussions that British and Austrian representations would be made individually at St. Petersburg, and that the Porte would have to be persuaded to accept a measure of reform. The more intransigent the Sultan, the harder it would be to sway the Tsar from a warlike stand. After a series of notes at the end of 1821, the Russians sent to Vienna an emissary from whom Metternich finally succeeded in eliciting a statement of the maximum Russian demands and also in amending them so that they might be accepted by the allies. In May, the Turks were finally induced to accept Metternich's reformulation of the Russian

33 Cited in Webster, *op. cit.*, p. 360.
34 Cited in Kissinger, *op. cit.*, p. 295.

demands, and the Tsar capitulated by rushing to resume diplomatic relations with the Porte. Through the subtle but unremitting pressure of Britain and Austria, the Tsar accepted a doctrine of self-limitation. He discarded the dictates of historic interest at the behest of legitimacy and the European Concert; in so doing he reversed the British hierarchy of values as exemplified at Naples. The general took precedence over the specific.

VI   The final triumph of the European Concert in the Greek question was but a prelude to increasing desuetude. The Spanish revolt had not been dealt with, and the Congress of Verona which opened in October, 1822 would see a British rupture with the Concert. They would not sanction interference in Spanish internal affairs, and they were finding it increasingly difficult even to attend the conferences of the Concert of Europe. The British attitude toward the international institution formed in 1815 had never been exactly the same as that of the continental monarchies. After 1822 it became even more unique. British insularity sanctioned a parsimonious view of cooperation with the continent. An island Power need intervene in world politics only when an "overriding danger" or a threat to its concrete interests develops. Castlereagh, therefore, could ignore Naples and Piedmont and refuse to consent to European interference in Spain.

At the same time an insular state can afford a remarkably poor memory. Because England was nearly invulnerable, she could forget the dangers of the Napoleonic period much more rapidly than the continental states. After Aix-la-Chapelle, Britain rapidly became oblivious of the need for continued general cooperation. By 1822 it was difficult to induce Britain to participate in the conference system on any terms, even the most innocuous. Verona was originally intended merely as a convenient ratification of the Tsar's capitulation over Greece; England would lose nothing from attending; she would gain a European imprimatur for her policy in the Near East. And yet, by 1822, "the *fact* of participation in *any* European Congress was becoming increasingly difficult to legitimize." [35]

It was not only the insular isolationism of Great Britain which made for a rift in the Concert of Europe. For all of Castlereagh's

35 *Ibid.*, p. 308.

conservatism, there was a political gulf between Britain and the three Eastern courts. Castlereagh was the keystone of a political arch uniting a British Parliament and European continent which were moving apart. The continental pier stood for continuing participation in conference diplomacy for general purposes; the keystone supported continuing participation in conference diplomacy for *specific* purposes; the Parliamentary pier increasingly balked at all forms of cooperation. When the trembling structure collapsed, Castlereagh's mind went with it. He committed suicide on August 12, 1822. The political cleavage which the final breakdown represented was summed up in the doctrine of nonintervention. Intervention was not an evil for an autocratic monarch who had learned Napoleonic tactics. His own regime enjoyed no constitutional limitations; it might, in theory at least, be altered at will. Domestic intervention *within his own regime* was the admitted privilege of every continental despot, but the British Constitution could not admit the right. Constitutional limitations circumscribed the powers of the British monarch and proscribed his personal intervention. To allot to a foreign royalty an authority not permitted to the British monarch was a slight in practice and an anomaly in theory. Thus political constitutions and political ideologies were important antecedents of the rift with the continent. Though the *content* of British government was conservative, its *form* was fundamentally liberal.

And yet, despite the eventual cleavage between Britain and the Continent, and despite the ultimate liberalization of France, the European Concert functioned admirably between 1814 and 1822. For the first time in modern history, an international institution operated to restrain conflict. The doctrine of legitimacy was the keynote of this cooperation, and in its various phases, it was accepted by the five great Powers. It represented an attempt, in the first place, to achieve international transformations through acceptance.[36] This effort was a novel one: the Napoleonic era did not conform to its maxims because Napoleon conducted a revolutionary diplomacy and mode of warfare. Since the Corsican's claims were universal and unlimited, they could not brook the limitations

[36] See *ibid.*, pp. 20-21 and Chapter 17. (The author is happy to acknowledge the influence which Professor Henry Kissinger's excellent study, *A World Restored*, has had upon his ideas here and elsewhere in this chapter.)

of legitimacy; Napoleon would act whether or not his actions were internationally "accepted." The eighteenth century did not adhere to its standards because self-conscious "acceptance" was unnecessary. "Acceptance" was a natural phenomenon in the old regime; it did not have to be secured; it was an immanent, not an explicit principle. Legitimacy became imperative only when acceptance was in doubt, and only when revolutionary tides had challenged the old order, did it become necessary actively to seek consensus. Metternich's diplomacy did not restore an older world; it built a new one. This mode of legitimacy was acknowledged by Castlereagh, though it was eventually denied by the British Cabinet. Whatever the objection to Troppau and Laibach, Castlereagh would not desert the Alliance, and though he would not sanction the methods used, the result was prospectively approved. From the British point of view the structure of legitimacy did not crumble until Verona.

The efficacy of legitimacy was even more marked in the case of Russia. In the negotiations of the spring and summer, 1822, the Tsar was brought to subject Russian traditional interests to the dictates of an international consensus. He would not intervene against Turkey without Allied consent, and when "acceptance" could not be attained, traditional policies were sacrificed. Legitimacy won an overweening triumph over the Tsar in the Greek question. Metternich, perhaps, made fewer sacrifices of interest at the altar of legitimacy than the other statesmen because Austria had fewer concrete interests. For the Austrian Chancellor, the Habsburg interests were not predominantly regional or historic; they were logical. Austria occupied a central position in post-Napoleonic Europe, and she depended upon maintaining the agreement of the flanks. Any disturbance of the equilibrium would rattle the Habsburg house, and this was precisely why Austria could not afford the luxury of concrete interests or spheres of influence. Since her interest was the universal one of general peace and stability in Europe, she could not ask in addition for areas of special consideration.[37] It followed that any disturbance of the European repose would constitute a direct threat to the entity of Austria,. and yet, even this overriding interest was sometimes subordinated to the general requirements of acceptance. The Spanish

[37] This statement is subject to qualification when applied to Italy.

revolt was a challenge in principle to the basis of Habsburg rule, but it was at least temporarily ignored when the Alliance could not legitimize intervention. Metternich made his real sacrifice at Troppau where, to maintain his British connection and the participation of Castlereagh in the structure of general agreement, he temporized on Spain. Metternich, for all of his vain pomposity did not ask of others what he himself was not willing to concede.

There was a second sense of "legitimacy" which emphasized method less than result. The form of legitimacy was acceptance; its content was the maintenance of conservative domestic institutions. Ultimately there was to be a conflict between the two senses of the term, but for eight years the contradiction was obscured. The French, with an occasional wavering over Piedmont, were won for moderate conservatism between 1814 and 1821; after 1822 reaction set in with a vengeance. They could, therefore, accept, and indeed, insist upon legitimate internal institutions; they could agree that the Concert should seek to preserve them. The British agreed in principle but not in practice. They wanted the maintenance of conservative institutions, but they could not agree that the Concert should have this as its primary function. Ethically, conservatism was just; politically, the Concert should do little about it. The Russians for a time shared an opposite conviction: ethically conservatism was bankrupt; politically, the Concert should seek to preserve it. Until Troppau, the Russians were potential incendiaries; their object was an international conservative mechanism which should set the conditions for domestic liberal reform. At Troppau, the Tsar abandoned his vague liberal sentiments and placed himself under the moral guidance of Metternich. In a very real sense Metternich ministered to the Tsar's moral conscience as the Baroness von Krudener enlivened his sense of religious exaltation. And yet in the end, it was the Tsar who exposed the internal contradictions of legitimacy. If legitimacy was a method, enshrining agreement, then nothing could be done to alienate the British, and the British would have become the determinants of the Alliance; if legitimacy was a result, enshrining conservatism, then the revolution in Spain had to be suppressed. The Tsar opted for the latter interpretation in October, 1822 and the British were driven from the Alliance.

VII The eight-year period after the Napoleonic wars witnessed a ruthless and efficient repression of the forces unchained by the French Revolution. Neither nationalism nor liberalism was permitted to disturb the European equilibrium. Nationalism was not visibly present in the revolts in Spain and Naples, and its first outbreak in Piedmont was rapidly dispatched. In Greece nationalism was an undoubted force, but as a result of the decision of 1822 it seemed that it would truly burn itself out "beyond the pale of civilization." Liberalism had also been checked by an international agency. The military revolt in the Kingdom of the Two Sicilies was put down by Austria acting under the international mandate of Troppau and Laibach; the military revolt in Spain was put down by France acting under the international mandate of Verona. Conservative internationalism extended even to the principles of domestic governance.

The temporary triumphs over liberalism and nationalism delayed the final impact of the Revolution. An international class of aristocrats and landowners briefly governed Europe, and the result was a unique conservative solidarity. The "natural" conservatism of the eighteenth century was rationalized into an explicit moral, social, and international code, and the conservatives tried harder than ever before to prevent divisions among them. If it is true that each major period of war and revolutionary change gives rise to antithetical tendencies—tendencies which seek to prevent subsequent war and tendencies which seek to cause it, then certainly, the first were concentrated in the eight years after Vienna. But the revolutionary tides could not be dammed forever, and eventually, neither domestic nor international dikes could contain the flood. When liberal and nationalist actors began to play on the world stage, the Concert of Europe would be profoundly affected. The Concert depended upon a conservative consensus, and its solidarity would be weakened when England and France adopted a more liberal attitude.[38] The Concert also depended upon

[38] Professor Albrecht-Carrié remarks: "From the long-term point of view and in regard to Europe as a whole, Britain and France had much in common; they represented, broadly speaking, what may be described as the liberal tendency in opposition to the conservative and reactionary emphasis that held sway in the Eastern Great Powers of Austria, Russia and Prussia." *A Diplomatic History of Europe Since the Congress of Vienna* (New York, 1958), p. 17.

an international consensus, and its effectiveness would be reduced when nationalist forces came to shape the policies of major Powers. The eighteenth century had been an age of internationalism, and the nineteenth century after the brief interlude of European unity, would be an age of nationalism. International institutions inevitably would suffer neglect and frustration in such a period.

This is not to say that the Concert was abolished in 1822. Once a habit of consultation has been established, it is difficult to break.[39] The Concert continued to function after 1822 but its activities were more directed to ratifying international facts than to changing them. In the years to come the Concert provided the official sanction for the Greek settlement, and for Belgian independence, but the threads of decision were fast escaping it. In 1818 the Concert was the *prima ratio;* in 1839 it was the *ultima ratio.* The uniqueness of the period after 1814 is that for the first (and perhaps the last) time, the conviction that war and its evils had to be eliminated was strengthened by a common ideological consensus. After the Napoleonic Wars, Russia, Prussia, Austria, France, and England could cooperate intensively for a brief period; after the Great War, a liberal France and England were soon confronted by Fascism in Italy and Germany; after the Second World War, the apparatus of cooperation foundered almost immediately on the ideological rock dividing the Western Powers from the Soviet Union.

Between 1814 and 1822, however, an international system of remarkable flexibility and power briefly functioned. The new international Concert operated to prevent domestic disturbance from causing international strife. It was able to regulate domestic affairs for international purposes, and the framework of consensus it provided ensured against disruptive actions by national actors. If the eighteenth century exemplified the most limited and moderate challenge to international stability, the functioning Concert displayed the most potent regulative agency for disturbing forces.

---

[39] Professor Artz takes a harsher view: ". . . the first serious experiment in international government ended in failure. It was not, however, without some far-reaching results; it introduced the idea of cooperation among a group of powers and of personal conference among a number of statesmen, and it established the idea of common interests among the nations. Unluckily there never grew out of the alliance any real machinery to prevent the great catastrophe that closed the nineteenth-century epoch." *Op. cit.,* p. 172.

The world has not witnessed equally stable systems in the time that has elapsed since 1822.

The Concert, moreover, introduced a new strand in diplomatic practice and technique. It could operate only if the objectives of states were more or less harmonious. It could prevent or inhibit conflict only if nations deferred to it. That it succeeded on both counts is a reflection of the enormous change in world politics that occurred after the Napoleonic regime. The consultative mechanism of the Concert was testimony to the new moderation of national objectives and efficiency of international techniques.

## chapter five

# THE TRUNCATED CONCERT

Despite the British divergence from the Concert in 1822 and afterward, the international institution was neither abolished nor destroyed. In truncated and spasmodic fashion it continued to function during the period 1822-1848. It no longer effectively controlled international developments, but it did pass eventual, if sometimes belated, judgment upon the course of events, and it did manage to hold Europe together in a framework of intermittent co-operation. In several respects it is surprising that this should be the case. As the incipient liberalism of France and England became overt and as the three Eastern courts continued their conservative legitimacy, one could expect the Concert to fall apart from internal division. How could reactionary and liberal states work together for international purposes? This query is reinforced when the assumptions of the prior functioning Concert are recalled. The Concert of Metternich and Castlereagh had worked because of a solidarity of idea, but the Concert of Metternich and Palmerston could hardly work because of a difference of idea. If conservative ideology was prerequisite to the success of 1814-1822, how could an ideological conflict conduce to co-operation in 1822-1848?

The answer in part was that the cleavage of ideas had not yet become total.[1] British liberalism was tempered internationally by the need to maintain a continental bulwark against France, the

---

1 See Gordon Craig, "The System of Alliances and the Balance of Power" in *The New Cambridge Modern History*, Vol. 10. *The Zenith of European Power, 1830-70*, (ed.) J. P. T. Bury (Cambridge, 1960), p. 266.

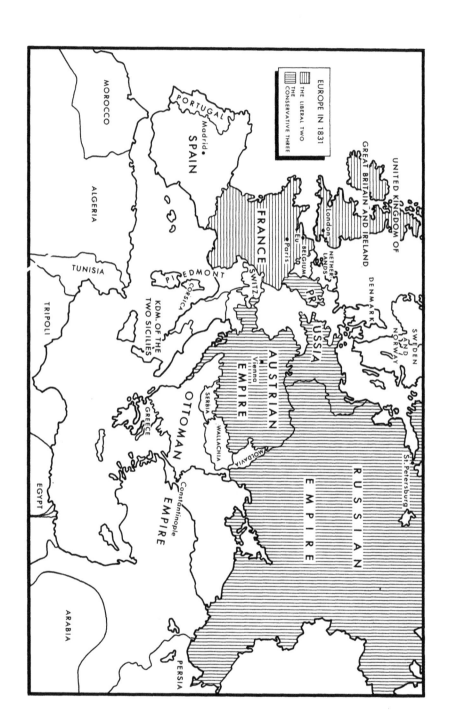

late antagonist of 1815. French liberalism expressed itself in revolutionary bursts and was not in this period a stable determinant of policy. But the failure of the ideological split to take the center of the stage was not the only reason for the continued if desultory work of the Concert. The Concert also had usefulness in the context of disagreement. The Concert was a mechanism which, logically speaking, was devoid of political content. Despite its legitimist background, the instrument of co-operation could be used for liberal as well as for conservative purposes. If Metternich could use the consultative mechanism for reactionary purposes, Palmerston might use it for more liberal ones.[2] The dominant diplomatic personality could turn it to his own ends. An international conference with its *point d'union* in London would have had a different outcome from a conference at Vienna or Petersburg. In this *dénouement* there is a paradox: Canning, that mediator between despotisms and democracies and follower of Burke, sought to end the method of periodic consultation: Palmerston, that avowed partisan of constitutional states, sought to revive it. The distinction was a difference over the political character of intervention and non-intervention. For Canning, intervention was a conservative doctrine, a means of support for reactionary regimes, and a method of undermining constitutional ones. Nonintervention on the other hand, was a liberal device. Since intervention was most likely to be used by the three Eastern courts to repress movements for constitutional reform, nonintervention was the correct policy for the incipiently liberal England. In the early stages of the Greek revolt, in Spain, and Portugal, and in the New World the potential interveners were reactionaries. Nonintervention in these circumstances was a benign and liberal doctrine flowing from the principles of 1688. England would not accept intervention in her own affairs, nor would she meddle in those of others. For Palmerston, intervention eventually became a liberal doctrine. Because revolutionary forces were in the ascendant, the conservatives could not maintain the dikes, and the political equipoise was reversed. The conservatives held the balance of forces in 1820, the liberals in 1830. In Greece, in Belgium and in Italy the liberals were the most likely intruders. Thus, the difference between Canning and Palmerston was as much

2 See Sir Charles Webster, *The Foreign Policy of Palmerston, 1830-1841*, Vol. 1 (London, 1951), pp. 80-81.

apparent as it was real. For the former liberal inclinations dictated nonintervention, while for the latter liberal sentiments required intervention. While Palmerston paid lip service to the principles of his master, Talleyrand is reputed to have said that "non-intervention was [for Palmerston] a metaphysical and political phrase meaning almost the same thing as intervention." [3]

As a result, the developing gulf between liberal and conservative principles (the former increasingly represented by England and France and the latter manifested by the courts of Russia, Austria, and Prussia) did not lead to the precipitate end of the Concert. While France and England began to use the conference system to legitimize liberal intervention, the conservatives did not withdraw from it. This fact is in itself surprising. If Canning had proclaimed nonintervention when he was sure that its instruments would be controlled by reactionaries, why would not the continental monarchs leave the Concert as it came under the sway of constitutional states? Nonintervention could be as much a conservative as a liberal doctrine. A part of the reason for continuing participation in the system of consultation was that the liberals in this period did not succeed in achieving the total control of the Concert mechanism which the conservatives had obtained in the past. Liberals did not win triumph over conservative forces in the period 1822-1848; they merely were able to contend with the reaction on a more equal footing. Thus the Concert never became the proprietary possession of the liberal camp, and the conservatives never had to give it up. What one finds in this span of twenty-six years is a limited struggle for the control of an international institution.

But it is more than this. Because neither group of states had attained political predominance, neither had the strength to act alone in all situations. Thus the contests within the Concert were not waged by war. Conscious of its own deficient strength, each group wished to win over the opposing faction to its point of view and wished to obtain the sanction of the Concert for its policy. Inevitably, the meetings of the great Powers were an odd combination of co-operation and conflict. Co-operation was necessary for the protagonists often hesitated to act alone; but conflict was intrinsic because of the difference in political attitude. The continued if restricted functioning of the international mechanism,

[3] *Ibid.,* p. 99.

then is testimony to the intermediate character of the age. In 1818 the Concert operated in a context of ideological harmony; in 1848 it perished in a context of ideological division; in 1839 it muddled through in a context of temporary compromise.

But the spasmodic working of the Concert cannot be attributed only to the moderation of the ideological conflict. It must be explained as well by reference to factors of historic interest. Only when the preoccupation with ideology became primary would the Concert falter. As long as liberal nationalism and conservative dynasticism did not between them dominate the international stage, co-operation was possible.[4] In the Eastern Question, an area of historic concern to both despotic and constitutional Powers, the lines of ideology were blurred. Castlereagh and Metternich were convinced that the Ottoman "Sick Man of Europe" could be treated and cured, and they sought to restore his vigor. Canning did not wash his hands of Turkey, but he could not resist the appeals of public opinion to do something for the Greeks. Anglo-French co-operation with Russia against the Turks was the result. Palmerston started out believing that Turkey would crumble, and his pro-Greek sentiments were well-known. Later, however, he became convinced that if the invalid were allowed to die, the ensuing Russian or French gains in the Near East would be intolerable.[5] The result was a violation of ideological frontiers in the East. Canning co-operated with Nicholas I in 1827 in an *entente* that was primarily liberal on the one hand, and governed by interest on the other. Palmerston opposed Thiers in 1840 as a result of an old fashioned conflict of interest. In this manner the promptings of interest led to temporary alliances across ideological boundaries and to temporary frictions within them. While in this period European diplomacy was often characterized by hostility between the Two (England and France) and the Three (Russia, Austria, and Prussia), there was no such thing as a monolithic liberal or conservative alliance.[6] Furthermore, the very prevalence of ques-

---

[4] Craig, *loc. cit.*, pp. 246-247.

[5] Webster, *op. cit.*, p. 82.

[6] Palmerston wrote in 1836 that the cleavage in Europe was "not one of words, but of things, not the effect of caprice or of will, but produced by the force of circumstances. The three and the two think differently and therefore they act differently." Quoted in Craig, *loc. cit.*, p. 246. See also Hajo Holborn, *The Political Collapse of Europe* (New York, 1957), pp. 34-35.

tions of concrete interest made the work of the Concert easier than it might have been. An important part of the moderation of the system of international relations of the eighteenth century was to be explained on the basis of the primacy of interest and the absence of conflicts of idea.

There was still another reason for the efficacy of the Concert in the generation after 1820. Though the fear of a resumption of war had declined since Vienna, it still had a profound hold on the European nations. The wars of Napoleon had been, or so the conservatives believed, revolutionary and eminently popular in character. Prolonged or general war, then, might lead to a new outbreak of revolutionary violence. Militarism was, from a certain point of view, to be as much feared as liberalism. The monarchs knew that their peoples would not fight wars of national liberation on behalf of conservatism and the old regime; in these circumstances a desperate war with a Liberal Power might be the engine of revolution in the conservative monarchies.[7] It was an odd paradox that those states who were best prepared to fight after 1814 were perhaps least disposed to do so. The Russian army was the largest in Europe, the Prussian military machine was on its way to becoming the most efficient, and the Austrian military was an effective professional force. But while Prussia was beginning to learn the lesson of Napoleon in its creation of the *Landwehr*, France seemed inclined to forget it. The Law Gouvion St. Cyr of 1818 provided for small annual conscription levy but it "laid down the basic principle of a small professional army, sedulously cultivating the *esprit militaire*." [8] The days of the *levée en masse* were apparently forgotten. The continental autocrats shrank from a general war not only because of its assumed incendiary impact, but because their forces had enough to do in dealing with insurrections at home. A new and general war in Europe would be an expensive luxury for an Austrian force that had to keep order in Italy and Hungary, as well as for a Russian or Prussian force that might have to do service in Poland. The fear of revolution reinforced the fear of war.

---

[7] See E. L. Woodward, "The Age of European Peace and the Character of European Wars," in Gordon B. Turner (ed.) *A History of Military Affairs Since the Eighteenth Century* (New York, 1956), p. 66.

[8] J. P. T. Bury, *France, 1814-1940* (Philadelphia, 1949), p. 25.

In the more liberal countries, on the other hand, armies were neglected because of an opposite ideological premise. Conservatism railed against war in the East as liberalism railed against armies in the West. The liberal philosophy prescribed retrenchment and a reduction of governmental activity, and the reform movements almost always demanded economy. In 1850 Cobden could state a premise of previously implicit British thought: "The progress of freedom depends more upon the maintenance of peace, the spread of commerce, and the diffusion of education, than upon the labours of cabinets and foreign offices." [9] The liberal philosophy, at this juncture, was primarily international only in its economics. Its political focus was domestic. It tended to divert attention from the international political issues which had agitated the Napoleonic generation. Despite what the conservatives believed, war was not at this stage thought to be a means of advancing the liberal movement. [10] The seeds of liberalism sown in the domestic soils of all European countries would germinate without external cultivation when the conditions were propitious. England neglected its army and consequently, "when the Duke of York died in 1827, he could not be given a military funeral, because, as Wellington reported, there were not enough troops in England to bury a field-marshal!" [11]

Despite their liberal attitudes, England and France could contemplate war with a cavalier spirit. For a period after the burst of revolutionary and reformist energy in 1830 neither France nor England feared revolution, nor were they afraid of the contagion of nationalism. Both could without great alarm envision a war of revolutionary consequence. Canning never ceased pointing out that if Britain entered into war, "she will see under her banners, arrayed for the contest all the discontented and restless spirits of the age, all those who . . . are dissatisfied with the present state of their own countries." [12] Canning could be abrupt, Palmerston bellicose, and Thiers unyielding. And thus there emerged a strange contrast be-

[9] Quoted in A. J. P. Taylor, *The Trouble Makers* (Bloomington, Indiana, 1958), p. 53.
[10] After the Revolutions of 1848, on the other hand, it was more difficult for France to resist liberal appeals for help. See Craig, *loc. cit.*, p. 263.
[11] George Macaulay Trevelyan, *British History in the Nineteenth Century and After (1782-1919)* (London, 1948), pp. 173-174.
[12] Quoted in Harold Temperley, *The Foreign Policy of Canning, 1822-1827* (London, 1925), p. 581.

tween Eastern and Western militarism. The more liberal states were hardly prepared for war and yet could posture and provoke, while the conservative states were ready and yet had to temporize. The West had will but no means, the East had means but no will. The end result was peace. Where warfare was impossible, diplomatic virtuosity was at a premium. Cobden inveighed against the "labour of cabinets and foreign offices," but his own doctrines made their work essential. Since warfare was unfeasible, the diplomatic virtuosity of an international Concert assumed a renewed importance.

I The international institution, however, did not have its old resiliency. Its operation was impeded and sometimes checked by the growing force of liberalism and nationalism. In its heyday from 1814 to 1822 the Concert had quashed the revolutionary legacy of Napoleon, and in the generation following the liberal and national movements often had their victories. While the functioning Metternichean Concert had dispatched revolts in Spain and in Naples, and contained the one in Greece, the Concert of Canning and Palmerston gave independence to Greece, sustained the constitutional cause in Portugal, and ratified Belgian freedom from the Dutch. The Concert continued to meet, but it had no single-minded purpose. When liberal and nationalist movements reached their apogee and ideological conviction was placed above the general peace, the Concert failed. First the Concert prohibited both freedom and war, later it allowed liberty but not warfare, and still later it succumbed to both.

Napoleon inadvertently set the stage for the national and liberal actors. Nationalism was initially a force in opposition to French hegemony, and liberalism was in the first place a force in favor of it. At the beginning the reactionaries were Napoleon's opponents, the liberals his friends.[13] It was not surprising then that after 1814 liberalism was strongest where French rule had been the most pervasive. Liberal sentiment existed in South Germany and North Italy, and even the Prussian monarch had to promise the granting of a constitution. But liberalism in these areas soon began to develop in alliance with nationalism. In Germany the Napoleonic administra-

[13] See Geoffrey Bruun, *Europe and the French Imperium, 1799-1814* (New York, 1938), Chapter Six.

tion had imparted an awareness of the benefits of unified and efficient rule. The Holy Roman Empire had been destroyed and the *code civile* applied to its succession states. The popular nationalism directed against Napoleon in the War of Liberation, partly peasant and partly agrarian in character, had been tinged with reaction. The popular nationalism directed against the resurgent conservatives in the years following was tinged with reformism, and had in part a bourgeois character. The nationalists of 1809 and 1813 were by and large not the nationalists of 1848. In Italy, the French Empire showed the advantage of a rule too liberal for the returning Austrians to accept. In the one case the French planted the seeds of German unity, in the other they engrained national revolution against the Habsburgs. In Germany the conservatives installed an enveloping system of oppression under the tender ministrations of Metternich. In the Habsburg realms the Austrian Chancellor encouraged national diversity.[14] This was in many ways a revolutionary policy, but it was an inescapable result of the conservative dilemma. The Habsburgs could not nationalize for fear of losing territory, nor could they centralize for fear of local resistance. In the end, Metternich believed that the centralizing tendencies of liberalism could be met by concessions of power to the periphery. He also seems to have thought that the growing German and Magyar nationalism could be countered by an even more localized nationalism. Joseph II had failed to centralize the monarchy; Napoleon had centralized it by force and Bonapartist liberalism; Francis II gave up the attempts at centralization altogether, since the efforts could have succeeded only at the expense of his political conservatism. Thus, the policy of historical revival of the provinces of the Empire served two purposes. It was conservative, and it weakened the overburdening German and Hungarian nationalism.[15] The discovery of Czech and Illyrian culture was supposed to be an antidote to Germanism and Magyarism. In the end, of course, Austrian catering to the minor nationalities postponed the national problem while intensifying it. It ensured that the Empire would not be split into two large blocks, but into smithereens.

Liberal and national movements elsewhere also owed much to the

---

[14] See A. J. P. Taylor, *The Habsburg Monarchy, 1809-1918* (London, 1948), pp. 42-43.

[15] *Ibid.*, p. 43.

period of Napoleonic hegemony. In France, Charles X, apparently feeling that Louis XVI's error had been in compromising with the revolution, set himself a course of unfettered royalism and religious exaltation. Under his hands the contradictions of the Constitutional Charter were revealed, and he determined to reassert royal power over the legislature. His ministers prepared new curbs on the press and a new and restrictive electoral law. In March, 1830 the issue was drawn with the liberals in the Chamber demanding that the king co-operate with a majority in parliament and dismiss the ministry. The reply was the dissolution of the Chamber and a new election in which the liberals strengthened their position. Thereupon the King resolved upon a *coup d'état* to deprive the liberals of their electoral strength, abolish freedom of the press, and institute a new Chamber which would be amenable to royal control.[16] The result was revolution.

The success of the "bloodless" July Revolution and the accession of Louis Philippe as "King of the French" paved the way for revolutionary outbreaks elsewhere. In Belgium an alliance of liberals and clericals carried through a revolution against the Dutch King. The Dutch had symbolized their opposition to Napoleon with a revolt in 1813, while the Belgians had evidenced their support by passive obedience. In Holland, French institutions and language were disdained, but in Belgium they were accepted. The difference in attitude toward the Revolution and Empire was heightened by other points of friction. The Belgians did not like the charter of the new monarchy, they were opposed to the burden of the Dutch debt, and they believed that Dutch Protestantism was diluting the Catholicism of Belgium. The regime of William I was not absolutely oppressive, but the liberal and clerical factions in Belgium were radical in their claims. Despite William's tardy efforts at compromise toward the end, the Belgians revolted at the signal from the French.[17]

Another area in which the French had exercised an important influence was touched by revolution in 1830. The Poles had received from the Russians a constitution even more liberal than the French Charter of 1814, but the Russians soon seemed bent on taking back

16 See Frederick B. Artz, *Reaction and Revolution, 1814-1832* (New York, 1934), Chapter 9, Part 1.
17 See George Edmundson, "The Low Countries," in *The Cambridge Modern History*, Vol. 10.

what they had given while the Poles were demanding more. The extension of the civil code to the Duchy of Warsaw had made a deep impression, and the Poles had not been willing to do reactionary bidding at the expense of the French Emperor. While Napoleon had not been able to raise them in nationalist passion against the leagued autocrats, they were only too willing to fight reactionary rule after 1815. The Polish Diet was hypercritical and therefore not often summoned, and finances remained in the control of Russian overseers. When revolution convulsed France in July, the Polish ferment grew. In November a group of students and soldiers acted. Constantine, the Tsar's brother and head of the Polish Army, vacillated and finally was drawn into negotiations with the rebels. He was allowed to leave to treat with the Tsar on behalf of the insurgents, but Nicholas thought only of total repression. Less than a year later a Russian army entered Warsaw and Polish liberty was extinguished.[18] The revolutions in France, Belgium and Poland were succored by outbreaks in Germany, in some of the Italian states, in Spain, Portugal, and in Switzerland, but only in the last three were the revolts successful. Nevertheless, it was clear that liberalism and nationalism were rising forces, and that if the old order had not been completely undermined by the events of 1830, it was significantly challenged by them. As liberal sympathy for the Poles and the Italians grew, it would be increasingly difficult to maintain the co-operation of the Great Powers. The conservative states did not go to war over France or Belgium, but they could scarcely permit the unification of Italy. The liberal states did not have to fight the autocrats to achieve liberal advance in 1830, but they might have to do so later on.

II The revolutions of 1830 were the hallmark of a new period of international relations. A Quadruple Alliance of constitutional states was formed among the Iberian states, France, and England in 1834 to counter the solidarity of the three conservative Powers manifested at Münchengrätz the previous year. Liberal constitutionalism was now not merely a domestic movement, it was coming to have significance for foreign policy as well. But despite the formalization of the ideological rift, the Concert did not grind to a halt as a result

18 See S. Askenazy, "Poland and the Polish Revolution," in *The Cambridge Modern History,* Vol. 10.

of the revolutionary tenor of the age. Indeed, Palmerston's accession as Foreign Secretary marked the re-entry of Britain into European councils. George Canning had ended the Concert in 1823; Palmerston revived it seven years later.

Canning had learned his political maxims from Burke, but his interpretation of the Burkean philosophy was novel. Burke had regarded the French Revolution as a rationalistic construction which violated the natural intimations of historical development. Accordingly, revolution was "foreign," conservative development indigenous. Canning turned this doctrine on its head. In practice, revolutionary change was for him a natural manifestation of historic processes — hence, to intervene to repress it was to violate an historical mandate. For Burke the reverse was true. Since Revolution was "unnatural," intervention might restore the interrupted historical tendency. Canning was a genuine disciple of his master in his acceptance of the results of historical evolution. He would change but only to conserve. He was for Catholic Emancipation, but also supported the Test Acts. "He opposed Parliamentary Reform and supported the suspension of Habeas-Corpus; he advocated Freedom of Trade and the eventual Abolition of Slavery." [19] But he differed from Burke in what he believed was historically ordained. For him revolution was the result of intrinsic process, and for Burke it was an excrescence. The doctrine of nonintervention which he took from Castlereagh and carried to its perfection was implicitly liberal. Intervention was thought to be a reactionary method of expunging liberal constitutions while nonintervention was a liberal doctrine designed to support them. When the Congress of Verona authored French intervention in Spain, Canning declared "come what may" he would not be a party to it. In so doing he consummated the rupture with the Concert.

But Canning's liberalism was tempered with restraint. He opposed both the systems of "simple democracy" and "simple despotism," and he conceived of England's role as that of mediator between the two. England's combination of monarchy and constitutionalism was to be commended to others, but in no case would Canning intervene to impose British institutions on other states. In this sense he represents a compromise between Castlereagh and Palmerston. The former was in sentiment a conservative, the latter a lib-

19 Temperley, *op. cit.*, p. 35.

eral. Canning was in between. Yet Canning's attitudes were more distinct from the former than from the latter. Castlereagh could not have publicized the maxims of his diplomacy for he sympathized too much with the old regime. On the other hand, Canning could publish his formulations for they emphasized the cleavage between England and the continent, between constitutionalism and despotism. Economic motives were no doubt important in the Anglo-Russian action to subdue the Turks, but the populace saw Greek freedom as a result. The English intervention in Portugal prevented a Spanish incursion, but it also sustained the constitutional cause. Canning was enormously fortunate in that actions of interest could be legitimized in liberal or constitutional terms. In the end, even he abandoned the strict interpretation of nonintervention. He intrigued at the Portuguese court, and the French, British, and Russian action against Turkey was interference pure and simple. It was, however, intervention in a case of overriding urgency and directed against, not in favor of, the Concert.

The death of Canning and the brief interregnum of Goderich and Wellington ushered in a reactionary interlude, and it saw a retreat in the constitutional cause. In November 1830, the Whigs came in with Palmerston at the Foreign Office. Strangely enough the liberal victories in France and England smoothed the way for co-operation with the Concert as well as among themselves. France had participated with Britain and Russia in the Treaty of London of 1827, which laid down the terms for the settlement of the Greek question, but at that time the object of her intervention had been territorial and domestic. Charles X's regime was losing popular support and needed a foreign policy success to bolster its position. After 1830, a liberal entente of the two Western Powers was restored for five years, but the Concert benefited as well. The successful revolutionary movements of 1830 had apparently frightened the conservative monarchs into a more moderate policy in Concert diplomacy. While it is difficult to imagine the conservatives presiding over the demise of their cause in Belgium or Greece in 1820, in 1830, they accepted Greek independence and Belgian freedom. Behind the new burst of Concert activity was conservative weakness, and the tide of reform being irresistible, the Concert yielded to it. Between 1830 and 1848 the Concert held pride of place, and nations gave way without deserting it. The French were humiliated over the Near East in 1840, yet they accepted the result in the Convention of the Straits in the following year.

The renewed co-operation established after 1830, however, did not extend to all spheres. Britain and France were often able to exclude the Concert from certain issues. While it was compelled to do constitutional bidding at the instance of the liberal Powers, the Concert was not allowed to act against the constitutional cause where it was well entrenched. England and France (to a lesser extent) acted to support the constitutionalists in Portugal and Spain. In neither case was the old doctrine of nonintervention applied. In the Quadruple Alliance of May 1934, England promised to aid the constitutional forces in Spain and Portugal with the Royal Navy. That threat in itself brought the capitulation of Dom Miguel in Portugal. In Spain, Don Carlos was more tenacious. Palmerston "relaxed the Foreign Enlistment Act to enable a volunteer military legion to be raised in England for service in Spain, which became the best aid of Isabella. He allowed arms and equipment to be exported to the constitutionalists and prevented their going to the Carlists. The British navy cut off Carlist supplies and occasionally bombarded their coast towns. Finally he lent the Queen Regent half a million pounds for military expenses. The Carlist movement lived on in the Basque provinces, but finally flickered out in 1839." [20] While the British and French were thus repudiating nonintervention in their private preserves, intervention by a European assembly would not be tolerated. Palmerston wrote in 1837: ". . . nothing but a State of Things in Spain of which at present there are no Symptoms, and which we fervently hope never will arise, could induce the British Government to become Parties to a European Congress for the Purpose of regulating the affairs of Spain. . . ." [21] In Greece also, Palmerston urged intervention upon individual states as a means of redressing constitutional grievances. He lectured Metternich on the despotic powers of King Otto, and he told Guizot that Britain, France, and Russia had pledged themselves to give a "real and *bona fide* Constitution" to Greece and that they had yet to do so. He proposed a joint intervention to France which would secure the desired object. As a result of Anglo-French action, the Greek gov-

---

[20] Harold Temperley and Lillian M. Penson, *Foundations of British Foreign Policy* (Cambridge, 1938), p. 103.

[21] Quoted in *ibid.*, p. 105.

ernment would be purged of the "Bavarian Camarilla" and prevented from "placing soldiers at free quarters, from poisoning brigands, from torturing prisoners, from conniving at 'the Slave Trade.' " [22] Direct intervention on behalf of the constitutional party was thereby sanctioned and avowed.

The Concert followed a checkered path after 1830. It dealt with the Belgian question between 1830 and 1833, but it failed to handle the Eastern Question in the latter year. The Continental Powers would acquiesce in liberal determinations in the West, but they would not give the maritime states the right to impose Concert liberalism on them in the East. In 1833, the French openly sided with Mehemet Ali against the Sultan, and the British were also not yet convinced that Turkey had to be maintained at all costs. The Eastern courts either wanted the Ottoman propped up or reserved to themselves the gains of partition. Münchengrätz was the signal of the breakdown of Concert diplomacy in the East. In effect it ratified the special position which the Russians had obtained as a result of Unkiar-Skelessi in the Ottoman Empire. The consequence of Münchengrätz in the East was the reaffirmation of constitutional unity in the West. England and France joined Portugal and Spain in the Quadruple Alliance of 1834. The Concert now seemed to be divided in half.

The defection of France from the liberal alliance after 1835, however, and the growing English concern with the Near East allowed the Concert to continue. In 1830 the liberal states had been able to use the Concert for their purposes in Belgium, but three years later the conservatives were not able to turn it to their purposes in the Levant. The result was a bifurcation of East and West. After 1835, however, France increasingly wooed the conservative courts, and with the domestic position of Louis Philippe secured, could afford to depart more frequently from the liberal entente.[23] This established a new link with the conservatives in the West; France often hesitated to back Palmerston's Spanish intrigues for fear of alienating the continental courts. After 1835, also, England began to despair of a liberal solution on Turkey. Turkey became a necessity if the British position in the Near East was not to be threatened. Any undermining or partition of the Ottoman would

22 Quoted in *ibid.,* p. 108.
23 See Craig *loc. cit.,* p. 247.

leave a greater Power in its stead, a Power more able to threaten British interests. Thus, after 1835, Britain began to look to co-operation in the East with the three conservative courts. Even Russia sought to protect the Ottoman against the onslaughts of his vassal, Mehemet Ali. As early as 1829, the Tsar had been won to a new policy toward his southern neighbor. "It was that a weak neighbor (Turkey) was better than a strong one, and that a speedy collapse of the Turkish Empire would bring in France and England to share the spoils. If, however, it gradually dissolved, Russia might absorb the 'lion's share.' " [24] Britain tolerated Unkiar-Skelessi. "The passage of time went to show that Russia did not seek to press her advantage while Britain reasserted a measure . . . of influence in Turkey: a commercial treaty in August, 1838, secured for her further advantages, putting a 3 percent limitation on Turkish customs duties, while the reorganization of the Turkish fleet was entrusted to British officers in 1839." [25] In this strange reversal of circumstance England began to work with the conservatives in the East while France co-operated with them in the West. The liberal alliance crumbled temporarily, and the Concert resumed its functioning in 1839.

Ever since Mehemet's attack on the Sultan in 1832, Mahmoud II had hungered for revenge. In 1839 he felt himself ready and in April launched an attack on Mehemet Ali's garrisons in Syria. The outcome was disastrous for the Turks, because Mehemet's son and commander, Ibrahim, won complete victory in June and the Ottoman fleet defected to the Egyptians a week later. The Sultan was left at the mercy of his princeling. The Powers managed to maintain their unity in a note to the Turks in July which reserved their rights to review any settlement, but a disagreement broke out between France and the other Powers over the extent of gains to be permitted Mehemet Ali. The French attitude was now quite different from the British. While Britain expounded liberalism in the West (in Spain) the French abandoned it; while the French sought liberalization or partition of Turkey, the British reneged on it. Mehemet Ali represented a force for progress in the Ottoman dominions, and his rebellion against the Sultan appealed to French senti-

[24] Temperley and Penson, *op. cit.*, p. 118.
[25] René Albrecht-Carrié, *A Diplomatic History of Europe Since the Congress of Vienna* (New York, 1958), p. 52.

ments. The French establishment in Algeria, moreover, confirmed
her interest in the Mediterranean and in Eastern issues. "France
[also] had maintained a close interest in Egypt ever since the time
of Napoleon, and the Egyptian army had been largely trained and
the Egyptian administrative services organized by Frenchmen. Mehemet Ali had responded by a policy which tended to be pro-
French and markedly anti-British." [26] When the other Powers proposed to pare down the Egyptian's gains to preserve the Ottomans,
the French demurred. The four other Powers, however, proceeded
to sign the Treaty of London of July 1840 which aimed to expel
Mehemet from North Syria and the Holy Cities. Thiers, who had
come to the Ministry in February, 1840 "represented at this time
the aggressive aspects of French foreign policy," [27] and would not be
likely to concede with good grace. But when Palmerston pressed the
terms on Mehemet Ali and the latter refused them, England intervened. Admiral Stopford pre-empted the French initiative and by
November had forced Mehemet to sign a convention submitting to
the Powers and returning the Turkish fleet. Louis Philippe found
an excuse to get rid of Thiers and prepared to accept the disagree-
able. At this stage the Tsar actually proposed to Palmerston an alliance directed against France, but the British minister would not
go that far. Indeed, his handling of the whole dispute, though reso-
lute, was affected by his feelings for France and his desire to cooperate with her whenever possible. Though the Treaty of London
of 1840 was signed without France, Palmerston was extremely cir-
cumspect in public. Nor did he permit the humiliation of Mehemet
Ali. The Sultan's vassal lost North and South Syria but was confirmed as hereditary pasha of Egypt and of Nubia.[28] When the final
Near Eastern settlement was reached in the Convention of the
Straits of July 13, 1841, France returned to the Concert. The Treaty
of Unkiar-Skelessi had expired the previous year, and the new convention replaced a bilateral agreement with a general European accord. The Sultan's "sovereignty rights" were recognized, and the
Bosphorus and the Dardanelles closed to ships of war. The French
and British took comfort from the former, believing this would re-
strict Russian access to Constantinople; the Russians were pleased

26 Bury, *op. cit.*, p. 58.
27 Albrecht-Carrié, *op. cit.*, p. 53.
28 Temperley and Penson, *op. cit.*, p. 123.

by the latter, believing that France and Britain could not menace Turkey or enter the Black Sea.[29]

The fall of the Whig ministry in September 1841 cemented the *rapprochement* with France which had begun three months previously. Aberdeen took the Foreign Office under Peel's premiership, and Europe sighed in relief at Palmerston's departure. Guizot seized the essence of what has been called, *la première entente cordiale*[30] when he pointed out "Peel and his colleagues were Conservatives who had become Liberals: we were Liberals who had become Conservatives." [31] Indeed, Guizot got along much better with Aberdeen than he did with Palmerston, and the generally moderate orientation of both countries facilitated co-operation with the Eastern courts. As late as 1847, Guizot was intriguing for the conservative cause in Switzerland.

The new friendship of France and England was more of sentiment than interest. Concrete frictions divided the two countries in Tahiti, in Greece and prospectively in Spain, but the leaders of policy were determined that a new effort at co-operation should be made. In pursuit of this course, Queen Victoria visited Louis Philippe at Eu in 1843, and it seemed then that a compromise had been reached on Spain. Aberdeen was willing to give up the candidacy of a Coburg prince, cousin of the English prince consort, for the hand of Queen Isabella if Louis would renounce the idea of marriage between Isabella and one of his sons. Later, when Guizot had second thoughts, it was apparently agreed that the Duc de Montpensier, son of the French monarch, could marry Isabella's sister, but only after Isabella herself had married and had borne issue. Despite a visit to England by Tsar Nicholas in 1844, the developing entente was not interrupted, and Louis Philippe returned the Queen's visit at Windsor. The monarchial solidarity thus congealed was helpful as a popular force, but "it is not too much to say that the intimacy between Aberdeen and Guizot was the most valuable asset in maintaining the Entente Cordiale." [32]

When Palmerston returned to the Foreign Ministry in 1846, he

29 *Ibid.*, p. 123.
30 By Raymond Guyot in his *La première entente cordiale* (Paris, 1926).
31 Quoted in R. W. Seton-Watson, *Britain in Europe, 1789-1914* (Cambridge, 1938), p. 230.
32 *Ibid.*, p. 237.

renewed the Coburg candidacy and refused to support the Eu formula of 1843. The French on their own part had been endeavoring to undermine the Eu agreement in order to permit a simultaneous marriage of the Queen with the Duke of Cadiz and the Infanta with the Duke of Montpensier. When the French found the English were backsliding, they pressed forward a *fait accompli.* In September, the two marriages were performed, and Palmerston was left out in the cold. Louis Philippe had not sought to deceive his English ally, but he was persuaded that Palmerston was already undercutting the earlier agreement. The result was a French victory, but ". . . it was an empty triumph; for the establishment of a precarious domestic influence in the troubled Spanish kingdom was hardly worth the determined hostility of the British Foreign Secretary and the rupture of the Entente which had been the mainstay of French foreign policy during the greater part of Louis Philippe's reign." [33] The breach with England threw France increasingly upon the mercies of the continental autocrats. Expansion in Algeria and cooperation with Metternich in Switzerland was scarcely to appeal to the majority of Frenchmen who wanted a liberal foreign policy.

In the period after 1822, the Concert of Europe had two bursts of activity; it dealt with Belgium after 1830, and it managed the Near East after 1840. In both cases it operated despite the existence of a liberal-conservative cleavage. The events described indicate that the Concert was no longer an instrument of conservative repression; it was sometimes called into action to perform a liberal service. When the tide of liberal reform was at its height, even the conservatives had to do liberal bidding, as in Belgium. In 1840-1841, however, after that tide had receded and historic interests had come to manifest themselves, the Concert was as much the property of the conservative Powers. England abandoned its liberalism when the integrity of the Ottoman Power was at stake, and France was compelled to go along.

The Concert continued to work and to ratify settlements between 1822 and 1848, but perhaps the signal characteristic of this era was the growing tendency toward separate action. Canning did not condone the Concert, and it was not the Concert, but France, England, and Russia together that liberated Greece from Turkish and Egyptian rule. After 1830 it was not the Concert, but England and

---

[33] Bury, *op. cit.,* p. 65.

France that maintained the constitutional cause in Portugal, and it was England that practically alone maintained it in Spain. Nor was the right to separate intervention an exclusive prerogative of the liberal Powers. The Concert did not decide affairs in Italy and Germany; they were settled by the direct or indirect intervention of Austria and France. Until 1839, Russia had a large measure of latitude in dealing with the Ottoman, and the treaties of Adrianople and Unkiar-Skelessi were evidence of that fact. In Poland the Tsar had effective predominance, and the resolution of the French chamber and the remonstrances of Palmerston were to no effect. By and large (and with the exception of Greece and later, Egypt) the maritime states reserved a unilateral right of intervention in the West, the continental Powers the right of interference in the East, and the two blocs shared interposition in the center. Austria maintained her predominance in Italy, despite French intervention, but Switzerland adhered to the federal and liberal cause in 1848, partly as a result of English support.

III   The Concert of Europe between 1822 and 1848 was a truncated Concert. It often functioned with the implicit opposition or abstention of some of its members, and it operated only spasmodically. The Canning era represented a transition between the effectiveness of the mechanism of Castlereagh and the refractoriness of the apparatus of Palmerston: under Canning it did not function at all. In many ways that it worked to any degree was a tribute to fortuitous circumstance. Canning believed that the Concert existed only to further reactionary purposes, and he would have been surprised to find it sanctioning and ratifying Belgian independence. Logically, one would expect that a new burst of revolutionary energy would cause division between the liberal and conservative realms and frustrate the operation of the Concert. Thus, if events of 1848 were to spell the demise of European cooperation, why did events in 1830 actually further it? The answer is not hard to give. The reactionaries of 1830, pressed from every side, could afford to give ground but only where their primary interests were not involved. Belgium could be conceded although Italy, Germany or Poland could not. But 1848 was to show that when revolutionary movements were centered in those very areas where the autocrats could not afford to yield, the Concert was destined to ex-pire. Whereas the revolutionary developments of 1830 forced the conservatives to yield and thus permitted a limited connection between England and France and the conservative states, the revolutionary developments of 1848 forced the conservatives to act and thus destroyed the Concert. Three possible situations could be imagined: the revolutionary tide could challenge but not undermine vital conservative interests, as in 1830; the revolutionary tide could overwhelm the conservative regimes and thus compel capitulation to the liberal states, as never occurred; the revolutionary tide could challenge and implicitly undermine vital conservative interests and thus demand wholesale international repression, as in 1848. In the first two cases, the Concert could function; in the last it could not. From the international point of view, the tragedy of the revolutions of 1848 was that they were potent, but not decisive.

Of course, the Concert could be used for variant ideological purposes. Where Canning despaired of its reactionary design, Palmerston employed it to advance constitutionalism. But it could oscillate between contending principles only so long as a real balance of force was sustained. Between 1822 and 1848, neither liberals nor conservatives had effective ideological predominance, thus, in principle, the Concert could be used for either cause. Each stayed in the game as long as the international institution was in balance. When it seemed that either camp might win the upper hand, the other prepared to desert. Canning had employed that tactic between 1822 and 1837; the conservatives might consider it after 1848. Disputes over the site of the *point d'union* were futile once command of the apparatus had been decided.

The real significance of the age between 1822 and 1848 was its intermediate character. The Concert functioned intermittently, and its ideological orientation was not finally determined. While conservatism had been dominant after 1815, conservatism and liberalism contended after 1822. Nor were all disputes ideological ones — conflicts of interest increasingly demanded the attention of the Concert and the issues of 1840-1846 were concrete or dynastic in character. The very existence of historic interest distracted attention from the ideological cleavage and made the work of international cooperation easier than it might have been. The material conflicts of the eighteenth century were reflected in a later age. And yet, the frictions of interest of 1840 were different from the frictions of

*Realpolitik* of 1860. *Realpolitik* implied the absence of any sense of limitation; cleavages of interest were mediated by an international institution. *Realpolitik* presumed that war was a proper means of regulating the relations among states, but conflicts of interest prompted diplomacy, not militarism. In this sense certain of the lessons of the Napoleonic Wars were not learned until after 1848. Before the French Revolution a minimal international consensus had prevailed in Europe: after it, a conservative consensus briefly held sway. It gavé way in turn to a more fragmentary consensus which temporarily united a Europe riven by ideology. The sense of limitation prevailed between Austria and France in their confrontation over Italy; it existed in the Near East when Mehemet Ali threatened to plunge the Powers into war; it prevented the fiasco of the Spanish marriages, the French intervention in Spain, the Russian intervention in Poland, and the British intervention in Portugal from leading to war. Interests were not pressed to their logical extremes.[34] Palmerston and Thiers may sometimes have acted as if they wanted war, but they were not ready to fight it. Nicholas, Metternich, and Frederick William III were better prepared, but they did not want it.

Ultimately, however, both camps had to face the consequences of a renewal of the liberal and national struggle. War could be avoided when the results of fighting would be worse than those of standing aside. But when conservative political principles or dynastic territorial principles were faced with radical challenge, war would be the lesser of two evils. When liberal political principles or national territorial principles were faced with absolute denial, war would become tolerable. When warfare for a political purpose became acceptable, the very bases of the Concert would be undermined. Indeed, the prime characteristics of the age after 1822 were the reverse. The Concert did not govern, it ratified. The international interest of peace, however, was placed ahead of the advancement of sectarian political ideologies. The ideological struggle was resumed, but it did not issue in war. After 1848, the Concert failed even to prevent war.

In this context, legitimacy was no longer the keynote of interstate relations. Legitimacy, as a conservative doctrine, had to make room for liberalism and nationalism. Legitimacy ʾas a creed of "accept-

[34] See Craig, *loc. cit.,* pp. 266-267.

ance" had to admit lapses in international co-operation and acknowledge separate action. Neither conservatism nor agreement dominated European relations. In the eight-year period after 1814 the salutary consequences of the Napoleonic Wars were displayed. Ideological unity was briefly restored and the horrors of war were uppermost in the minds of European statesmen. After 1822 the contrary tendencies of the period of war and revolution began to appear. The ideological unity was shaken, and the dangers of war were no longer primary. It seemed that an observer, witnessing the revolutionary upheavals of 1848 would predict that the forces of the French Revolution and Empire would come to final fruition in the generation to follow, and that the system of international relations would be, once again, transformed.

For the moment, however, peace and a modicum of stability prevailed. The Concert was strong enough to preclude warfare among major states as a reliable alternative of policy, though it no longer regulated the conditions of domestic existence in conservative and liberal countries. The challenges to the international system were not so severe as to require an omnipotent Concert, for war and revolution were not essential requirements of either conservative or liberal policy. The conflicts between the two camps, moreover, were muted by pursuit of territorial gain in the Near East and North Africa. Ideology and interest frequently diverged; a direct confrontation of liberals and conservatives did not materialize. International outcomes could be held within conventional limits.

The stability of the system, however, did not conceal its distinct features. International ambitions and modes of action were once again altered. A political competition between ideological rivals resumed, but it was a competition that neither camp wished to end in war. The issues of reform of reaction, thus were not carried to extremes. Diplomatic techniques bore witness to the limitation of objectives. Together the Concert and traditional diplomacy handled the disputes of the age, and they did not permit radical solutions.

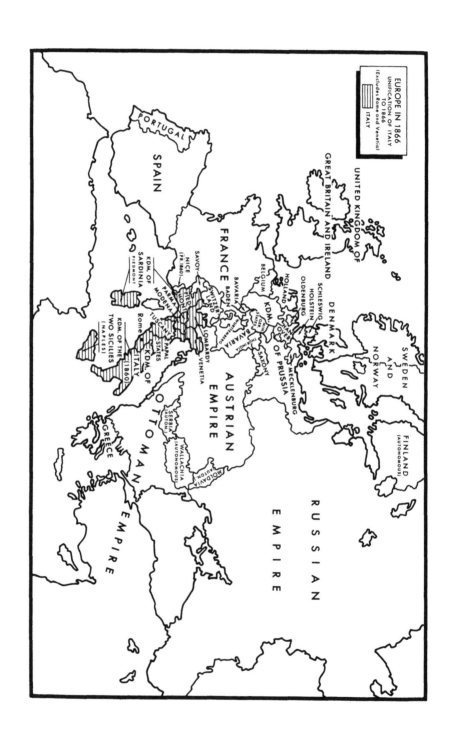

EUROPE IN 1866
UNIFICATION OF ITALY
TO 1866
(Excludes Rome and Venetia)

ITALY

PORTUGAL

SPAIN

FRANCE

GREAT BRITAIN AND IRELAND

UNITED KINGDOM OF

DENMARK

SCHLESWIG
HOLSTEIN
OLDENBURG
HANOVER
MECKLENBURG

KDM. OF PRUSSIA

HOLLAND
BELGIUM
BAVARIA
BADEN
SWITZERLAND
SAXONY
NASSAU
HESSE CASSEL
HESSE DARM.
WÜRTTEMBERG

SWEDEN
AND
NORWAY

FINLAND
(AUTONOMOUS)

KDM. OF
SARDINIA
(PIEDMONT)

NICE
(FR. 1860)
SAVOY
PIEDMONT
PARMA
MODENA
TUSCANY
PAPAL
STATES
Rome
LOMBARDY
VENETIA

KDM. OF
ITALY
(1860)

KDM. OF THE
TWO SICILIES
(NAPLES)

AUSTRIAN
EMPIRE

SERBIA
(AUTON.)
WALLACHIA
(AUTONOMOUS)
MOLDAVIA
(AUTON.)

GREECE

OTTOMAN
EMPIRE

RUSSIAN
EMPIRE

## chapter six

# THE SHATTERED CONCERT

I The revolutions of 1848 ushered in a period which was neither liberal nor conservative, yet was paradoxically a period in which political ideology was of great importance. The results of 1848 were equivocal in that neither pure liberalism nor the old legitimist conservatism triumphed. As one writer has remarked: "The success of the revolution discredited conservative ideas; the failure of the revolution discredited liberal ideas." [1] If liberalism and conservatism were both rejected, how can one explain the demise of the Concert? Until 1848 the causes of friction within the international alliance had been conflicts of political ideas, and it could be assumed that when the ideological struggle was resumed domestically, it would lead to such division that conservatives and liberal revolutionaries could no longer coexist within the Concert. But this was not what happened. The revolutions did not lead to a heightened conflict of liberals and conservatives which was destined to destroy the international mechanism — rather, the two antagonists destroyed each other. And the very end of the old cleavage might be assumed to promote the solidity of the Concert. If it had not worked well in

[1] A. J. P. Taylor, *The Course of German History* (London, 1954), p. 68. The author does not claim here that liberal and conservative ideologies ceased to be of importance after 1848; rather, that they both had to be defended by new means. Professor Pouthas takes a different view. The 1848 revolution, he says, "brought about the end of a world. Being the practical application of an ideology that sprang from the French Revolution and the First Empire, it can be said, by its failure, to have exhausted that ideology. Thus it is an end rather than a beginning, for subsequent events were the fruit of different ideas." Charles Pouthas, "The Revolutions of 1848" in *The New Cambridge Modern History*, Vol. 10 *The Zenith of European Power, 1830-70*, J. P. T. Bury (ed.) (Cambridge, 1960), p. 414.

a context of ideological division, might it not work when the antagonists were removed? Here is the problem of 1848-1871: the ideological split in its old sense was undermined, but the result did not give a new lease on life to the Concert. Instead, it shattered it.

The end of the old liberal and conservative alliances did not mean, however, a decline in the influence of ideology. Instead, it turned ideology to new purposes. The success of the liberal revolutionists of 1848 discredited the old legitimacy once and for all. Previously, tradition had been the sanction of conservative regimes, and historic tenure the justification for legitimate rule. After 1848, however, the conservative synthesis was toppled, and the conservatives had to find a new *raison d'être*. Previously usage was reason enough, but now a more concrete justification had to be given.[2] After 1848, the conservatives, no longer able to ignore popular sentiments, had to rationalize their rule in some terms acceptable to the population. Thus, in one of the strange outcomes of history, the conservatives whose formal doctrine enjoined absolute rule, had to pay lip service to popular opinion. If they were to maintain their grip on the reins of power after 1848, they had to swallow a portion of the liberal doctrines of their late antagonists. Conservatives had to appear to espouse liberal causes, if only to sustain their domestic position. In short, the result of the revolutionary outbursts of 1848 was not a refurbished and virile conservatism, contending on equal terms with a revolutionary liberalism because the revolutions did not lead to a new and more powerful conservative alliance against all measures of reform. Instead, the conservative alliance, because it was temporarily defeated, fell apart under the hands of liberalism, and it was the error of Tsar Nicholas that he did not realize this fact soon enough. So fundamental was the challenge to conservative existence, that each conservative state could not afford to waste its energies defending the others; it had to concentrate on defending itself. In 1850 the Austro-Prussian alliance crumbled; in 1854 Austria and Russia went their separate ways. The political challenge of 1848 was far different from that of 1830. The challenge of 1830 was directed at the general forces of conservatism; the challenge of 1848 was directed at the existence of separate conservative regimes.

[2] See James Joll, "Prussia and the German Problem, 1830-66" in *The New Cambridge Modern History*, Vol. 10 (Cambridge, 1960), p. 500.

The existence of Austria, Prussia, or Russia was not at stake in 1830, but it was a generation later.

Thus, the very thoroughness of the liberal conquest set the conservative regimes quarreling among themselves. Because the very existence of conservatism, at least in central Europe, depended upon the recognition of certain liberal demands, the erstwhile conservative regimes hired liberal ministers, paraded a façade of representative institutions, and espoused the national cause. They had to outdo each other in their lip service to liberalism in order to justify their rule. They could, of course, have become fully-fledged liberal and representative governments, but that would have undermined their conservative character, and liberalism then would have won final triumph. Short of that disastrous result, they could offer memorials to liberal sentiment and work for the national cause. Nationalism was a perverse doctrine which lent itself to conservatives as well as liberals. Its origins were French, and they were as much manifested in the enlightened despotism of Napoleon as in the decrees of the National Convention. The impact of Napoleonic victories and reform upon the body politic of Europe had awakened the hatred not so much of the liberals as of the agrarians.[3] The nobility resented Napoleon because of his transformation of the old regime, while the petty landowners and peasants were offended because of the Napoleonic regimentation. For the latter, it was French centralization, the obliteration of localist particularism and the *Gleichschaltung* of inconsistent historic privilege that made for alienation. The War of Liberation was genuinely popular in that it had no specific class character. But the nationalism which was manifested in the popular groundswell against Napoleon created the very sentiment against which it was first directed. Centralization and co-ordination had been the disadvantage of French rule; but the nationalism which spurned the French was itself a centralizing phenomenon. French centralization had been rejected, but only to make way for German centralization.

In this sense, nationalism had intrinsically a much greater appeal than liberalism. Of course liberals rapidly became converts to the national cause as well, and, indeed, it could be argued that if po-

---

[3] See Robert C. Binkley, *Realism and Nationalism, 1852-1871* (New York, 1935), p. 69.

litical liberalism expresses itself in the demand for representative and constitutional government, it must delimit the territory over which government is to be exercised. If the people are going to run their affairs through representative institutions, they must constitute themselves as a governing unit for that purpose. Hence, it was not surprising that liberals became nationalists. But if this was the case, nationalism became a vertical movement while liberalism retained its peculiarly horizontal character. Nationalism appealed to elements of all classes;[4] liberalism remained essentially a middle class phenomenon. Thus, nationalism, if properly handled, could become a conservative device more easily than liberalism. When liberal reform was the order of the day, the conservatives could sometimes raise the national question as a means of distracting attention from the political position which they could not abandon. This was the process inaugurated in 1849. It would be rash· to say that the conservatives were ever true proselytes of nationality. They had resorted to the national tactic in 1809 and in 1813, but only in the gravest emergency. They resorted to it after 1849 and again because of dire necessity. One cannot believe that Schwarzenberg, Bach, Manteuffel, and Bismarck were convinced nationalists for in truth they espoused nationalism as a device.[5] Manteuffel and Bismarck would gladly have returned to the old system of legitimacy and the conservative alliance had that been possible. Since it was impossible and since the liberals had taken the lead in the national question in the Frankfort Parliament of 1848, the conservative regimes of Prussia and Austria could only reclaim their hold on public sentiment by pressing forth nationalism under the aegis of conservatism.

Much has been written about the failure of the liberal and national revolutions of 1848, but in fact, they were more successful than is often believed.[6] They were so successful that they demolished the edifice of traditional conservatism and forced a new conservative synthesis. But the new reactionary program would be very

---

[4] See *ibid.*, pp. 69-70.

[5] Bismarck, for example, referred to the movement for national unity as "the German swindle."

[6] Mr. Hallgarten points out the difficulties of realizing both the liberal and national creeds in 1848. The first required opposition to the Prussian state; the second absolute dependence upon it. G. W. F. Hallgarten, *Imperialism Vor 1914* (Munich, 1951) Vol. 1, pp. 117-121.

different from the old. Conservative legitimacy and dynastic rule had fostered a kind of internationalism both domestically and externally. The national groups within the conservative empire should subject their interests to the overriding good of the monarchy and the state. The conservative states themselves should subject their interests to the overriding good of international legitimacy. In the heyday of Metternich, legitimacy was an international as well as a domestic creed. It regulated the relations among states and placed reliance upon conservative solidarity against the revolution. The old conservatism, in other words, fostered an international consensus, and it prescribed the international Concert. The new conservatism, on the other hand, by enshrining nationalism and separate action, subverted the international institution. Though the nineteenth century world was not aware of it yet, nationalism and internationalism were antithetical.

But it was not merely the theoretical bases of the new conservatism which were in conflict with the pre-existing order, the prime national question of the age set Austria and Prussia against each other. If the *kleindeutsch* solution were reached, Prussia would benefit, and the Austrians would lose their position in Germany; if the *grossdeutsch* concept prevailed, Prussia would be overwhelmed in an "Empire of seventy million Germans" directed by the Habsburgs.[7] If Germany were unified without the Austrian Empire, Austria would suffer; if Germany were unified with the Austrian Empire, Prussia would be overborne. Thus, as the conservatives in Prussia and Austria were forced to take over the cause of German national unification, their ancient alliance vanished. Not only was nationalism opposed to internationalism, in the circumstances of 1850 and after the Prussian version of nationalism was at odds with the Austrian variety. The Erfurt Union, the humiliation of Olmütz, and the Austrian defeat at Dresden were the concomitants of the Austro-Prussian struggle for separate nationalist conceptions, conceptions rendered necessary by the liberal strength of 1848. When Prussia and Austria vied for predominance in Germany, they were engaged in a struggle to provide a new *raison d'être* for a conservative regime, and in a real sense the conservatives were fighting for their existence. No genuine co-operation was possible between them until unification was in process and the Magyars had come to dom-

7 See *ibid.*, pp. 120-121.

inate the foreign policy of the Austrian Empire.[8] The Concert might regulate nationalism in Belgium, but it could never regulate nationalism in Germany.

The revolutions of 1848 not only transformed the conservatives, but altered the liberals as well. "The success of the revolution discredited conservative ideas; the failure of the revolution discredited liberal ideas." Liberalism and liberal nationalism came to the forefront in 1848 — they had their chance, and they failed. By 1849 a new reaction was in the ascendant. The constitutionalists did not hold power in Austria, the liberals did not hold power in Prussia, and the republicans did not hold power in France. The liberal onslaught, seeming to depend upon continuing revolutionary ferment, could not govern under conditions of order and domestic peace. Thus, the liberals, because of their impotence, had to forge a new alliance. They had to unravel the secret of conservative stability and use it for their own purposes. The liberals and the conservatives delivered simultaneous knockout blows against each other in 1848, and to succeed in the future they each needed the other's Sunday punch. As the conservatives pondered liberal tactics, the liberals rethought conservative strategy. In France, as elsewhere, liberals had to compromise after 1848.[9] The liberal-conservative situation in Europe was asymmetrical: conservatives used reformist tactics in Central and Eastern Europe to reinsure themselves, liberals were not always able to hold power in the West, regardless of technique. In France in particular, the Second Empire under Louis Napoleon did not mean liberal rule in conservative garb.[10] The Empire had no specific class character and no party to support it. As Professor Farmer writes: "France, [Louis Napoleon] believed, had no graver need than for a secure political order, and the Legitmists, Orleanists, and republicans, each in turn, had proved incapable of providing for this need. No alternative remained but the rule of a

---

[8] As early as 1856 Bismarck was writing: "In the not too distant future, we shall have to fight for our existence against Austria and . . . it is not within our power to avoid that, since the course of events in Germany has no other solution." Quoted in Gordon Craig, "The System of Alliances and the Balance of Power," in *The New Cambridge Modern History*, Vol. 10 (Cambridge, 1960), p. 268.

[9] See Paul Farmer, "The Second Empire in France" in *The New Cambridge Modern History*, Vol. 10 (Cambridge, 1960), p. 442.

[10] A work which emphasizes Louis' liberal sentiments is Professor Roger Williams, *Gaslight and Shadow* (New York, 1957).

sovereign standing above these factions, who would give expression
to the wishes of the mute mass of the nation, more desirous of the
blessings of a stable government than of the triumph of any particular party." [11] His object was the reconciliation of those who favored "progress" with those who favored "order." In this sense Bonapartism had a different import in 1852 than in 1805. Napoleon I
was unquestionably the heir of revolution. Domestically, he protected the bourgeoisie, and the conservatives could not abide him.
Napoleon III, on the other hand, did not aim to protect any single
class. His policies at different periods catered to the farmers, the
business magnates, the clericals, the conservatives, and even the
workers. He was not the heir of revolution because he endeavored
to stand above it. Revolutionary liberalism was a much weaker reed
in France in 1848 than it had been in 1792. In the East the conservatives made appeals to the general population to consolidate
conservative rule, while in France the Empire made appeals to the
general population to consolidate general rule. Class government
was no longer possible in France. The liberals were only one strand
in the Bonapartistic synthesis.

But Louis Napoleon was, perhaps more than his conservative adversaries to the East, the prisoner of his domestic support. Though
his sentiments were mildly reformist, he could not always manipulate his backers in the direction of reform. And the policy of general appeals suffered from internal contradictions. There was no
imperial party to sustain him when these appeared. In the final
analysis his policy toward Rome did not conciliate the clericals, the
conservative empire failed to please the conservatives, and the liberal empire failed to appease the liberals. Lacking "natural" domestic solidarity, the Emperor had to create it through foreign success. "In his nebulous conception of his mission, the restoration of
the diplomatic pre-eminence of France was to be the counterpart to
the resolution of the embittered dissensions within the nation." [12]
But Bonapartism in foreign relations held equivalent contradictions. On the one hand Louis wanted to restore the liberal *entente*
with England which Guizot had broken, and it seemed for a while
that Palmerston and the French President could work together as
closely as Guizot and Aberdeen before the affair of the Spanish mar-

---

11 Farmer, *loc. cit.*, p. 448.
12 *Ibid.*, p. 461.

riages. He also sought to aid the national cause in Europe, to make nationalism work for him rather than against him. In both cases he correctly diagnosed his uncle's failures. On the other hand, he was a Bonapartist and thus pledged to undo the territorial settlement of 1815. A Bonaparte would perforce move toward France's "natural frontiers." This was the real tragedy of the Second Empire: in both internal and external affairs a policy of "general appeals" might end up pleasing no one.[13] The liberal *entente* with England, consummated in Italy, was ruptured over aggrandizement of Nice and Savoy, and the adventures in Mexico and on the Rhine were scarcely designed to reassure the insular antagonists of the first Bonaparte. At the same time the conservatives were estranged. Austria looked rightly upon the French Emperor as the architect of Italian unification, and support of the Pope hardly diminished the offense. Prussia would not pay Napoleon's price (*pourboire* would perhaps be a better word) on the Rhine. External success might have smoothed internal discontents, but it was not always forthcoming.

Thus the impact of the revolution and counterrevolution in 1848-1849 smashed the framework of international co-operation. The conservatives in Germany, shaken to their roots, gave up the apparatus of conservative co-operation and each went his separate way. The revolutions of 1848 had shown that all conservative states could not co-exist in the face of growing nationalism; when this was realized, the conservatives turned on each other. Previously the Concert had faltered when charged with the task of bringing about co-operation of different ideological camps. After 1848 it could not bring about the co-operation of a single ideological camp. French liberalism was also transformed. It was forced to accept imperial trappings and to yield to Bonaparte. It could not sustain itself without the emperor. If French liberalism could work only by donning Napoleonic garb, how could the co-operation with an England which needed no such disguise possibly continue? Paradoxically, the more liberal Napoleon's foreign policy, the more repressive his domestic institutions; the more conservative and expansive his foreign policy, the more liberal his internal institutions. Co-operation with England could not really have gone beyond the plunder of Savoy.

[13] See A. J. P. Taylor, *The Struggle for Mastery in Europe, 1848-1918* (Oxford, 1954), p. 67.

If the simultaneous discrediting of the old liberalism and the old conservatism in 1848-1849 had really obliterated ideology as a factor in European relations, a restoration of the Concert might have been possible. When states are not animated by ideological hostilities and a framework of limitation exists, an international institution can operate. In one sense, the international ideological hostility was eliminated by the events of 1848. No longer did the conservatives have as their primary objective the eradication of the liberal movement and the transformation of its national proponents, and no longer did the liberals have as their primary objective the total defeat of the conservative doctrine and the metamorphosis of its dynastic protagonists. Neither group could afford to fight the all-out ideological battle for each was challenged within. Self-confident nations can afford to fight for principle: fearful ones must protect their own existence. France, Prussia, and Austria began to protect themselves after 1848, and in this sense the ideological contest did not mean an end of ideological belief, and the notion of *Realpolitik* did not convey the absence of idea. *Realpolitik* was not an objectiveless casting about for policy, motivated only by material considerations; it was more properly the use of all available means to advance a specific objective. The Franco-Austrian War of 1859 which has been declared "incompatible with any known systems of international morality" [14] is a prime example of *Realpolitik,* but it was fought to secure the national unification of Italy. The Austro-Prussian and the Franco-Prussian wars may have been deliberately provoked by Bismarck, but they were wars to maintain conservative Prussian hegemony in a national Germany. *Realpolitik*, then, did not signalize a new age by virtue of its nonideological character, rather it marked a new epoch by virtue of its employment of every means to secure a given ideological end.[15] Conservatism and liberalism were not abandoned in the age of *Realpolitik*. They were simply pursued in a revolutionary fashion. The old conservatives would never have conceived of using liberal or nationalist means to achieve reactionary ends, but Radowitz and Schwarzenberg did.[16]

---

14 *Ibid.,* p. 112.

15 Professor Hajo Holborn points out in *The Political Collapse of Europe* (New York, 1957), pp. 43-46, that if *Realpolitik* implies the absence of ideology, Bismarck cannot be called an adherent of *Realpolitik*.

16 Radowitz wrote his wife in 1849 that an attempt must be made to see "whether

The old liberals would not have thought of using conservative or aggrandizing means to achieve liberal ends, but under the Second Empire they did. *Realpolitik* did not end the Concert by drowning the flames of ideology; it did so by revolutionizing the methods of ideologues. The truncated Concert had not been able to control the ends of states, though it sometimes regulated their methods; the shattered Concert not only failed to control ends, it lost control of means. Although warfare had not been an internationally acceptable device before 1848, it was sanctioned and blessed afterwards.

In one respect this was a surprising *dénouement*. While the conservatives of 1840, fearing the revolution, had been hesitant to wage war, the conservatives of 1860, even more fearful of the revolution, were ready to wage it. Again, however, the adoption of warfare was a measure of the revolutionary devices the conservatives were now willing to use. In 1840 their very existence had not been in jeopardy, and they could disdain controversial tactics. In 1860 their survival was at stake, and war might protect it. *Realpolitik*, in this sense, is the mark of conservative desperation. The adoption of revolutionary liberal and national causes and the espousal of potentially revolutionary militarism held great dangers, because a fraudulent reformism, stage-managed from behind the scenes by the conservatives, might suddenly become genuine. The conservatives were fighting fire with fire, and they were necessarily afraid of general conflagration. *Realpolitik* depended upon a controlled unleashing of what otherwise might become an unchecked chain reaction.

In France the policy of Bonapartism also acknowledged the rebirth of militarism. Liberalism had fallen in 1848 because it was powerless to defend itself. The liberal-conservative revolution of Louis Napoleon would advance ideological causes by means of war. Italy had failed to liberate itself first in 1820, then in 1830, and finally in 1848. In 1859 French armies would provide external aid. In the end Italy was united not by the unanimous acclamation of Mazzini but the armies of Louis Napoleon, Garibaldi, and Bismarck. Cavour was another liberal who would countenance conservative intrigue and use militarism for liberal, and nationalist purposes. While neither liberals nor conservatives embraced militarist doc-

---

our government could be led along a path which will not make the so-called German party its most bitter enemies at a time when a life- and death struggle against the democratic party is beginning." Quoted in Joll, *loc. cit.*, p. 500.

trines before 1848, afterwards both had to do so. And the Concert which had prevented war between major powers for more than thirty years was incapable of preventing it after 1848.

Russia and England were special cases. Neither was touched by revolution in 1848, and as a result neither had to become an apostle of *Realpolitik*. Nicholas retained at least until the Crimean War his belief in the conservative alliance against the revolution, and he acted as the policeman of the alliance when he suppressed the Hungarian revolution for the Austrians in 1849. The theme of conservative solidarity was played incessantly by the Tsar when Austria and Prussia fell to quarreling over Germany, and he proclaimed that he would support "whichever Power was nearest to the treaties (though he characteristically added that he did not understand what these were)." [17] When the Prussian monarch threatened to prevent federal execution in Hesse, the Tsar backed Austria, and the Prussians had to accept defeat at Olmütz. The Tsar refused to make a third in the new Holy Alliance which was there proclaimed "so as not to provoke a western alliance in return." [18] Russia believed that just as the alliance had protected the Habsburg monarchy in Hungary, it should protect Russia in the Near East. The fallacy of this mode of reasoning did not emerge until 1854, and when it did, the conservative alliance was exposed as a chimera, and Russia became a convert to *Realpolitik*. The Crimean War was for Russia what the revolutions of 1848 were for Austria and Prussia in that both led to new domestic and international policies — reform domestically and self-protection internationally. The emancipation of the peasants was the Russian equivalent of Prussian liberalism and Austrian constitutionalism, and just as Austria and Prussia were pursuing antagonistic policies of self-protection in Germany, Russia had to protect herself at the Straits. In 1856 she exchanged the lofty ambition of conservative solidarity against the revolution for the more limited and desperate one of winning back what she had lost at the Congress of Paris.

England was not affected by the revolutionary ferment of 1848. The repeal of the Corn Laws had been conceded by Peel in 1846, and a period of Victorian Whig-Liberal ascendancy was approaching. England could still afford to judge international issues in terms

[17] Taylor, *Struggle*, p. 37.
[18] *Ibid.*, p. 44.

of black and white since her liberalism was untainted by *Realpolitik*. The difference of English political complexion from that of the continent in 1848 is made clear by one British historian: "When, in the weeks that followed, the barricades were rising in city after city, and the princes of Europe were flying from their palaces, or hastily signing new constitutions, while class was arming against class, and race against race in the wild confusion of universal overturn, the British people looked on at a spectacle that could not fail to interest, but scarcely seemed to concern them. . . . It was difficult to understand what was going on across the Channel, but there was satisfaction in the thought that we were not as other nations." [19] Because of the triumph of Whig-Liberalism,[20] Britain had little to fear from conservative *revanche,* and the British liberals, conscious of their own strength, did not have to make political compromises with the opposition.[21] Indeed, British policy and attitude became increasingly distinct from that of the Continent after 1848. Even Louis Napoleon had to appease the French conservatives and Catholics with a policy of intermittent clericalism and aggrandizement. Palmerston, Russell, Gladstone, and Bright had to make no such concessions in England. With the failure of continental liberalism in 1849, England became a uniquely enlightened member of the European family of nations. British enlightenment and political advancement led to a consummation of liberal tendencies which had been evident earlier. A state favored by a benign political constitution must choose its national associates carefully. America's consciousness of her advanced liberty led her to reject a continuing association with European states during the nineteenth century; Britain's awareness of her constitutional uniqueness led her to avoid a continuing connection with the Continent during the second half of the nineteenth century. But there were two responses following from the condition of superiority — one was isolation, to avoid contamination; the other was intervention, to correct the misguided.[22]

---

[19] George Macaulay Trevelyan, *British History in the Nineteenth Century and After (1782-1919)* (London, 1948), pp. 294-295.

[20] See David Thomson, "The United Kingdom and Its World-Wide Interests" in *The New Cambridge Modern History,* Vol. 10 (Cambridge, 1960), p. 338.

[21] The British conservatives never had to be revolutionized because of their genius in accepting empirical reform. In some instances it was the conservatives themselves who took the lead in reform movements. See *ibid.,* p. 338.

[22] Professor R. W. Seton-Watson notes that "the principle of intervention in con-

For Great Britain, Palmerston and later Disraeli represented the second tradition, Cobden and Gladstone the first. Palmerston was ready to assert the principle of "Civis Romanus" in the Don Pacifico affair of 1850, and Russell intervened to help the birthpangs of Italian unity a decade later. The Crimean War was intended as a lesson to the reactionary rulers of Europe, and on the British side it was fought as much for military adventure to vindicate British prestige as for the balance of power.[23] When Austria and Prussia seized Schleswig from the Danish king, the English reverted to isolation. They stood by again on the sidelines when Prussia humbled Austria and France. British isolation meant that they would follow a separate course in international relations. John Bright repudiated a British obligation to right the wrongs of humanity: "It is not my duty to make this country the knight-errant of the human race. What a notion a man must have of the duties of the . . . people living in these islands if he thinks . . . that the sacred treasure of the bravery, resolution, and unfaltering courage of the people of England is to be squandered in a contest . . . for the preservation of the independence of Germany, and of the integrity, civilization, and something else of all Europe!"[24]

Thus the European Powers were bound to act separately and often against each other. Triumphant English liberalism confirmed an isolationist and spasmodically interventionist policy in regard to the retrograde continent. The revolutions of 1848 had failed in

---

tinental affairs, habitually practised by Palmerston, was now carried farther than ever before. It doubtless had an underlying psychological explanation in what may be called the 'cocksureness,' the moral certainty of the mid-Victorian era, when infallibility was quite as much a political as a religious dogma, when it was assumed by so many excellent people that British liberal and constitutional doctrines were a sure panacea for every ill and justified almost any interference, and when at the same time it was assumed even more confidently by the Radical interventionists of the Manchester school, that Free Trade was the perfect economic remedy and was destined to triumph everywhere." (*Britain in Europe: 1789-1914* [Cambridge, 1938], p. 357.) Professor Trevelyan includes these revealing sentences about the British Exhibition of 1851: "The unfortunate Europeans, having failed to master our secret of combining liberty with order, were invited, as a consolation prize, to come and admire the peace, progress and prosperity of Britain." *Op. cit.*, p. 295.

23 See Trevelyan, *op. cit.*, p. 302.

24 Quoted in A. J. P. Taylor, *The Trouble Makers* (Bloomington, Indiana, 1958), p. 62. The Crimean War, of course was the event which transformed England from interventionist to isolationist. See Craig, *loc. cit.*, pp. 269-270.

Europe and they were superfluous in England. Russia had experimented with a traditional conservative policy until the *Realpolitik* of her erstwhile allies proved her downfall in the Crimean War. Thereafter, she was converted to *Realpolitik* for the purpose of recouping her losses at the Congress of Paris. She considered several times a revolutionary alliance with France to undo the Vienna settlement in Italy and in the Near East. This pursuit of a radical policy by a conservative state was emblematic of the times. Prussia and Austria, despite their temporary rapprochements, were determined by the events of 1848 to vie for hegemony in a united Germany, and no lasting co-operation could be developed between them until after the Peace of Prague and the *Ausgleich* of 1867. Both Powers considered revolutionary alliance at different times to advance their opposed purposes: Prussia with England or France, Austria with France. The Concert could no more have prevented a struggle between them than it could have squared the circle.

In this atmosphere of inward turning hopes and fears, the Concert could not continue. While the Treaty of London of 1852 restrained the Prussians in Schleswig-Holstein and confirmed the succession of Prince Christian over the duchies, it did not go beyond personal union, and it reserved the rights of the German Confederation. The five Great Powers were party to this treaty, and it was negotiated while Britain and Russia were still participant in general European affairs and before the conflict of Austria and Prussia over Germany had reached substantial proportions.[25] But if the Concert temporarily succeeded in regulating Danish and German rights in the duchies, it failed soon afterward.[26] Despite continuous negotiations in Vienna, the international mechanism did not prevent the Crimean War. Its failure is all the more remarkable in light of the fact that the Russians accepted the four Powers' Vienna Note of 1853, and withdrew from the Danubian principalities when asked to do so in 1854. "Russia's withdrawal left the western allies at a loss. They had gone to war in order to check Russia's aggression on Turkey; and this aggression had ceased. They were thus faced with the problem — how to check an aggressive Power when it is not being aggressive?"[27] Nonetheless, the war proceeded in the Crimea

[25] See Binkley, *op. cit.*, p. 163.
[26] See Taylor, *Struggle*, p. 142.
[27] *Ibid.*, pp. 66-67.

while diplomacy continued at Vienna. The allies (France and Britain) took Sebastopol in September, 1855 but did not know what to do with their victory. "The intrigues of November, 1855 were a fitting end to a war in which diplomacy had only occasionally been interrupted by battles." [28] Surely, the Crimean War was one which could have been prevented by diplomatic contact, had there been a climate of moderation. As it was, Napoleon opted for disturbance, and the British, in the mode of the Don Pacifico affair, wanted a prestige triumph. In March, 1854 the cause of war had been Russian occupation of the principalities; in August, 1854 she withdrew from the principalities, but the war, having been declared, had to continue. The Crimean War was completely unreal, and the Concert should have prevented it, but it did not. [29]

Instead, the Powers met at Paris in 1856 to deal with the remnant issues. For the first time since 1815, the Concert had failed to prevent a war among the major Powers, and now it could only deal with its results. For fourteen years afterward the Concert not only failed to prevent war, it did not even ratify the evil which war caused. At Paris, the Danubian principalities were granted autonomy, and the Black Sea was "neutralized," a polite phrase for the demilitarization of the Russian Black Sea fleet. Prussia was kept out of the negotiations until the very last moment as the result of a British protest against her neutrality; she was admitted only as a signatory of the Straits Convention of 1841 and then only after Lord Clarendon had vigorously condemned her policy before the other four Powers.

After Paris the Concert collapsed. The Great Powers did not interfere to prevent or to ratify the unification of Italy in 1860 and the cession of Savoy and Nice to France. Indeed, the proposal for a European Congress on the affairs of Italy which Russia broached in March, 1859 was regarded by Austria as a signal for aggression. The

---

[28] *Ibid.,* p. 79.

[29] Professor Craig writes: ". . . it is important to note that that curious conflict marks a significant turning point in European history. Behind it lay forty years of peace; before it stretched fifteen years in which four wars were fought by the great powers of Europe, with the result that the territorial arrangements of the Continent were completely transformed." *Loc. cit.,* p. 267. Both he and Professor Robert Binkley view the Crimean War, and not the Revolutions of 1848, as the real turning point in European international relations. See Binkley, *op. cit.,* p. 179.

Concert failed to deal with the frictions caused by the Polish revolt of 1863, and Napoleon's abortive project for a Congress was
designed to reawaken discontent, not to stifle it. Since the revolt
had fizzled in Poland, a Congress might stir it up again. What the
French Emperor wanted was a conference that would serve the
policy of liberalism and adventure. Diplomacy might accomplish
the same result as revolution or warfare. The mere fact that such a
proposal might be made indicates the new international tenor: the
past objectives of the Concert had been pacification and agreement;
the future objective (*après* Napoleon) was to be revision and disruption. After 1863 the Concert's failures multiplied. It could not repeat its success of 1852 on the Danish question; in 1864 Austria and
Prussia acted against the German Confederation and against Europe
when they invaded Schleswig. In 1866 Prussia was allowed to
humble Austria without challenge. In 1870 Prussia defeated France,
and totally upset the balance of material power in Europe. Still,
Prussia was not hailed before the bar of the Concert. *Realpolitik*
had shattered it.

II  The events of 1848-1870 transformed the international system.
They revealed the crisis and failure of "federative polity." [30]
After 1814 there was a progressive decline of ideological international policy in Europe. The conservatives of 1814 had opted for a
policy of principle, and the Concert had regulated the affairs of the
Continent for a brief eight-year period. The liberals and conservatives after 1822 still pursued general ideological policies, but instead of advancing the interests of a united and conservative Europe, they each sought to advance the interests of their own ideological group. Their conflict, however, was moderated by a minimal
international consensus, and warfare was exorcised. In 1848 liberalism and conservatism exploded against each other and the result
put an end to general international policy. No longer would conservatives place their faith in the solidity of the conservative alliance; no longer would the liberals advance in a solid phalanx
against the reaction. Conservatives still desired to protect themselves, and liberals still wanted help against the Northern Courts,
but neither group would act in unison. General interests were now
pursued by "special" policy. This was a surprising turn of events.

30 See Binkley, *op. cit.*, p. xix.

The ideological struggle engendered by the French Revolution was expected to determine European politics for the entire course of the nineteenth century. ". . . In 1848 men did not expect new manoeuvres of the Balance of Power. They looked forward to a greater war of religion, with the Holy Alliance on one side and the revolution on the other." [31] It was strange to find "the decline of revolutionary spirit in the most revolutionary decades of European history. Marx and Engels were more profound judges than their contemporaries; and they expected the revolutions of 1848 to be followed by other and more violent explosions. They turned out to be altogether wrong. In the first years of the twentieth century, violent revolution seemed more remote from every great European country than it had ever been." [32] If the anticipated had occurred, the final conflict of ideological antagonists would have brought the demise of the Concert just as surely as the mutual exhaustion of 1848. The total bifurcation of Europe into a powerful liberal alliance and a resurgent conservative bloc would have meant the end of international co-operation; as it happened, co-operation ended as a result of the collapse of the two adversaries. And the very frailty of both conservatives and liberals demanded a desperate grasping for revolutionary straws; not until the conservatives and liberals were once more secure in domestic opinion could a more moderate external policy be followed. Because of the failure of Prussian conservatism in 1848 Bismarck had to unify Germany under conservative leadership. Because of the failure of Carlo Alberto's liberalism in 1848, Cavour had to unify Italy under liberal leadership. If liberalism could not be advanced without force, it would be advanced with it. Militarism, essentially a revolutionary device, came to play a new role in European relations after 1848.

The Crimean War provided the keynote of the previous age. It was fought by professional armies and its hallmark was a fusty inefficiency. "That age enjoyed a blessing of which ours has known too little — freedom from competitive armaments. It could scarcely then expect military efficiency when war came at last." [33] Very dif-

---

31 Taylor, *Struggle*, p. xx.

32 *Ibid.*, p. xxxiv.

33 Trevelyan, *op. cit.*, pp. 305-306. See also Professor Binkley who remarks: "The inefficiency of the European military estabishment was merely the counterpart of the bygone efficiency of its diplomatic establishment." *Op. cit.*, p. 174.

ferent were the Austro-Prussian and Franco-Prussian wars of 1866 and 1870 respectively.[34] The Prussian army had modeled its tactics most nearly on those of Napoleon I, and it was the closest approximation to a citizen army in all Europe.[35] Moltke followed Napoleon's pattern of emphasis upon speed and mobility as well as upon the massing of forces. While his Austrian and French opponents sometimes succumbed to old eighteenth-century notions of "superior position," Moltke stressed time above place. He realized that two separate armies might be moved more quickly than one great one, and even more than Napoleon he was willing to achieve concentration on the battlefield itself.[36] He was learned in the lore of topography, and his use of roads and railroads to heighten mobility was based on the principle behind Napoleon's own lightning marches. Though Moltke realized the value of an inner line of operations, he was not averse to flanking, concentric movements which would envelop his foe. The Austrians at Königgrätz had the interior lines, but they were unable to prevent two Prussian armies from joining and threatening flank and rear. The Prussians, after some hesitancy, also came to accept Napoleon's stress upon artillery, and the engagement at Sedan, which broke the back of the Second Empire, showed the impact of massed artillery fire.[37] The Prussians had various other advantages over their enemies. The Austrians had a muzzle-loading rifle which was no match for the Prussian needle gun, and although the French had the breech-loading *chassepot*, numerically French forces were often inferior to the Prussians, and they did not use their artillery properly.

The supremacy of the Prussian army in both contests was due to

---

[34] Captain Liddell Hart remarks: "The forty years from 1830 to 1870 saw a greater change in the means of warfare, both on land and sea, than during the whole previous span of modern history—or all of previous history. Most of the change was concentrated, at least in the sense of being demonstrated, within the last decade of the period. The technical, tactical, and strategical developments during the wars of this decade foreshadowed the operational trend, and social form, of warfare in the next century." "Armed Forces and the Art of War: Armies" in *The New Cambridge Modern History*, Vol. 10 (Cambridge, 1960), p. 302.

[35] See Alfred Vagts, *A History of Militarism* (New York, 1937), p. 221.

[36] Hajo Holborn, "Moltke and Schlieffen: The Prussian-German School," in Edward Mead Earle (ed.), *Makers of Modern Strategy* (Princeton, 1948), p. 178.

[37] Maj. Gen. J. F. C. Fuller, "The Period of German Consolidation, 1861-1871," in Gordon B. Turner (ed.), *A History of Military Affairs Since the Eighteenth Century* (New York, 1956), p. 189.

superior organization and speed, made possible by the adaptation of new techniques to the art of warfare. The contrast between the Crimean War and the two adventures of Prussian militarism could not have been more marked. The Crimean War had its antecedents in the eighteenth century, the Prussian wars in the battles of Napoleon. The Crimean War was declared in March 1854 but the decisive battle was not fought until eighteen months later. The Austro-Prussian War did not even wait for a formal declaration. Hostilities began in earnest on June 21, 1866 and the decisive battle of Königgrätz was fought less than a fortnight later. The Franco-Prussian War began on July 15, 1870 and Sedan occurred on September 2nd. The new technology had revolutionized warfare and ultimately diplomacy. Decisions came so fast that neutral Powers could no longer sit on the sidelines waiting to enforce armed mediation. No longer could a Power wait until war began to find allies because allies were of no use unless they were pledged and ready when war commenced. "The system of Metternich . . . had no general alliances and few particular treaties." But "at the end of the nineteenth century all the Great Powers except Great Britain were involved in formal alliances." [38] The Powers which mobilized first would have a great advantage, so when war seemed certain, allies would have to urge speedy mobilization upon each other. The presumption of pre-Sadowa was diplomacy first, war second; the presumption of post-Sadowa was almost the reverse. Diplomats were given their chance, but when war seemed near initiative passed into the hands of the soldiers.[39] While the elder Moltke, however, would not prejudice the political issue by military measures, his nephew reversed priorities. ". . . as chief of staff [he] had to inform William II in August, 1914, that the strategic plans of the general staff had deprived the government of its freedom of action." [40] The Prussian army had refurbished Napoleonic strategy. "Its victories of 1866 and 1870 revolutionized military thought. After 1871 every continental Power adopted the Prussian system of universal military service for three years." [41] Prussia had shown that the *levée en masse* might even be turned to conservative purposes.

38 Taylor, *Struggle*, p. 1.
39 See Liddell Hart, *loc. cit.*, pp. 312-313.
40 Holborn, *loc. cit.*, p. 181.
41 Taylor, *Struggle*, p. xxiv-xxv.

Yet, the extinction of ideological alliance after 1848 did not have only unfavorable effects. As it turned out, the *Realpolitik* of post-1848 was but a prelude to renewed cooperation after 1871. Certainly, the Concert of Europe could not act as a unit when it was riven by ideology. If the revolutions of 1848 had marked only a beginning of clashes of ideas, the Concert would not have long survived. A sharpened conflict of united conservatism with united liberalism in the nineteenth century would probably have led to the same kind of antagonism as that between liberal and Fascist Powers and liberal and Communist Powers in the twentieth century. From the international point of view, the total triumph of conservatism or liberalism would have been preferable to a continuing standoff. Thus the triumph of *Realpolitik* and the demise of the split between adherents and antagonists of the French Revolution permitted, in theory at least, a general reformulation of international connections. That 1848-1871 was an age of conflict is not to be explained by the traditional ideological cleavage, rather in terms of the desperation ensuing from the failure of traditional ideology. Not until the conservatives had learned to master revolutionary tendencies by stealing their thunder, not until the liberals unraveled the secret of traditional conservative appeals would a new moderation prevail. Bismarck placed conservatism on a new foundation by utilizing the seemingly liberal (but actually Bonapartist) device of universal suffrage and representative institutions, while Cavour placed liberalism on a new foundation by using the conservative tactic of monarchy, diplomatic intrigue, and military force. As a result of the mutual failure of 1848, the liberals began to learn something about material power, the conservatives something about the power of ideas. Ideas and material power, taken singly, had each foundered in 1848, but taken together, they would succeed after 1871. When the necessary learning had taken place, liberals and conservatives could get along much better. The ends of international relations had not changed, but the policies used to realize these ends brought ideological antagonists closer together. No one doubted that Bismarck was a conservative, or that Cavour was a liberal — however, the policies of the two were similar. Once the conservatives began to use revolutionary policies, there seemed less reason for revolution. As they used liberalism, the German liberals capitulated; as they used nationalism the German nationalists capitulated. Once the liberals began to flex their muscles, to learn the technique of intrigue, to appeal to traditional symbols, there was less *raison d'être* for conservatism. The French conservatives were hampered by Louis Napoleon's return to *le roi soleil's* policy of historic expansion, weakened by his Catholicism, and undermined by his policy of adventure for its own sake. The conservatives might rail over the unification of Italy but it redounded to the interests of the House of Piedmont. What Carlo Alberto failed to achieve as an independent monarch Victor Emanuel gained in alliance with liberalism.

The real tragedy of the system after 1848 was that the necessary learning could only be accomplished at the expense of others. In order to raise a bulwark against revolution, Bismarck had to neutralize it, but it could only be neutralized at the expense of Austria. In order to raise a bulwark against conservatism, Napoleon had to defuse it, but it could only be defused at the expense of Belgium, Luxembourg, South Germany, Mexico, or Savoy. Liberals seemed to advance at the expense of liberals, conservatives at the expense of conservatives. Only the Crimean War and the Franco-Austrian War retained a prior ideological flavor. After 1871, liberals and conservatives attained a new self-confidence, and did not have to scramble to maintain their separate existence. Bismarck continued to fear the social peril, but he held it in check for the generation after Frankfort. The conservatives in France were, despite the revolutionary republic and the Commune, partially numbed by the Second Empire. They could not unite to form a monarchical system after 1871 and the Third Republic eventually emerged. English liberals had triumphed even without *Realpolitik*. The new self-confidence after 1871, the partial merger of political policies permitted a strange new Concert to function. Once again, the question of sheer existence having been settled, the statesmen of Europe could turn to more lofty causes. Because of the ideological *détente* the preservation of peace could take on a renewed importance. Peace is to statesmen of all countries a secondary object to be sought only after self-preservation is assured. The consolidation of 1870 and after permitted the states of Europe to dwell on secondary issues once more.

III    In an important sense the struggles of 1848-1871 put an end
       to the conflict of ideas generated by the French Revolution.
While revolution and counterrevolution were the orders of the day,
international compromise was hard to find. Both liberals and conservatives feared for their lives. Thus liberalism and conservatism
had to fight each other; if a liberal regime were allowed to exist it
would pose a threat to the political constitution of conservative
regimes; as long as conservative regimes remained in the saddle,
liberal governments could not feel completely secure. Liberal and
conservative tides swept across Europe and touched almost all nations; revolutionary or counterrevolutionary war would have an
even more profound impact. If the ideological conflict had continued to determine European relations after 1848, pure liberal regimes
fighting pure conservative regimes, the peace would have been
rapidly broken; the Concert of Europe might not have survived the
blow. The events of 1848 and after did not end ideology as a factor
in European politics, but they made conflicting ideologies tolerable
politically. After 1871 liberals and conservatives, while still wary,
did not have to have deathly fear of each other. Once the conservatives had taken over a modicum of the liberal-national program,
they insulated themselves against revolution. Once the liberals had
taken over a measure of conservative symbolism, they insured themselves against counterrevolution. As the domestic position of each
group improved, its international position could become more cooperative. Liberals and conservatives had to contend before 1848,
but not after 1871. While the Concert might have failed in the context of ideological division, it could reappear when the need to
wage the ideological struggle disappeared.

Even the conservatives were able to make peace with one another.
After the Austro-Prussian struggle for hegemony in Germany was
decided in 1866, Austria rapidly made her peace with the new
Germany. Within Austria the new centralization of Bach had given
rise to a struggle of German and Magyar nationalism for control of
the Empire. If Germany had been unified under Austrian leadership, the German influence would have triumphed; the failure of
German nationalism led the other "master" nation, the Magyars,
to assume control. The *Ausgleich* delivered the Empire into the
hands of the Magyars, and they in turn thrust Austria's interna-

tional policy into the hands of the new German Empire. *Gross-deutsch* would have submerged the Hungarians, but *kleindeutsch* saved them. Soon after 1866 the Magyars brought a new *rapprochement* of the enemies of the Austro-Prussian War. Russia reinsured its position by repudiating the Black Sea clauses of the Treaty of Paris in 1870, a symbolic act which received the *post hoc* imprimatur of the London Conference in 1871. With the emergence of the Third Republic in France, the liberal alliance was in principle restored, though the cooperation of England was limited by her "splendid isolation." But the force of the old ideological accords was weakened by the events intervening after 1848. Disraeli would opt as often for Germany and Austria as for France; Bismarck would work as often with the English statesman as with the Tsar. Bismarck was the focal point of European relations after 1871, and the refurbished Concert of Europe was truly a "Bismarckian" Concert. In terms of material power, Germany was dominant on the Continent, and in terms of diplomatic subtlety, Bismarck was Metternich's equal. The Concert after 1871, thus, had a different character from the Concert of 1815. The three great Powers of Austria, Russia and England had shared the stage at Vienna, and Castlereagh, Alexander, and Metternich the diplomatic limelight. The multilateral Concert was reinforced by power and diplomatic *savoir-faire;* the Bismarckian Concert had a particular *point d'union* — Berlin — and its leading strings were firmly in the grasp of the German Chancellor.

The international system of 1848-1871 was unlike those which immediately preceded it. It had a Renaissance flavor; Machiavellianism abounded; and there was a profusion of great "political architects." The state became a "work of art" in Burckhardt's terms, and any materials or methods might be used to fashion it. The result was not quite a return to Cesare Borgia, but the respect for treaties, the appeal to the Concert were noticeably lacking. Wars were as often provoked for overriding political objects as the result of genuine tension. Prussia and Austria did not want to fight each other, but they had to do so. The liberal alliance, on the other hand, did not have to fight Russia, it wanted to do so. In all countries, domestic sentiment was more and more becoming a determinant of national policy. Palmerston, and "Civis Romanus" appealed to a latent jingoism of English public sentiment, Napoleon to a similar phenomenon in France. Even Bismarck's wars against France and Austria had a popular cast. The wars of the period violated historic canons. The Crimean War violated Navarino and the Straits Convention of 1841, though it seemed to conform to ideological principles; the Franco-Austrian War of 1859 shattered the previous standoff in Italy, though again ideology played an important part. But the strange outcome was not wars of ideological character, but those which violated them. While one might expect Austria to fight against France, or England against Russia, one was surprised to find that the major conflict of the period was Prussia's struggle against Austria. The tentative links between France and Austria, France and Russia, and Prussia and England at various times would have surprised the ideologue. It was a paradox that at the very point that the ideological struggle was being carried to its height and jeopardizing the domestic positions of both liberal and conservative regimes, international alignments were violating all ideological canons. *Realpolitik* did not mark an end to ideology, but it represented the most realistic and ruthless pursuit of it.

In the end, the shattering of the Concert of Europe produced a highly unstable international system. There was no supervisory institution to regulate the disruptive actions of European states, and the actions themselves took on a more desperate and unlimited character. The direct confrontation of interests, propelled by the danger to domestic regimes, involved Europe in four important wars. Nations seemed unable to limit their ambitions, and wars did not issue from unredressed international grievances: they were provoked on purpose to placate discontented fractions of society. War did not occur because it could not be averted, but because it was necessary. The Concert itself became a vehicle of disturbance.

The distinctiveness of the system of *Realpolitik* can be seen in its characteristic ambitions and policies. For the first time since the first French Empire the governing classes were fighting for their own existence. All means were used to advance that end, and combinations frequently violated ideological lines. Warfare, chicanery and intrigue were the staples of diplomacy, while the Concert failed to ensure peace. The transformation of the role of ideology did not produce a return to the Balance of Power. Rather, the unlimited means employed harked back to the desperate struggles of the Thirty Years' War or to the Italian city-states of the Renaissance.

# chapter seven
# THE BISMARCKIAN CONCERT

I The Franco-Prussian War of 1870-71 marked the close of a diplomatic era. Ideology had been a determining force in European relations prior to 1871, but it was not after 1871. The Concert of Europe, having declined into suspended animation, was revived. Liberalism or movements tending in a liberal direction had held the center of the stage in a host of European countries before 1870; they were challenged though not displaced by labor and socialist movements afterward. While public opinion had not been a voice to reckon with in the molding of foreign policy before 1870, it was an insistent harangue after that time. War was thought to be a revolutionary device until the Austro-Prussian and Franco-Prussian wars, but afterward it was believed to be a tolerable means of policy. Permanent alliances had not been necessary in peacetime before 1871, and nations had relied on the Concert or themselves alone. However, alliances were a necessity after victory came to depend upon speed of mobilization. Imperialism which had not been a decisive component of the European system since the first Napoleon, came to be the signal characteristic of the pre-1914 age.

With these manifold changes, it is perhaps surprising that the system of international relations after 1871 retained any similarity to the systems which preceded it. That it did so is tribute to the staying power of the older classes. Despite the progress of liberal reform, the conservatives did not lose the reins of power in East and Central Europe. In the new Germany universal suffrage was used to elect a Reichstag with a few powers, but ministerial responsibility or parliamentary government was not established. In the Federal

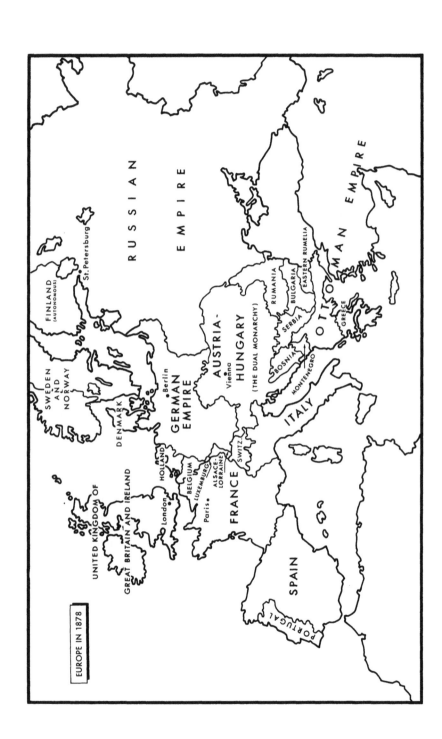

EUROPE IN 1878

FINLAND
(AUTONOMOUS)

St.Petersburg

R U S S I A N      E M P I R E

SWEDEN
AND
NORWAY

DENMARK

Berlin

GERMAN
EMPIRE

AUSTRIA-
HUNGARY
Vienna
(THE DUAL MONARCHY)

RUMANIA

BULGARIA

EASTERN RUMELIA

SERBIA

BOSNIA

MONTENEGRO

GREECE

O T T O M A N   E M P I R E

HOLLAND

BELGIUM

LUXEMBURG

ALSACE-
LORRAINE

SWITZ.

UNITED KINGDOM OF

GREAT BRITAIN AND IRELAND

London

Paris

FRANCE

ITALY

SPAIN

PORTUGAL

Council, or Bundesrat, Prussia was in a minority, but usually obtained her way. The successes of 1866 and 1870 forced the liberals to compromise, and Bismarck maintained his grip on domestic as well as international politics.[1]

In Austria the situation apparently was reversed. The failure of the Habsburgs to carry through the unification of Germany under conservative auspices gave German liberals a new lease on life. After Sadowa, Francis Joseph made two compromises: he delivered Hungary into the hands of the Magyars and Austria into the arms of the German liberals. The first bargain remained until the collapse of the empire; the second was taken back after ten years. The Constitution of 1867 had prescribed the responsibility of ministers to parliament, but in the 1880's the Emperor was able to make them accountable to himself. The four-class system of elections redounded to the interests of the professional and propertied elements, but the liberals were never able to take full advantage of this fact. The Church and the Monarchy eventually prevented the realization of liberal middle class rule.[2]

In Russia and the Ottoman Empire liberalism was a farce. Neither constitution nor suffrage was allowed to disturb the tranquillity of these eastern regions. In both countries a "westernizing" liberal influence was temporarily felt, but in neither did it affect the main character of the regime.[3] In Turkey there were occasional admirers of the English parliamentary system. In Russia the abolition of serfdom in 1861 and the establishment of local government bodies, the *zemstvos*, in 1864 reflected the more liberal attitude of the times. And yet, the liberal advance of the late eighteen-sixties and eighteen-seventies was misleading in Central and Eastern Europe. Fundamentally, the old conservatives maintained their previous control — Bismarck, because he had stolen liberal thunder; Francis Joseph, because of German liberal weakness and the growing Magyar ascendancy; Alexander II because of his entrenched position. Despite the French Revolution the old regime had not been discarded.

In the West and in Italy, liberal regimes were the order of the day. Universal suffrage was taken over from the Second Empire in

---

[1] See A. J. P. Taylor, *The Course of German History* (London, 1954), pp. 116-118.

[2] See A. J. P. Taylor, *The Habsburg Monarchy* (London, 1951), p. 141.

[3] C. J. H. Hayes, *A Generation of Materialism, 1871-1900* (New York, 1941), p. 73.

France, but it no longer operated as it had for Louis Napoleon. As long as labor and socialist movements were undeveloped, universal manhood suffrage, enfranchising the peasantry, was a conservative device. With the Commune and the growth of working class sentiment, however, universal suffrage would no longer favor the Right. In England, the restricted franchise even after 1867 guaranteed a generation of middle class rule. Thus, the changed atmosphere of the age did not rule out the older classes: liberals and conservatives were still at the helm of state. The nature of liberal and conservative government, however, was much changed. No longer was ideological advancement the program of either group. The impact of the revolutions of 1848 had been the jettisoning of Messianism. Existence became the pre-eminent concern of each regime. After 1871 the challenge to each had been partially or largely overcome. Bismarck obtained kudos by realizing an important part of the liberal-national program; Francis Joseph secured himself by temporary concession to the liberals and permanent concession to the Magyars. The Habsburgs had an option which was not open to Bismarck: failing to unify Germany, they could still play the German liberals off against the nationalities. By encouraging conservative national groups within the empire, they could avoid the retreat which Bismarck would have been forced to make if he had not won the day at Königgrätz. In the end, of course, either policy was futile; concession to the liberals would immediately reduce the Emperor to the status of constitutional monarch; concession to the nationalities would eventually split the empire apart. After 1867, however, the second seemed the more remote evil. In Russia, the Tsar had repaired the losses of the Crimean War when he denounced the Black Sea clauses of the Treaty of Paris. At the same time the Western liberal regimes were secure. The English had never been in danger; the French were better able to handle the conservative-royalists after 1878 than they had been during the Second Empire. In one sense, 1871 brought the period of *Realpolitik* to an end. *Realpolitik* had been necessary only so long as the regime itself was in jeopardy; it could be overthrown when greater security of tenure had been attained.

It is perhaps surprising then, that an age of ideology did not succeed the age of *Realpolitik*; once primary goals had been achieved, it was proper to turn to secondary ones. And yet, the struggle between the liberal *entente* and the "three Northern courts" was not resumed. The reason was primarily that no regime had the discretionary latitude that it once possessed. During the revolutionary period and shortly afterward ideological victory had been almost identical with internal stability: conservative solidarity was the only safeguard against the revolution; revolutionary liberalism was the only protection against conservative onslaught. During the eighteen thirties and forties, however, the security of regimes and the promotion of ideology were dissociated. Liberals and conservatives could live and let live and even work together in the Concert of Europe. At this stage ideology was no longer vital. After 1871 the capabilities available to European regimes were not sufficient to permit a renewal of the ideological struggle. Bismarck's internal alliance with the liberals forbade a conservative *revanche* against the revolution. Austria, which had to make an even greater obeisance before the liberal altar in the years 1867-1879, could hardly make recourse to the Holy Alliance. Even the Russian Tsar felt popular impulsions toward more liberal or nationalist policies, and could not embark upon a policy of unregenerate monarchical solidarity. In France the Third French Republic was too shaky to embark upon ideological crusades and in England liberal government was thought to be so advanced as to be incapable of realization anywhere else. France could not advance liberal causes; England would not deign to do so.

What emerged was a way-station between the *ancien régime* and *Realpolitik*. Under the latter the object of policy had been the survival of separate regimes; under the former the object had been the aggrandizement of individual regimes. The new system aimed to protect and secure the state regime. Survival was not at stake, but the internal and external threats were great enough to rule out wholesale aggrandizement. The European conservatives were never sure enough of their own position to attempt an attack on their ideological adversaries. As the liberals had not been able to destroy the conservatives in 1848, so the conservatives gave up the idea of undermining the liberals after 1871. By this time each group had consolidated its position, and the total destruction of either was out of the question.

The limitations of domestic sentiment also ruled out an ideological crusade. In France, Germany, and Austria-Hungary the leading political group could remain in power only by seeking support of a particular class. Bismarck could not parade his conservatism when in alliance with the National Liberal Party; Taafe could not pledge bleak reaction when he was trying to lure the masses with the bait of universal suffrage. Both liberalism and conservatism were largely class phenomena; when the support of a single class was insufficient the old ideological appeals could no longer be used. Thus, instead of a new confrontation of Holy Alliance with the Revolution, the conflict of ideas evaporated. In its place both liberal and conservative regimes turned to nationalism to find the necessary social cement. For the liberals, nationalism was a means of preventing left-wing success and conservative revenge.[4] The laboring classes could hardly press for a drastic change in the existing social order when they were deifying the presently constituted nation-state. The conservatives could hardly turn back the clock when nationalism taught them to revere the state as it was. For the conservatives nationalism was an antidote to liberalism and socialism. Where reactionaries were in control, nationalist doctrines would legitimize and sanctify an existing order against liberal or social change. But working class appeals were often played as a descant to conservative melodies. In the conservative countries, social legislation was a weapon against the liberals, and in both France and in England, the less liberal groups were partisans of social legislation. Thus, the political strength of both liberal and conservative regimes was partially equalized: the liberals relied upon their own predominant middle-class backing and upon the appeal of nationalism; the conservatives played the nationalist theme and also pandered to the working classes.

The result of the political equipoise domestically was a more favorable international climate. For practical purposes ideology had been eliminated as a divisive factor in international politics; the security of domestic regimes was not so precarious that revolutionary or military expedients were necessary measures of insurance. The regimes which were losers in the period of *Realpolitik* were almost as well entrenched afterward as the victors — Sedan could be blamed on the clericals and the conservative coterie; the *Ausgleich* furnished a pattern of using the nationalities against the liberals.

[4] See Harold D. Lasswell, *World Politics and Personal Insecurity* (Glencoe, Illinois, 1951), pp. 48-51.

Revenge against Germany, for both France and Austria, was a secondary aim simply because the existence of their separate regimes did not depend upon it. International conflict usually results from desperation or from supreme confidence. In the first case war is necessary; in the second it can be afforded. A very insecure regime, wages war because it has no alternative, while a very secure regime does so because it does not fear for the result. The wars of the eighteenth century were, for the most part, the product of security, and the wars of the nineteenth were products of insecurity. Between 1871 and 1890 Europe happily fell between the two stools into moderate anxiety. Warfare was, temporarily at least, undesired and unnecessary, and the Concert re-emerged to protect the peace.

But the Concert of Bismarck was not like the Concert of Metternich and Castlereagh. The victors over Napoleon I shared a common political conviction about domestic and international society, and they abhorred revolutionary war. They agreed on the tenets of conservatism, and they were willing to go to great lengths to prevent a new revolutionary assault on the ancient liberties of Europe. The very fury of past war reinforced the conviction that no such period of violence could be tolerated again. Hence, the architects of Vienna, Aix-la-Chapelle, and Troppau had a firm bond among them. The diplomats who presided over the defeat of Napoleon III had no such solidarity. They were not united by a common political ideology, and their only agreement was on the tactic of nationalism (a policy bound to raise trouble in the future). Nor were they convinced of the futility and danger of war. If any deduction was to be drawn from the Prussian campaigns against Austria and France, it was that wars were quickly decided, leaving the vanquished little worse off than the victor.[5] They did not promote revolution or civil disorder; they did not have to leave lasting estrangements. After Waterloo war seemed intolerable, but after Sedan it was found to be supportable. And this was not all. The creators of the

[5] Captain Liddell Hart writes: 'Soldiers everywhere assumed that future great wars would be decided as quickly as in 1866 and 1870 — and worked on that assumption. They would have been wiser to have paid more attention to the lengthy last phase, and also to the four years' Civil War in America. For this foreshadowed the future of war more truly — although Moltke is said to have discounted it as a case of 'two armed mobs chasing each other around the country, from which nothing could be learned.'" "Armed Forces and the Art of War: Armies" in *The New Cambridge Modern History*, Vol. 10 *The Zenith of European Power, 1830-70*, J. P. T. Bury (ed.) (Cambridge, 1960), p. 327.

European Concert had discarded the system of Balance of Power because it would not function quickly enough. One could not wait for the balance to be overturned; the Concert had to act at the first threat to the peace or to the domestic order. But the presumption of the statesmen of Vienna was that action could still await the fact — something had to happen before the Concert should be called into operation. Here the later successes of Prussian militarism pointed a different lesson: since wars were won or lost in a matter of weeks or months, even the Concert could not act fast enough. It would be too late to convene a Congress after war had begun. The nation which mobilized first would have a great advantage and the Concert might find itself with a *fait accompli*. The Concert might prevent a war through prior negotiation, or it might pare down the gains of war through subsequent diplomacy; but it could not, in and of itself, intervene militarily while the contest was in progress. The interventions authorized at Troppau and Verona could not be duplicated a half-century later. Thus, peacetime military alliances absorbed a portion of the Concert's task. Because the Concert could not act quickly enough, military allies, not Concert intervention, would bear the brunt in the first instance. Separate action thereby partially replaced a multilateral instrument.

Thus, the Concert had to function as much through the alliance network as through formal institutional means. The Concert was formally convened to consider questions of first importance only twice during the twenty years after 1870.[6] In spirit, however, it was present in the complicated alliance negotiations which most often were used to settle international disputes during the period. And the eclipse of ideology as a dominant factor in world politics did not permit a return to the balancing theories of the *ancien régime*. In the eighteenth century material power was to be kept divided, and the assumption was that the cardinal sin was to seek to concentrate it. In the Bismarckian system material power was to be accumulated in the hands of the Concert directorate, and the cardinal sin was to lodge power elsewhere. When a challenge occurred, the directorate would seek to consolidate its strength by additional alignments. The potential disrupter would at the same time be assured that it had much to lose from separate action and something to gain if it remained within the multilateral-bilateral framework.

[6] At London in 1871 and at Berlin in 1878.

The Bismarckian Concert differed from the Metternichean Concert also in that it was largely dominated by a single Power and a single intellect. The material strengths of Russia, Austria, and England were not far apart in 1815, and the diplomatic finesse of Metternich, Castlereagh and the Tsar was of a piece. Since neither a single army nor a single mind could dominate Europe, agreement became the keynote of Concert operation. Metternich, above all others, realized this truth, and he labored long though sometimes vainly to bring other Powers to accept limits on their actions. Few were coerced to do international bidding. Most were persuaded to do so. Bismarck, on the other hand, did not need to persuade, cajole or flatter. Germany's powerful central position ensured a hearing for the Iron Chancellor. Instead of bland inducements, he would stir up a war scare, pass army bills, and conclude new military alliances. Germany was powerful enough to force peace down the throats of recalcitrant Powers, and Bismarck was not above doing so. Furthermore, a genuinely multilateral agreement was often beyond his patience. But Bismarck's methods were not dictated by temperament alone. Without alliances, mobilization plans and a large army, multilateral agreement could never be enforced. Metternich could put agreement first and loiter on the question of means; Bismarck had to put means first and defer agreement.

There was still another important difference between the old and the new Concert system. After the Napoleonic wars, France, the defeated Power, had been rapidly admitted to the Concert if not to the Quadruple Alliance. She had lost territories to the Coalition, had been forced to accept Allied occupation and to pay an indemnity, and her new internal regime had practically been installed from without. Yet the French people, having on the whole accepted the defeat, did not force the restored Bourbon regime to embark on a war of revenge against the Allied victors. In terms of the Vienna settlement and the second Treaty of Paris, the Treaty of Frankfurt in 1871 was not a Carthaginian peace, and in terms of the accepted practice of the old regime, it was not humiliating at all. Under the *ancien régime* vast tracts of territory changed hands. Typically, however, a victor would not demand too much and a defeated Power concede too little. With the growing mobilization of popular sentiment in the latter part of the nineteenth century, however, peace settlements became ever more difficult to agree upon. Pressed on by national opinion, winners would have to demand more, losers to concede less. The seizure of Alsace-Lorraine would not have been a decisive obstacle to friendship with Prussia in 1814, and in 1750, it would have been even less a barrier. In 1871, however, Bismarck's demand for Alsace-Lorraine was perhaps the greatest blunder of his diplomacy, for it meant that France could not effect a *rapprochement* with Germany, however sincerely she repudiated a war of revenge. In 1884 and 1885 Bismarck and French statesmen cooperated for colonial purposes, and the German Chancellor would probably have liked to erase the blot on Franco-German relations if France had permitted it.[7] But a fundamental *détente* seemed out of the question. France, in a fashion, returned to the Concert of Europe after 1871, but she could never still her animosity for Germany. Gambetta, far less bellicose than the French conservatives, epitomized the French attitude toward the captured province when he said in 1880, "Think of it always, speak of it never."[8] France, then, could not play her accustomed part in European diplomacy after 1871, and because Bismarck feared for French intentions, a central purpose of his policy was to divert French energies to colonial expansion and to prevent France from finding an ally which could be used to win territory on the Rhine.

II  Thus, the Bismarckian Concert, a precarious combination of force and volition, rested upon the tenuous foundation of a common agreement upon nationalism as the basis of international policy. The growth and development of popular government and the extension of suffrage were potent factors in the new nationalism. In liberal countries, middle-class rule produced a bourgeois identification with the nation-state. In short, the middle class took a proprietary interest in and lent a proprietary support to the liberal regime. Popular sovereignty became a nationalist force. In the conservative countries, the extension of suffrage hoodwinked the gullible and gave nationalist support for the conservative cause. Liberal trappings were accepted in the place of liberal rules. The feeling of

[7] William L. Langer, *European Alliances and Alignments, 1871-1890* (New York, 1950), Chapter Eleven, esp. pp. 297 and 301.
[8] Quoted in René Albrecht-Carrié, *A Diplomatic History of Europe Since the Congress of Vienna* (New York, 1958), p. 167.

identification with the state regime was similar to that in liberal states.

But while popular government and suffrage reform added new reserves of power to the fund of the regime, it did not adequately channel and direct that new power. The old assumption had been that national government would be pacific government;[9] the masses would give new support to the political leadership, but in exchange they would demand a greater control over the conduct of international and domestic affairs. If the citizenry were bolstering the position of the regime with one hand, they were checking and directing it with the other. As it turned out, however, the checkrein was mythical, for instead of prescribing a policy of peace and international restraint, the masses increasingly opted for expansionism. In some cases they forced national aggrandizement on an unwilling regime, or demanded glory where the regime would have been satisfied with repute. The tragedy of the last quarter of the nineteenth century was popular support of government without corresponding popular control of government.

The new nationalism and the new imperialism were in part the result of a new kind of personal and collective insecurity. In the *ancien régime* the individual had had few civil or political liberties, but he had a certain amount of personal autonomy. Within the scope of historic social duties, the peasant, the artisan, and the *petit bourgeois* had a measure of independence and power. During the phase of cottage industry, the laborer retained a good deal of control in the production and marketing of his commodity. In the period of merchant capitalism, the worker still retained his ascendancy in production but began to lose it in marketing. Finally, in the phase of industrial capitalism, not only did marketing become a social instead of an individual function, but production did so as well.[10] By the third quarter of the nineteenth century, a sense of powerlessness was descending upon the laborer in an increasingly industrial civilization. Important reserves of independence had been appropriated by the then highly technical functions of production and distribution. No longer could the individual in any sense pro-

[9] This doctrine was formulated by Kant and popularized by Mazzini.

[10] For the preceding the author is indebted to the lectures of Professor Louis Hartz of Harvard University.

vide for himself by his own efforts. His efforts were geared to a machine technology, and his work did not provide direct sustenance since it had become merely a unit of exchange. The range of labor autonomy was curtailed while cultural standards were being raised. The net impact seemed to be a reduction of individual control over personal environment and a simultaneous increase in the standards demanded in that environment.[11] Individual power was diminished while individual responsibility was increasing. The moral conscience was elevated to a high point, while the ability of living up to that conscience was lowered. It is small wonder that many individuals turned to collective autonomy as a substitute for their lost personal autonomy. Thus was the flagging independence of the individual to be restored by the appeal of group independence. At the same time the tension between the highly developed standards of an industrial civilization and the reduced capacity to fulfill them introduced an element of the irrational. Personal or collective aggression, or insanity was a means of escaping the disparity between precept and fulfillment.

Thus liberalism emerged ultimately as an ambivalent social system that freed the individual of the political and civil oppressions of the old regime, while substituting a social restraint of its own making. The dissatisfaction of the ordinary working man with *laissez-faire* industrial society had two outlets: the one was socialism or economic reform; the second was submersion in the national collectivity. World War I proved that the second was more compelling than the first. But merely rendering obeisance before the nation-state was not enough. The nation was not merely given more power, but was required to exercise that power. The nation was forced to do what the individual was incapable of doing. When it appeared that the ordinary form of coalescent or unificatory nationalism was insufficient, expansive or integral nationalism became an overriding impulse.[12]

Where the process of industrialization was at work, a demand for nationalism emanated from the social order, sometimes fostered by the regime in power. In liberal states it was a tool to be used against movements for social reform, whereas in conservative

---

[11] See Sigmund Freud, *Civilization and Its Discontents* (New York, 1930).

[12] See Hayes, *op. cit.,* p. 252, and W. L. Langer, *The Diplomacy of Imperialism, 1890-1902* (New York, 1951), pp. 94-95.

states it was a device to nullify liberal gains.[13] Where the conservatives could not espouse liberalism, they espoused nationalism. But unlike the liberals, who might in principle remain content with coalescent nationalism, the conservatives most often had to favor expansive nationalism. The erection of a political boundary around each nationality was an anathema to the conservatives for it spelled an end to multi-national empire. For domestic reasons the Habsburgs, though they had the most to lose, had to concede more to this form of national expression than did the other conservative monarchies. The Russians could not tolerate it because of the western frontiers, and the Germans could not abide it because of Poland. Hence, it was natural for the conservatives to think in terms not of nation determination, but of national expansion. Nationalist imperialism might secure their domestic position where nationalist localism would undermine it.[14]

Thus the Bismarckian Concert, operating on the rickety structure of nationalism, had to admit a new wave of imperialism. In this context it is difficult to see how it could have functioned at all. The answer was partly that the safety of individual regimes was not yet dependent on the imperial course, and nations could still be persuaded to limit their imperial ambitions by means other than war. Imperialism was an ancillary aid, not an absolute requirement. The previous generation had seen an all-out struggle for security, and even among the defeated Powers that security had temporarily been won. In France the empire had discredited itself, but the benefit ultimately was conferred on a liberal-republican regime, and in Austria the Habsburgs stimulated particularist nationalism as an antidote to liberalism. In the long run this policy sealed the fate of

[13] This is not meant to signify that nationalism was only a manipulative tool in the hands of governing classes. It was a genuinely popular phenomenon which attracted adherents from all classes.

[14] Significantly, Professor Hayes writes: "'Conservatives' and 'reactionaries,' who in Metternichean times had been almost as chary of 'nationalism' as of 'revolution,' were now in the van of every ultra-patriotic movement — economic nationalism, imperialism, etc. — and by the 1880's they had an unusually large and loyal clientele. Liberals (with the capital letter) might be dwindling a bit in number but not in patriotic fervor, and many of them — National Liberals in Germany, Liberal Unionists in Britain, and majority of Radicals in France and Italy—were approximating in this respect the attitude of contemporary Conservatives. Apparently they had to do so to retain popular support." *Op. cit.*, p. 252.

the Empire, but in the short run it kept the regime in power. Though Francis Joseph did not sit on a stable throne, he was the last of the European monarchs to embark on a policy of imperial expansion. The readiness to yield at the behest of the Concert was illustrated at the Congress of Berlin in 1878. Russia, to be sure, was too weak to take on the armies of Europe after the stumbling before Plevna, but at the same time Alexander II realized that to yield was not to place his crown in jeopardy. A humiliation cannot be borne by a regime which is fighting for its domestic life, although it can be endured by one which has a semblance of domestic support. In 1888 the Russians backed down again, and settled for a purely nominal sop to their ruffled prestige. The election of Ferdinand of Coburg as prince of Bulgaria was declared illegal. The Russians consented to the "bigger Bulgaria" and conceded their failure to influence it. The English in their turn yielded before the Franco-German entente of 1883-85 and backed down on the Penjdeh crisis of 1885. Even Bismarckian Germany did not always come out on top. In the "war in sight" crisis of 1875, the Concert informally functioned to forbid a preventive war launched by Germany against France. Whether Bismarck's intentions extended this far is doubtful, but the rebuff was real nonetheless.[15]

But the effectiveness of the Bismarckian Concert was not only due to a more secure domestic position in the major countries; it also followed from the nature of early imperialism.[16] Ultimately the

[15] See the discussion of these separate incidents in Langer, *op. cit.*, and A. J. P. Taylor, *The Struggle for Mastery in Europe, 1848-1918* (Oxford, 1954).

[16] The causes of imperialism have been much debated. The Marxian approach has been quite generally discredited and its place has been filled by neomercantilist explanations. (See Langer, *Diplomacy*, pp. 74-75.) Professor Hayes, in a masterly synthesis, however, points out that these accounts do not come to grips with the fact that political imperialism generally preceded tariff restriction in the latter half of the nineteenth century. He remarks: "The fact remains, nevertheless, that the founding of new colonial empires and the fortifying of old ones antedated the establishment of neo-mercantilism, and that the economic arguments adduced in support of imperialism seem to have been a rationalization *ex post facto*. In the main, it was not Liberal parties, with their superabundance of industrialists and bankers, who sponsored the outward imperialistic thrusts of the '70's and early '80's. Instead, it was Conservative parties, with a preponderantly agricultural clientele notoriously suspicious of moneylenders and big business, and, above all, it was patriotic professors and publicists regardless of political affiliation and unmindful of personal economic interest. These put forth the economic arguments which eventually drew bankers and traders and industrialists into the imperialist camp." *Op. cit.*, p. 220.

development of imperialism was a force in favor of conflict because there had to be squabbles about the division of limited territory. A repetition of the eighteenth-century imperial wars seemed to be in the offing. But the immediate impact of imperialism was more salutary. At the beginning imperialism tended to direct attention away from European questions without leading to new conflicts in Asia or Africa. During the Bismarckian ascendancy most energy was devoted to a solution of European and related Near Eastern questions. The developments outside Europe received much less attention.[17] This emphasis reflected the obvious fact that European issues were paramount, but at the same time showed that imperialist frictions overseas had not yet become important. "Prior to 1875 not one-tenth of Africa, the second largest continent, had been appropriated by European nations. By 1895 all but a tenth of it was appropriated. . . ."[18] In the first decade of imperialism, European nations could expand almost limitlessly without coming into collision with one another. In one sense Africa and Asia provided escape valves for European tensions for a ten-year period. Setbacks in Europe were not so important as long as they could be easily recouped by expansion elsewhere. Russia was not alarmed by the crisis of 1887 because she was bent on new adventures in Asia. Britain could stomach her reverses in the Congo and Afghanistan because of advances in other areas. Before 1890 there was colonizable territory left to be seized and possibly taken without bringing on a war between imperial competitors. After 1890 the territory overseas was rapidly being divided and further attempts at expansion were destined to bring one Power into direct conflict with another. During the period of the Bismarckian Concert, imperialism was on the whole a beneficent phenomenon reducing European hostilities without creating important ones in Asia or Africa. After the Bismarckian Concert, imperialism was a disastrous movement that instead of reducing conflict, fomented it.

This was partly the reason for the success of the Concert. Nations could afford to yield to the dictates of an international mechanism as long as they were not required to do so too often. Bismarck's diplomacy was adequate to handle European disputes in part because it did not have to handle many in Asia or Africa. Nations

17 The Congo Conference of 1884-1885, of course, remains an exception.
18 Hayes, *op. cit.*, p. 236.

could limit their ambitions to Europe alone as long as they knew that they would not have to limit them in all other areas. Thus, the domestic position of a host of European regimes never had to face the ultimate test because it never had to submit to Concert governance over all major international actions. If imperial as well as European questions had been hailed before the bar of the Concert, domestic politics might have ruled out compromise. The Concert had to deal only with those portions of diplomacy that produced friction, and that many questions did not reach this stage is to be accounted to the early workings of imperialism.

III In the end Bismarck's alliance system tied up all major Powers on the Continent with the exception of France. The technique was unique. Agreement was not patiently worked out at a multilateral Concert. Instead, counterbalancing alliances were formed within the context of a single system. Bismarck did not seek to drive offending parties from the central coalition, but to bring them into it, paralyzed by the spidery filaments of alliance obligations. Potentially aggressive Powers sought Bismarck's support, his price being in practical terms the maintenance of peace. The decline of the ideological factor in European alignments could not be better illustrated than by the combinations of 1887. On the one hand Bismarck had separate linkages with Prussia's erstwhile ideological *confrères*, Austria, and Russia. Through the Triple Alliance he was bound to Italy, a state of more liberal complexion. Still more amazing were the two Mediterranean Ententes which pledged Austria, Italy and Britain to maintain the status quo in the Mediterranean and at the Straits. Imperial questions and questions of special interest had come to overshadow the older dictates of ideology. Theoretically, Britain should not have departed even temporarily and indirectly from her policy of "splendid isolation" to ally with continental powers, least of all with unregenerate Austria. Practically, the question of the Near East in 1887, as in 1877, had overborne previous ideological sentiments. Isolation, like liberalism, had basic ideological roots.

There was still another reason why ideology did not play an important role after 1871. The conflict of ideas was compromised because it was a futile struggle on both sides. The ideological issue was partly spent during the truncated Concert because of the growing strength of the two antagonists and because of the waning fervor of both conservatism and liberalism. At once, there seemed to be less need to fight the battle, and it was a harder battle to win. These conditions were present after 1871. Revolutions — even the revolution of 1848 — had receded from view, and the Commune of Paris did not give them a new lease on life. More important perhaps, liberal and conservative regimes were either equally weak or equally strong. Weakness in each case ruled out an ideological assault on the other camp, while strength guaranteed that if an attack were launched it would not succeed. But there was an important difference between the Bismarckian and the truncated Concert. In 1840 the methods and policies of the two groups had been distinct. Liberalism implied a particular political and constitutional program, and conservatism indicated its opposite. By 1871 the programs and policies of each were blurred. Anticlericalism was a policy of conservative Germany during Bismarck's *Kulturkampf* as well as of more liberal Italy. France and England could hardly object to Bismarck's economic policies which were liberal until 1879.[19] The Republicans in France quickly became "opportunists," studiously overlooking the social question, and seeking to attract Orleanists and members of the conservative peasantry.[20] In all countries nationalism ceased to be the rallying cry of the liberals and became the property of all classes. It was characteristic of the times that Bismarck, who truly aspired to *Junkertum,* could be reviled by the class he aided most and find his allies among the National Liberals. Liberal and nationalist paraphernalia was a means of protecting conservative institutions though it was not realized by either the conservatives or the liberals who rushed to swallow the bait. The domestic *rapprochement* in liberal as well as conservative countries facilitated an international *détente.* Bismarck, who had taken over a part of the liberal-national program, was liberal enough for the English and sometimes even for the French. But he sought fundamentally to revive the Holy Alliance, and his basic aims were congenial to those of the Eastern Courts. Again, a single *point d'union* for the Concert becomes understandable. Bismarck, who wooed the liberals with universal suffrage, a façade of parliamentary government, and a liberal economic program at one time and who appeased the Junk-

---

19 See A. J. P. Taylor, *Bismarck* (London, 1955), Chapter Six.
20 See J. P. T. Bury, *France, 1814-1940* (Philadelphia, 1949), p. 153 ff.

ers and industrialists with tariffs on grain and industrial products at another, was ideally suited to link Eastern and Western Europe.[21] In 1815 any one of the great statesmen might have spoken for Europe for they were all equally agreed on the conservative cause, but in 1871 Bismarck had to speak for he alone could hold Europe to-gether. The first European Concert was genuinely multilateral in its functioning; the Bismarckian Concert operated under a single exec-utive. The ideological issue did not re-emerge after 1871 because it was compromised through the intercession of the "honest broker" of Berlin.

IV  The Concert, however, was a fragile instrument, the success of which depended on an atmosphere of moderate tension and a measure of domestic insecurity. If a secure position had been at-tained, self-confident expansion would have ensued, if domestic chaos had beckoned, the peace would have been sacrificed. The delicate equilibrium between these two extremes was hard to main-tain, and eventually it collapsed. The domestic and international entanglements which followed Bismarck's fall were a compound of total security and total anxiety. Internationally, the German Reich was approaching the zenith of its power relative to other states, and if action had to be taken, it could be risked. Domestically, the imperial regime was losing support. Like the American Republicans of the latter part of the nineteenth century, the Germans had to "wave the bloody shirt." The new emphasis upon nationalism, im-perialism and "world policy" was a token of domestic complica-tions. In 1890 Bismarck's policy had failed to produce a majority in favor of the imperial regime, but Caprivi and Hohenlohe suc-cessively embarked upon "new courses" hoping to find new support. Caprivi alienated the industrialists and the Junkers by his ties with the Social Democrats. Hohenlohe lost support of the provinces by reversing the *Kulturkampf* and allying with the Centre.[22] It followed that there was no longer a majority in Germany to support a con-servative or even a Bismarckian policy; but there was a majority to support a nationalist policy. "World policy" was created for domestic reasons.

But Germany was not the only Power which made a credo of ex-

[21] See Taylor, *Bismarck*, Chapter Eight.
[22] See Taylor, *Course of German History*, pp. 138-146.

pansive nationalism. The other conservative states, Russia and, later, the Dual Monarchy, embraced the new imperialism. Their uncertain domestic position made a flexible international policy more difficult. A regime resting firmly on the favor of a majority can tolerate reverses, though it does not enjoy them, whereas a regime having more tenuous claims can scarcely admit defeat. Imperialism, then, was a much more desperate expedient where events were quietly sapping the strength of the political leadership. The conservatives, as in the period of *Realpolitik* were always falling between two stools. They no longer enjoyed the buttress of historic sanction which had sustained them for so long; they did not yet enjoy the panoply of popular support. Nationalism, a doctrine capable of catering to all classes, seemed the solution.

Even the liberal states of England and France, however, could not overlook the imperialist drive. They did not always follow imperial policies in order to garner domestic support, although this was sometimes the case. They submitted to the imperial wishes of the electorate already supporting them. Broadly speaking, imperialism was initially a doctrine propagated by the masses in liberal states and by the elite in conservative states. (Later, of course, it came to be the property of all segments of society.) But the momentum of imperialism was different in Western Europe. France and England were the most successful imperial nations, yet, they perhaps had less need to be so. Each had minor imperial skirmishes, and the British proved the reality of their intentions by fighting the Boer War, the French by conquering Indo-China. Still, failure was not disaster for the liberals and compromise was often possible. Egypt was compromised in 1904. France backed down at Fashoda and the British faced an "abortive continental league" between 1894-97 [23] and fought the Boers unaided and with the passive opposition of Europe two years later. Liberal regimes could "accept" defeat or face isolation, and they could afford to make compromises. Socialism turned out to be a much more pliable opponent than the old conservatism had been. This in part marked the difference between 1850 and 1900. During the period of *Realpolitik*, the liberals (in France) were almost as unsteady as the conservatives in Central and Eastern Europe. Fifty years later, the liberals had come much closer to solving the problem of domestic support while the conservatives saw the Bis-

23 See Taylor, *Struggle,* Chapter Sixteen.

marckian "solution" fall apart in their hands. At the turn of the century, conservatives still had to scramble for adherents, and they often scraped their knees. The liberals were a more self-confident group. Compromise on imperial questions was always a possibility for the liberal states, but it was more and more difficult for conservative ones. The unfortunate deduction from previous militarism was that compromise need not be tolerated. Sedan and Königgrätz conveyed the false impression that war was an acceptable policy, applicable after diplomacy had made routine attempts to end the crisis. No nation need bear slights to its honor when it could redeem itself at such little cost on the battlefield. While war was held to be a terrible revolutionary instrument in 1814, it was palatable fare less than a hundred years later. The elder Moltke came to believe that "in contrast to the wars of 1859, 1864, 1870-71, future wars were likely to last for many years." [24] But Count Alfred Schlieffen, his successor, believed that decisive wars were still possible, and his famous plan of 1905 was designed to give, in the shortest possible time, total victory to Germany even in a two-front war. In two or three months the war in the West would be over. Ferdinand Foch saw the possibility of a war of "immobilism" but he rejected it as an inferior form. Fundamentally, he believed wars of the future would consist of "the battle maneuver, where one supreme effort, a decisive attack, achieves surprise and victory. . . ." [25] Even the generals of the pre-War age thought that decisive wars would still be fought; wars of attrition would not be tolerated ". . . when the existence of a nation is founded upon the uninterrupted progress of commerce and industry. . . . A strategy of attrition will not do if the maintenance of millions of people requires billions." [26] Quick, painless wars would be fought if only because they would have to be fought, and wars rendered innocuous by the progress of civilization became politically tolerable.

[24] Hajo Holborn, "Moltke and Schlieffen: The Prussian-German School," in Edward Mead Earle (ed.), *Makers of Modern Strategy* (Princeton, 1948), p. 188.
[25] Stefan T. Possony and Étienne Mantoux, "Du Picq and Foch: The French School," in Earle, *op. cit.*, p. 225.
[26] Count Alfred Schlieffen, quoted in Holborn, *loc. cit.*, p. 187.

V The Bismarckian Concert marked a distinct system of international relations; it was not a return to the Balance of Power, but rather to its opposite. As an international institution, its foundations were not ideological but technical. It was not because certain basic ideas had come to have general acceptance that the Concert worked, but because certain divisive ideas had been blunted and smoothed. The absence of disagreement passed for the presence of agreement. The new Concert, moreover, operated with new techniques. International conferences were no longer the usual mode of settlement — precautionary alliances, military posturing, and the creation of new alignments during an impending crisis also served to impose an enforced calm on troubled waters. The international mechanism did not wait until a single nation had managed to tip the scales of the Balance of Power, nor did it wait even for a conference to be convened to deal with an overt threat. It made bilateral or multilateral arrangements before calling a conference. Once peacetime alliances were the order of the day, they could be checked only by other peacetime alliances. The novel Concert succeeded in its time because of the modest security of European regimes and the preoccupation with domestic questions. At the same time, the imperial movement, which became so frantic in the last decade of the century, actually contributed to the European peace by distracting efforts elsewhere. Through it all, the nations of Europe were rebuilding for war, the probable outcome of "world policy," but they also were reassuring themselves that warfare would not disturb the progress of European civilization.

The Bismarckian international system, therefore, represented a temporary interlude of stability between periods of conflict. The disturbing elements in the system operated beneath the surface, and as long as nationalism and imperialism did not disturb the European repose, they were factors for stability and peace. There was no need to initiate disruptive measures as long as domestic stability was assured by national imperialism overseas. The Bismarckian Concert could deal effectively with residual issues. New alliances or military postures might be conjured up to prevent a European crisis from getting out of hand. In the longer run, however, the Concert was not flexible enough to counter all disturbance, and its dependence upon alliance structures was an additional factor for rigidity. Equally important at a certain point, imperialism would return to haunt European capitals. Then new disruption would challenge an increasingly crippled Concert, and international outcomes would exceed traditional limits.

There can be little doubt that the Bismarckian system represented a novel mode of conducting international relations. Once a degree of domestic security had been won, the policy-making elites could view.diplomacy with a degree of equanimity. But changes in the technology of warfare made rapid action imperative, and rapid action meant increasingly action of separate states or alliances. As the Balance of Power gave way before the Concert, the Concert itself was too cumbersome an instrument in an age of quick, decisive engagements. While objectives were held within bounds, techniques perforce, were becoming more unlimited.

## chapter eight

# IMPERIALIST NATIONALISM

I The fall of Bismarck marked the end of an epoch of international relations. This was not only because Bismarck's personality and brilliance were conducive to the operation of the previous system, but also because the assumptions of that system themselves were being undermined. Fundamentally, the Bismarckian Concert had worked because the political elites in each major country could afford to let it work. There were no issues, as in the previous period of *Realpolitik,* which demanded action against the international framework. The conservatives, by pre-empting a portion of the liberal-nationalist creed, had won a new place for themselves in public esteem. The liberals, by humming the nationalist strain, managed to distract attention from the need for social reform and to neutralize the left-wing radicals. Liberalism had been initially an attack upon the state; nationalism prevented any further attacks. Thus, liberal elites in England and France, and conservative elites in the Eastern courts were in a secure position during the Bismarckian aegis.

At some point, however, the bargain permitting traditional classes to govern reformist societies came unstuck. The bargain lasted twenty years, before events began to discredit it. Socialist movements emerged to challenge bourgeois-liberal ascendancy in the liberal states; liberal and socialist movements became increasingly dissatisfied with conservative rule in the conservative states. By the very nature of the case, the Bismarckian synthesis, which allowed the conservatives to use liberal methods against the liberals and social methods against the socialists, was the first to crumble. Indeed, it

149

had always had the character of a *tour de force*. The conservatives had to deal not only with those in favor of social reform, but with those in favor of liberal reform. Bismarck's techniques of governance, involving the harassment and coercion of the chambers, would not work as the sentiment in favor of parliamentary government increased. The Iron Chancellor's mutterings in 1890 about the need to scrap the federal constitution suggest that the old theories of government were becoming out of date. And yet, Bismarck himself never divined the answer.

After Bismarck's fall, his successors were able to come to grips with the problem. The working classes were pacified by new labor legislation,[1] and they were appeased by the powerful economic upswing. It was not accidental that Bernstein revisionism appeared in a context of vast economic advance. The National Liberals were further propitiated by protective tariffs and by a benign government attitude toward mergers, cartels, and trusts. In the end the National Liberals became the party of big business. Even the Conservative agrarians were succored by new tariffs on grain. Perhaps more important than all of these was the conciliation of the middle stratum of German society. The salaried group, the petty tradesmen, the clerical white collar classes had always been the bulwarks of the policy of national greatness. When industry and agriculture hesitated to support colonial ventures in the past, the *Mittelstand* had urged them on.[2] After 1890 the economic factors leading to imperial expansion were overpowering; [3] what the middle sectors demanded on political and prestige grounds, the magnates desired on economic bases. The disaffection of the agriculturalists, the Catholics, and the workers was not sufficient to divert Germany from the path of *Weltpolitik*. And in the end it is no great exaggeration to state that "the two parties of the masses were transformed, as the liberals had been, into agents of the Reich, and the reign of William II ended in 1918 in a situation in which the Centre and the Social Democrats became the political mouthpiece of the army, the defenders of the great estates and of great industry, and the upholders of the 'na-

---

1 See C. J. H. Hayes, *A Generation of Materialism, 1871-1900* (New York, 1941), p. 211.

2 See G. W. F. Hallgarten, *Imperialismus Vor 1914* (Munich, 1941), Vol. 1, pp. 206-208.

3 See *ibid.*, pp. 257-262.

tional' cause."[4] National greatness and the large navy unquestionably helped to dispose of the products of a 'hothouse' economy. In the final analysis, however, the development of imperialist nationalism had more than economic roots. It was the means of overcoming the Bismarckian dilemma. Opposition parties could not be won by parliamentary maneuvering, but they could be captured for a policy of German expansion. Expansive nationalism was an anodyne for the pains of social and political grievance. In the end it proved so potent that parties whose objectives were ecumenical in character virtually adopted nationalist platforms in their stead.[5] The clericals voted for the large temporal navy; the Marxists supported the bourgeois war. This policy served to, in Eulenburg's phrase "satisfy Germany without injuring the Emperor." But it also held William II prisoner in the nationalist course. When, in 1908, the Kaiser tried to patch things over with England, the German public rebuked him, for once started on the imperialist course there was no turning back.

In Austria expansive nationalism was also the means of keeping the Habsburgs in power. The conservative rulers of the Dual Monarchy had given latitude to the subject nationalities to assuage Sadowa. The defeat for the dynasty should have meant concession to the liberals, when actually, it meant cultivation of the subject peoples. But this tack could be followed only so far: at some point this method of maintaining Habsburg rule meant the dissolution of the Empire. When the Balkans were "put on ice" in the Russo-Austrian bargain of 1897, external issues could no longer be used to assure internal solidarity. Domestic solidarity existing in the face of international disputes dissolved with the settlement of these problems. Thus, minus the external problems that forced internal cohesion, domestic strife again commenced. In 1907, the emperor made a final attempt to submerge particularist nationalism and liberalism in a new democracy. The universal suffrage which was to inaugurate this democratic stage was supposed to square the circle: it was asked to produce a majority for the Empire on the one hand and for the Habsburgs on the other. Universal suffrage would unite the peoples of the monarchy and obliterate their national differences. It would also maintain Francis Joseph on the throne. Neither objec-

[4] A. J. P. Taylor, *The Course of German History* (London, 1954), p. 140.
[5] See Hayes, *op. cit., passim.*

tive was really achieved. The Christian Socialist and Social Democratic parties broke down into their national components. Nor was universal suffrage a reactionary device: by the early years of the twentieth century, the enfranchisement of the peasant and the working man failed to prop up monarchy, but instead acted to undermine it. In these circumstances the reversion to expansive nationalism was the only means of holding the realm together under Habsburg control. "Like an elderly man whose powers are failing, the Habsburg Monarchy sought to recover its youth by a display of virility." [6] The restoration of the external threat was conveniently accomplished by the Russian return to European affairs. Checked in the Far East by the Japanese in 1905, the Russians began to eye the Balkans. Serbia began to be portrayed (incorrectly) as the "Piedmont of the South Slavs." Expansion at the expense of either (or both) would distract attention from the internal instability of the Habsburg dominions. In other words, the remedy of particularist nationalism was conceived to be integral nationalism even though the impact of integral nationalism would be to provide grounds for future localist nationalism. As if the Austrians did not have enough of a nationality problem without aggrandizing other nations, they affected to believe that Serbia should be partitioned with Bulgaria and that Bosnia and Herzegovina should be formally annexed. An Austrian "mission civilatrice" was added to its French counterpart. In Austria and Russia the process was similar — expansive nationalism was an alternative to genuine political and social reform and as political concessions were taken back, imperialist ones had to be given in their place.

Thus, imperialism was not simply a movement of the liberal middle classes.[7] It was as much (and certainly more in the conservative states) a tactic of reactionaries. The conservatives were increasingly out of step with the political and social ideas of the communities they ruled.[8] Aristocrats still dominated the state.[9] They could not concede liberal reform for that would have ended their pre-eminence, but they could concede imperialism. A reversion to

[6] A. J. P. Taylor, *The Habsburg Monarchy* (London, 1951), p. 214.

[7] See Hayes, *op. cit.*, p. 220.

[8] See Maxwell E. Knight, *The German Executive, 1890-1933* (Stanford, California, 1952), Table 9 and pp. 22-23.

[9] See *ibid.*, Table 15.

the most blatant form of nationalism might discourage liberal or socialist attacks upon the state.

In the liberal states, the elites in power were also having their troubles. In England, the mild social reform inaugurated by Disraeli had been abandoned by his successors, and the grievances of the working classes and the Irish went unredressed. There were occasional demands for a substitution of "Social Reform at home for Imperialism overseas,"[10] but the dominant upper- and middle-class factions aimed at the reverse. Indeed, Rosebery for the Liberals, and Salisbury and Chamberlain for the Conservative-Unionists pressed hard for an imperialist course. The result was an overwhelming tide of public sentiment on behalf of imperialist expansion. The failure to make social reforms may perhaps have initially weakened British liberals, but the evocation of imperialism enormously strengthened them. One historian goes so far as to say: "There is surely some room for argument that popular pressure was more important in the growth of imperialism than was the action of the ruling classes."[11] British elites stabilized their position by gratifying the imperialist demand, a demand which they in part originated but which reverberated constantly thereafter.

In France the Opportunist Republicans had to find a means of nullifying attacks from the conservatives on the right and the radicals on the left.[12] Nationalist imperialism was a possible instrument for this purpose, but in France the imperial question was irrevocably tied with the issue of *revanche*. Nothing should be done overseas which might weaken France in her major confrontation on the Rhine. Imperial expansion would be tolerated so long as it could be accomplished without exertion.[13] When Jules Ferry suffered a minor

---

[10] George Macaulay Trevelyan, *British History in the Nineteenth Century and After (1783-1919)* (London, 1948), p. 427.

[11] William L. Langer, *The Diplomacy of Imperialism, 1890-1902* (New York, 1951), p. 80.

[12] See J. P. T. Bury, *France, 1814-1940* (Philadelphia, 1949), p. 171.

[13] Professor Langer writes for example: "French statesmen generally had no use for the colonies and were passionately opposed to further expansion. So long as their eyes were riveted on the German menace, and their thoughts concentrated on the lost provinces, it was regarded almost as treason to suggest the dissipation of French forces outside of Europe. France, it has been said, was suffering from 'acute national myopia'; while gazing at the blue line of the Vosges, she became entirely blind to world movements." *European Alliances and Alignments, 1871-1890* (New York, 1950), pp. 285-286.

reverse in Tonkin, however, he was denounced as a "tool of Germany" for thus exposing France. Clemenceau even went so far as to accuse the Cabinet of treason. In such circumstances imperialism was not a very effective prophylactic against social discord. These conditions prevailed for some time, but eventually gave way to more general imperialist sentiments. Imperialist nationalism acted against Dreyfus, solemnized the Franco-Russian alliance and supported French action in Siam. Even when the Radicals came to power at the very end of the nineteenth century, the imperialist trend was not abandoned, though it was pursued with less heat. Delcassé was prepared to yield at Fashoda and to negotiate outstanding differences over Egypt, though he was of course interested in the prize of Morocco. The Radicals did not succeed in establishing stable government in France, however; they did little to advance social reform, and in the end were forced back on the imperialist path. Liberal government in France, it seemed, could not be maintained without nationalism.

The final result, then, of the insecurity of both liberal and conservative elites in their respective countries was a general rush for national expansion and imperialism. But there was a difference between the two. For the conservatives; nationalist imperialism was a more desperate expedient than it was for the liberals. The conservatives, haunted by the spectre of political reform or revolution, were afraid that they might not maintain themselves in power. Aehrenthal could not compromise Austria's expansionist aims for he believed that the monarchy itself depended upon expansion. Bülow or Kiderlen would not compromise Germany's bid for "world policy" for the conservatives had no majority in Germany; the only majority they could find was a majority for nationalism. Nor could the Russians contain their imperialist ambitions. Even the disastrous lesson of the Russo-Japanese war did not convince them that expansion was bankrupt; it served merely to channel their expansionist urges into different areas. The conservatives' persistent refusal to acknowledge a liberal solution domestically forced them to use nationalism as a legitimizing principle. It is not accidental that the conservative states, perhaps more than the liberal nations, found it impossible to back down in July and August of 1914.

The liberal elites were not as uneasy in the citadels of power as their conservative brethren. They wished to postpone social reform wherever possible, but they did not confront revolution or abrupt reformation at every turn. Under the liberals in England and the radicals in France limited progress was made in the social field. Nationalism, then, was not as vital to liberals as it was to conservatives. At the same time the liberals, precisely because of the amount of political and economic reform which they had allowed, had succeeded perhaps to a greater degree in nationalizing public sentiment. As new classes were admitted to the nation, nationalism became an almost universal phenomenon.[14] Even proletarians embraced the nationalist symbolism. The fears of the liberals were exaggerated, for when a share in power was offered to the reformist classes, their reformist desires collapsed in a welter of nationalist fervor. Still, liberal elites were probably less the prisoners of national forces than conservative cliques. Left to themselves the liberals might have been able to compromise on the eve of World War I.

II Even the development of nationalist imperialism might not have led to war if colonizable territory had been generally available. The imperialist movement, as we have noted, did not originate in 1890, but began in the previous decade. For a time at least, Bismarck encouraged colonial acquisitions by European Powers, particularly France, as a means of distracting them from the more vital issues at stake in Europe itself. French energies which otherwise might be concentrated on regaining Alsace-Lorraine could be harmlessly discharged in Africa. Russian eyes might be diverted to the Far East in order to hide the potential conflict in the Balkans. In the short run, imperialism was a beneficent phenomenon because it provided an outlet for aggressions that otherwise might vent themselves in Europe. In the long run, however, unbridled expansion was disastrous. Very roughly, the imperialist movement proceeded in three stages. In the first stage, it began the colonization of overseas areas; conflict was limited in this stage by the vast tracts of land available for pre-emption. In the second stage, overseas territories were rapidly being divided up, and conflicts over

14 Nationalism and imperialism were linked. As Professor Langer points out: "During that score of years [1890-1910] the competition in the acquisition of territory and the struggle for influence and control was the most important factor in the international relations of Europe." *Diplomacy*, p. 67.

extra-European real estate became characteristic. Skirmishes in North, East, and South Africa, and in the Far East were representative of this stage. In the third period, imperialism turned inward upon itself, as it were, and the drive for expansion continued within the confines or on the fringes of the European Continent. The defeat of Russia in Siberia undid the Austro-Russian agreement in the Balkans. The failure of France at Fashoda suggested an adventure in North Africa. England's own inability to hold the line in Europe and the Far East at the same time involved an end to "splendid isolation." Imperialism now could only be continued with outside support. Bargains were thus concluded for imperial purposes in Egypt, Persia, and in the Far East. Germany's pursuit of "world policy" and a great navy became more ominous as the sources of colonizable territory disappeared.[15] The habit of successful expansion in the past undermined the possibility of successful compromise in the present. It was difficult to persuade successful imperial Powers to compromise or give way when tradition had habituated them to the opposite. This was an intrinsic weakness of the Bismarckian synthesis: Bismarck had urged European states to find outlets for their hostilities outside of Europe, and had thus implicitly admitted that hostilities could not be settled, but merely deflected. How was it possible then to demand compromise when deflection was out of the question? Under Bismarck, European questions had been settled in part because of the imperialist "safety-valve," but the "safety-valve" was only a means of European agreement. After 1905, the so-called "safety-valve" was the prime factor in European disagreement, and no heritage of compromise on imperial questions was available to moderate the conflict.

Not only was precedent lacking, the mechanism for enforcing it was also absent. As we have seen, the Concert of Europe in the Bismarckian period was as much a function of the alliance system as it was of the habit of periodic consultation. The crisis of 1887 was as representative of the first method as the Congress of Berlin was of the second. In both cases a recalcitrant Power (Russia) was brought to accept a "European solution" of its problems, and it finally swallowed the pill that was presented. Solutions reached under the Bismarckian Concert acquired a certain legitimacy. The problem of the period of imperialist nationalism was that the mech-

[15] See E. L. Woodward, *Great Britain and the German Navy* (Oxford, 1935).

anism of Concert governance had broken down. No longer was consultation the function of the Concert; no longer did the Concert operate informally through the alliance system; no longer were Concert mandates legitimized for all concerned.

Military developments of the latter part of the nineteenth and early twentieth centuries had made the consultative mechanism inoperative. Even more than in the Bismarckian period, international effectiveness depended upon swift action. A meeting of the Concert presumed a fluidity of alignments; it presumed open questions and the uncertainty of national responses to them. The function of the Concert would be to air the issues, compose an international coalition, and take action in the proper direction. But the difficulty of Concert operation after 1890 was that the requirements of decision and action could not be met simultaneously. By the time an international decision had been worked out, the aggrieved party might already be prepared to take action against it. International decisions, then, by postponing  the final question of the means of enforcement, allowed the offender to make his own preparations and to initiate offensive operations on his own. All sides presumed that an enormous advantage would fall to the Power or group of Powers which could assume the initiative, and the hesitation involved in making decisions, therefore, tended to augur in favor of the nation whose decisions were already made. Conversely, the overemphasis upon action undermined the basis of political or international decision. States harassed by their respective militaries could scarcely linger over the details of political formulae — they simply did not have time to smooth ruffled feelings. Essential political positions had to be adopted hastily or they had no chance of being carried out. In this fashion, political and military *desiderata* almost became reciprocal quantities — to pay attention to political factors was to slight military ones, to exalt military questions was to pass over political ones. The pressures of military plans in 1866 and 1870, as we have seen, were not sufficient to deprive political leaders of their freedom to decide, but the pressures of military plans in 1914, however, left little enough room for political negotiations. Where the offensive becomes all important, and speedy mobilization necessary to assume it, politics is at a disadvantage.

The consultative mechanism of the Concert of Europe, then, was a luxury which too few military staffs could afford. But consultation was not trammeled by military factors alone. Consultation also depended upon the existence of open-ended alignments. That part of Bismarck's Concert mechanism dependent upon a reformulation of alliances when crises arose was undercut shortly after his fall from power. Even Bismarck had not pledged himself irrevocably to Austria-Hungary, and he would not choose finally between the Habsburgs and the Romanovs in the East. But if Bismarck had not committed himself to allies, neither had he permanently estranged outsiders. France could be wooed by a temporary colonial *entente;* England might be brought in on questions affecting the Straits or the Mediterranean. Allies and external Powers were kept in a state of tolerable uncertainty, and the categories of "friend" or "enemy" had not yet been definitely applied. When an emergency occurred, then, the German Chancellor might meet it by balancing between allies, luring uncommitted states into temporary connections, and proposing new army bills. In Bismarck's mind, formal alliance with one Power did not preclude *entente* with others — indeed, the two devices were often countervailing. After 1890, a pattern of closed-end alliances began to develop on the European continent. The Franco-Russian Alliance of 1894 made it more difficult for Germany to cooperate with Russia even though Germany continued to tender support to the Tsar in the Far East. But no longer could Russia seriously be proposed as an antidote to Austria-Hungary, no longer was Russia a prescription which the German doctor could himself administer. The disadvantage of the new alliance combination from the German point of view was that it required the partial amalgamation of interests of the two powers. As the Kaiser found out after Björkö, the Russians could not consider only themselves, they also had to consider France. Neither Power then could be played in accordance with national interests. Both had to be played in accord with international interests. It was almost as if the number of players in the game had been reduced, and bishop and knight had been fused.

But the "free hand" situation which ensued allowed some flexibility. The Germans still believed that they might have the best of the two possible worlds — balancing in favor of Franco-Russia at one juncture and on behalf of England at the next. Neither could really be used as a limitation upon Austria-Hungary, but each could be used as a limitation on the other. When the circle was squared and the Triple Entente forged, the players had been fused into two. The flexibility of strategy, the flexibility of players no longer existed.[16] Again it seemed that the conditions of militarism were at fault. The requirements of offensive war demanded precise mobilization plans and their integration with the similar plans of allied states. But if war plans had to be formulated well in advance of hostilities, the coordination of operations with allies also had to be worked out in peacetime. This meant that alignments had to be delineated in advance. Thus the very preparation for the crisis determined the form the crisis would take. Even where political understandings were tentative, military plans were concrete.[17] When the challenge finally issued, it did not lead to new combinations formed to deal with the threat at hand, but merely called into operation pre-existing combinations.

Equally important, the Concert did not propose solutions which could be legitimized for all concerned. Legitimacy of Concert decisions had been secured in the past largely through two devices. The first was an overwhelming array of force mobilized against the unruly Power. The second was a real concern for its position and a desire to find a means of accommodation which it could with dignity accept. The first discouraged action against the Concert; the second made submission palatable. In 1887 Russia could hardly act on the secret terms of the Reinsurance Treaty while faced with the opposition of the second Mediterranean *entente*, although the willingness of influential members of the Concert to have the Sultan declare the election of Ferdinand of Coburg illegal made it easier for the Russians to back down. Legitimacy in the sense of "acceptance" was still operative.[18]

At the end of the nineteenth century, however, the Concert became a feeble reed for the promotion of legitimacy. The division

---

[16] A fleeting flexibility was demonstrated in the case of the Balkan Wars. Professor Woodward writes: "The cooperation between Germany, Great Britain, and France during the three Balkan wars impressed and indeed surprised the statesmen and diplomatists of Europe. The Concert of Europe had at last taken form. London was the centre of action, and throughout the most critical periods a conference of Ambassadors of the Great Powers met under the presidency of Grey." *Ibid.*, p. 398.

[17] See A. J. P. Taylor, *The Struggle for Mastery in Europe, 1848-1918* (Oxford, 1954), pp. 437-438.

[18] See Henry A. Kissinger, *A World Restored* (Boston, 1957), Introduction.

of Europe into two camps prevented the creation of an overpowering coalition against any untoward act. International offenders could count on as much support as might be mobilized against them, and the Concert itself merely became a contending party. In 1906 at Algeciras the Concert could not force the French out of Morocco or sustain a French protectorate. Neither the French nor the Germans were "forced" to yield. The rebuke to Germany was not sufficiently authoritative to prevent German action to reverse the decision. The real purpose of Bülow had been to shake or destroy the Anglo-French entente, instead, Algeciras had strengthened it. But this outcome could not be forced down German throats. The Concert of Europe had operated traditionally to make war unthinkable, and had organized such an overwhelming display of force that a recalcitrant state quickly abandoned all ideas of war. But this was not true in 1906: Algeciras did not make war less likely, but instead made war more likely. It registered the existence of a Franco-German quarrel without being able to settle it. Neither side was finally dissuaded against the use of force. ". . . [Morocco] was a true 'crisis,' a turning-point in European history. It shattered the long Bismarckian peace. War between France and Germany was seriously, though remotely, contemplated for the first time since 1875; the Russians had to envisage for the first time honouring their engagements under the Franco-Russian alliance — and did not like the prospect; the British contemplated military intervention on the Continent for the first time since 1864." [19]

Nor was the Concert present, except in name, on the count of legitimacy. A signal characteristic of the old system had been the concern for the general interests of Europe. The decisions of the Concert acquired a certain legitimacy in part because they did not reflect simply the configuration of national interests. The positions adopted on Belgium and Mehemet Ali, the stand on the Treaty of San Stefano, the final position on Bulgaria in 1887 — all these had eventually been "accepted" even by those Powers sure to lose the most. Concern for the general peace or ideological solidarity had lent a *de jure* quality to Concert action. In 1906, however, this characteristic was absent. The Concert no longer operated in behalf of Europe; it merely coincided with the national interests of the

19 Taylor, *Struggle*, p. 441.

most powerful alliance system.[20] The Concert itself began to take on
an *ex parte* flavor. In this context, "legitimacy" could not attach
to Concert decisions. Decisions, once taken, might be undone
when the injured party could firm up his alliance partners.

In this context, the alliance system itself replaced the Concert. As
we have seen, the partial amalgamation of alliances with the Concert mechanism had begun under Bismarck. But for the great German Chancellor, alliances had been a tool not an object. They
served to implement more general interests. By 1906, the reverse
obtained, and the Concert was subordinated to the respective alliance combinations. This meant fundamentally that not general interests but only separate national interests, as reflected in the two
great military coalitions, had partisans. The Concert was reduced
to an amphitheater in which the two protagonists might vie for supremacy.

III The ability of the Concert to prevent a major clash between
European states was weakening at the very moment when
war was assuming dangerous proportions. The lessons of 1866 and
1870 were being learned too well. The short war seemed the only
war, and this proposition received support from many quarters.
The examples of the Boer War and the Russo-Japanese War were
cited only in proof of pre-existent notions. The latter was evidence
in behalf of brevity, but the failure of cavalry was not noticed.
Trench warfare was illustrated in the Boer conflict and even before at Plevna, but the military staffs managed to overlook it. The
growing invisibility of armies as demonstrated in South Africa and
in Manchuria was not deemed applicable to European wars.[21]

The generals believed in the primacy of offensive operations as
in 1870, and they believed, as in 1870, that a future conflict would
be quickly decided in favor of the offensive force. France and Germany readied mass armies for the decisive battle. Strategists from
both countries accepted the offensive, but they used it in different
ways. For Foch, the offensive represented the supremacy of the will,
*"Victoire = Volunté";* for Schlieffen, the offensive meant the suprem-

---

20 This statement must be qualified in respect of the general cooperation in the
Balkan crises.

21 See Alfred Vagts, *A History of Militarism* (New York, 1959), p. 353.

acy of the plan. In these different conceptions, the French were the closest disciples of the elder Moltke: "No plan of operations reached with any certainty beyond the first encounter with the enemy's main force." [22] They believed that the Franco-Prussian War had been lost because of French inflexibility. Though the French were inclined to praise, rather than to criticize Moltke's generalship, they thought the French army had not taken sufficient advantage of his mistakes. The lesson seemed to be an emphasis upon the offensive without rigid adherence to plan. For Schlieffen, planlessness was a luxury. The Germans believed they would have the numerically inferior force; and that a deficiency in numbers could only be compensated by a single-minded execution of a plan designed to maximize simultaneously German strengths and Franco-Russian weaknesses. The wheeling operation through the low countries to turn the French left wing was the result. Even with fewer men, however, Schlieffen expected victory in a short period. A month would be sufficient to place German troops on the Somme, and short months later German forces would be operating south of Paris. French armies would be thrown "against their own fortresses and the Swiss frontier." [23] German forces would then be free to deal a death blow to the Russians in the East.

The military staffs placed such emphasis upon a short war in part because they thought civilians would not support a long war. Schlieffen was convinced that a protracted struggle was "impossible at a time when the existence of the nation is based on an uninterrupted functioning of commerce and industry and when by a quick decision the machinery brought to a stop must be started again. A wearing-out strategy cannot be undertaken at a time when the maintenance of millions calls for billions." [24] Economic mercantilism might permit a long and arduous conflict, whereas economic liberalism would not. Liberal-minded parliaments were willing to authorize large armies partly on the assumption that they would be able to decide a war quickly. The prolongation of war would impinge upon the civilian sector and destroy the network of world economic

[22] Quoted in *ibid.*, p. 347.
[23] Hajo Holborn, "Moltke and Schlieffen: The Prussian-German School," in Edward Mead Earle (ed.), *Makers of Modern Strategy* (Princeton, 1948), p. 192.
[24] Quoted in Vagts, *op. cit.*, p. 349.

relations, while a short war, on the other hand, would be politically and economically tolerable. Civilians rushed to embrace the military opinion that the war would be won in a matter of months.

More than this, the coincidence of Darwinian theory and the moderation of the wars of 1866 and 1870 led to the conclusion that war might positively be desirable. Wars, it was argued, were an essential element in national solidarity, a means of moral purification, and essential in the development toward perfection. "The path of progress is strewn with the wreck of nations. . . . These dead peoples are, in very truth, the stepping stones on which mankind has arisen to the higher intellectual and deeper emotional life of to-day." [25] "War, said Treitschke, consolidates a people, reveals to each individual his relative unimportance, sweeps away factional hostilities and group selfishness, and intensifies patriotism and national idealism. When two nations are at war, each comes more fully to know and respect the other, and the exchange of good qualities is made easier." Finally, it was claimed, "war begets various individual virtues — valour, industriousness, inventiveness, orderliness, 'habit of obedience,' 'cleanliness,' 'temperance,' 'moral stamina,' 'spiritual enlargement.' " [26] The advantages of war might be stressed all out of proportion to its disadvantages because the military toll was not expected to be costly. The Austro-Prussian War afforded a convenient rationalization for strife without appreciable cost. In human and material terms, the war was bearable, and in political terms, the settlement was lenient. It might, therefore, be repeated.

The assumptions concerning militarism underwent a sea change after 1870. The lessons of the Napoleonic Wars had been that war and revolution were inseparable. In destructiveness, the Napoleonic conflicts bore a grim message. The continued fear of revolutionary militarism restrained conflict in the two decades following 1830 even after an ideological cleavage appeared in the ranks of the Concert. The lessons of 1866 and 1870 were almost the opposite. Wars would not be as strenuous as the battles in the Crimea, to say nothing of approaching the fury of Napoleonic campaigns. The

[25] Karl Pearson, quoted in Francis W. Coker, *Recent Political Thought* (New York, 1934), pp. 448, 449.
[26] *Ibid.*, p. 449.

secular trend seemed to be toward the humanization of warfare; the new technology would make it even more painless.[27] It is not surprising then, that restraints failed to function, and that the nations of Europe entered lightly into war in July and August 1914.

The system of international relations prevailing at the turn of the century was similar in surface respects to the system of the eighteenth century. Superficially, it seemed that the use of war as a regulatory mechanism was the same, in that the balance of power system in Frederician Europe had not prevented war. Rather, war served to maintain the balance between states. Similarly, it might be argued, war was the means of adjusting the balance at the end of the nineteenth century. In actuality, however, the two cases were not comparable. The *ancien régime* had never permitted war to destroy the system, and war was never carried so far as to imperil the existence or viability of one of the essential members of the system. War was used only to restore the balance, not to overthrow its foundations. The limitations upon war in the eighteenth century reflected the quasi-medieval social organization which characterized domestic society. War could not be total because populations would not lend total support. The limited international polity was predicated on a limited domestic polity. In the period of imperialist nationalism, on the other hand, international limitations were frustrated by the absence of domestic limitations. Total support was demanded and received in both liberal and conservative states; while the international system received no help from domestic restrictions. More than this, the mechanism Mazzini believed would limit conflict in international relations turned out to

---

[27] Captain Liddell Hart shows how wrong this picture was: "When armies became bigger in scale, wars tended to become more comprehensive in scope. They imposed greater demands on industry, which became more closely geared to military needs. Armies became less manageable, and this handicap, in conjunction with the greater quantity of trained man-power available in reserve, tended to make wars longer in duration. War became less politically controllable — at all stages, from inception to completion. In the first place, universal conscription tended to precipitate war, as the dramatic calling-up of the nations' men from their civil jobs produced a state of excitement and disturbance prejudicial to diplomatic efforts to avert a conflict, and also because the machinery of mass mobilization and deployment was so dependent on keeping rigidly to time-table. That effect was very clearly seen in the outbreak of war in 1914." "Armed Forces and the Art of War: Armies" in *The New Cambridge Modern History*, Vol. 10 *The Zenith of European Power, 1830-70*, J. P. T. Bury (ed.), (Cambridge, 1960), pp. 312-313.

be a catalyst of antagonism. Mazzini believed that popular government would make for a "moral" foreign policy. Arguing after the
manner of Kant, Mazzini held that peoples would forbid the cyni-
cal warlike policies which had been the stock in trade of despots. In
this view Mazzini turned out to be quite wrong, for in the conservative states, the people lent considerable support to the imperialistic policies of their governors without exacting in return a
real control of policy. In the liberal states, the people could not
be disregarded in the formulation of foreign policy, although they
did not insist upon a pacific course in diplomacy. They were as
bent on expansion as their cabinets and foreign offices. The mobilization of public sentiment in support of the nation revealed an
important difference between the latter parts of the eighteenth and
nineteenth centuries. The old regime had not been able to manipulate national symbols persuasively enough to avoid revolution, nor
had the old conservatives succeeded in convincing their publics
that support of the "legitimist nation" would bring social and political reform. Those who believed in the existing national basis
were overborne by those who believed reform could not come
without altering the legitimist basis of the nation. In the late nineteenth century, the situation reversed, the political leadership was
able to persuade the great majority of people either that reform was
not necessary, or that it could be accomplished within the existing
national framework. In 1914 nationalism took precedence over
revolution; in 1789 revolution took precedence over nationalism.

The balance of power system of the *ancien régime,* then, could
not operate a century later, since the internationalism of the old
order was quite different from the nationalism of the imperialist
age. But the social context was not the only factor differentiating
the eighteenth-century system from that of a hundred years later.
The technical facts of militarism in the two eras were very different.
Alliances, the devices for directing militarism, existed in both periods. But they operated in a wholly dissimilar fashion. Alliances
were usually concluded in the eighteenth century only after the
balance had already been upset, they were for limited purposes, and
they did not specify the details of military cooperation. They were
the prime means by which the balance was redressed. At the beginning of the twentieth century, however, alliances were no longer
tools to refashion the balance; they were the mechanism by which

the conflict would be carried on. In the old regime, the nature of alignments was determined by the crisis at hand, and similarly, alliances were composed for the purpose of dealing with a specific problem. In the imperialist regime, alignments were determined antecedently, and they could not be altered for the purpose of dealing with the specific case. Eighteenth-century alliances were fundamentally a means of preserving the system, while twentieth-century alliances were basically a means of waging war, regardless of the system.

Nor was there more than a superficial similarity between imperialist nationalism and the truncated Concert. In both periods a bipolar tendency existed: Triple Alliance confronted Triple Entente in the first decade of the twentieth century, as liberal nations had opposed conservative states during the eighteen forties. But the bipolarity was different in the two cases. In the era of Palmerston, the tendency of liberal states to work together and against conservative states was not carried so far as to disrupt the Concert. The fear of war was so great that cooperation among ideological foes was not impossible. The conservatives did not assume that war was an effective way of disposing of liberalism; the liberals did not believe that social reform could be advanced only by military action. The very solidity of liberal and conservative powers discouraged action on either side. War would probably not work, and its consequences might be unfortunate for both sides. In this situation, the Concert had to be retained as a means of accommodation. The bipolarity of Triple Alliance and Triple Entente was quite different. The efficacy of war as a means of policy, and its relatively moderate political impact had been shown in the Austro-Prussian War of 1866. Defeat of an opposing Power or group of Powers might be obtained without tremendous cost, and further, defeat itself could be risked for its political consequences might be reduced to a minimum. The two forces which operated against war and on behalf of the Concert in the eighteen forties took an opposite direction in the eighteen nineties. With the adoption of war as an important potential instrument of policy, the Concert declined in inverse proportion.

IV Perhaps the most surprising outcome for a century habituated to revolutionary conflicts was the decline of ideology in the years before World War I. For nearly half a century, the alignments of Europe were largely determined on ideological grounds, but after 1848, sentiment was no longer a prime governing factor. The two alliance systems of the first years of the twentieth century violated ideological canons. Italy was linked in the Triple Alliance with the Dual Monarchy and Germany; Russia was linked in the Triple Entente with Britain and France. The need for allies to pursue the imperial quest and the need for military security outweighed the revolutionary issue. Nationalism, an ideology on which all Europe agreed, dwarfed the liberal-conservative split and towered over the liberal-socialist issue as well. In 1914 it became all-determining.

The first World War reintroduced an ideological antagonism, and in so doing it harked back to the Napoleonic Wars. The conquests of Napoleon had enormous social significance in terms of the forces to which they gave rise. For a considerable period after 1814 European development was conditioned by the struggle between those who wished to extend the Napoleonic victories and those who wished to confine them. In a somewhat similar fashion, World War I gave rise to a division between those who wanted to fight the war over again, and those who did not want to fight at all. Like the Napoleonic campaigns before it, the Great War was an enormous force in European society, vastly altering former assumptions about the most desirable social organization. Before the war German liberals had believed that capitalism and liberal government were the ideal forms of social life, after the war, an important fraction of the middle class no longer accepted this view. The war inflation, accentuated by the inflation of 1923, led salary earners and those who lived on fixed incomes to desert liberal ranks. The grand inflation wiped out the fortunes of the *rentier* class and transformed it into a potentially revolutionary instrument. The industrial capitalist, meanwhile, earned unwonted windfall profits from his war industries. As one fraction of the middle class suffered from capitalism, another enormously profited from it. This inequity split the ranks of the middle class when middle-class government became a possibility for the first time in German history. The refusal of the erstwhile middle-class salary earner to be proletarianized ruled out socialism or Communism, and at the same time the discrediting of the industrial bourgeoisie ruled out liberalism. Again, it seemed that only nationalism could hold German society together. But the nationalism which emerged as a new ideological challenge after 1919 was far different from the old imperialism. Under the empire, nationalism was primarily a device of winning liberal support, and only secondarily was it designed to take the wind out of the sails of the Social Democrats. After 1919, however, nationalism had to be joined with militant social radicalism. It had to appeal to the pauperized lower middle class, to the workers, to the returned soldier as much as to the more respectable bourgeoisie. This new brand of nationalism was to create a new ideological antagonism in world politics. Ideology was not a factor in international relations at the turn of the century, although the impact of the war gave it a new and terrible importance.

The international system of imperialist nationalism, thus, introduced a concatenation of instability. Its own unstable effects created new ones, and a new period of war and conflict ensued. The alliance system turned out to be incompatible with an effective Concert. The disruptive inputs of national actors could not be mediated or restrained by a powerful international institution, and imperialism eventually became a major force for conflict. The competing demands made by nations on the international environment could not be satisfied simultaneously, and the attempt to satisfy them could lead only to war, the outcomes of which could not be tolerable to all participants.

The goals and tactics of diplomacy in the system of imperialist nationalism had superficial similarities to those of the *ancien régime*. Imperialism, military alliances and the pursuit of power and glory were common manifestations of both systems. But the imperial expansion of the eighteenth century was a demonstration of domestic confidence, not desperation. And the wars of the old regime might be handled with restraint and compromise. At the end of the nineteenth century, however, the very existence of domestic regimes was bound up with the imperial course, and warfare, far removed from the patterns of interminable maneuver, was foreordained to drain the substance of the nation.

## chapter nine
# INTERLUDE BETWEEN WARS

I The Great War ushered in a new period of international relations, but its lineaments were not immediately clear. An observer, surveying the world situation on the eve of peace, might well have seen the results of that war to be the irrevocable triumph of liberal institutions and democratic government. Even before the war liberal ideas were making inroads in conservative as well as liberal states: suffrage reform was progressively conceded, written constitutions were proclaimed, and it was increasingly difficult for the conservatives to avoid full liberal government.[1] With the war the decadent Austrian, Russian, and Ottoman empires toppled. Woodrow Wilson insisted on concluding peace with German liberal representatives, not with the Kaiser. Aside from Russia it seemed that liberal-democratic government had been ensured in the major states of the world.

A general devotion to the liberal-democratic myth might have smoothed the path of the League of Nations, but several European peoples had changed their minds on the desirability of national expansion and war. "The idea that there should be no wars between the nations of Europe and of the World, from being a mere eccentricity of the Anglo-Saxons, was being entertained as not a wholly absurd hypothesis by millions of European citizens. The belief that war was wrong and should be avoidable has never been more widely held."[2] The shift in attitude was testimony to the impact of the war.

[1] See C. J. H. Hayes, *A Generation of Materialism, 1871-1900* (New York, 1941), Chapter Two, Section 2.

[2] R. B. McCallum, *Public Opinion and the Last Peace* (London, 1945), p. 1.

As long as wars were believed to be healthy ventures in "discipline," "moral purification," and "spiritual enlargement," anti-war sentiments could not flourish; as long as nationalism and patriotism were placed above all other determinants of foreign policy, war could not be ruled out. Yet, there was a sense in which it seemed that publics of several countries had learned the lessons that Kant and Mazzini claimed to be self-evident. Republican regimes would not tolerate war for the populace would be the first to suffer. Popular sentiments might be educated, and the doctrines of the two theorists might be realized after 1919.

Liberal institutions could be the more trusted after 1919 because they had been democratized. Domestic tension and uncertainty had lain behind the general adoption of nationalist policies at the turn of the century. Although liberals as well as conservatives had played the imperialist theme as a means of avoiding domestic reform, at the end of the war liberals could no longer postpone concessions to the left. The Labour Party became the main opposition party in Great Britain and in France the *Cartel des Gauches* governed briefly after 1924. The left had attained a respectability that prevented sectarian liberals from employing nationalist symbols to deny the left a share in political power.

Even more important was the strand in Wilsonian thinking which sought a world "made safe for democracy, by democracy." [3] A world united by a single ideological code would be more likely to remain at peace than one riven by diverse ideological strands. In this sense peace heralded the prospective triumph of Mazzini's reasoning. The Italian nationalist had believed that only states organized on liberal and nationalist principles could remain at peace with one another. Mazzini was proved wrong after 1890 when it was demonstrated that the popular will often preferred expansion to peace. After 1919, however, liberal governments, so it was thought, would entertain no such sentiment. Ideological unity would finally put an end to the conflicts of ideas engendered by the French Revolution. Pacific liberal governments could function in a harmonious atmosphere.

As events unrolled, however, these hopes proved to be vain. Liberal government was not established everywhere. Liberals were challenged initially by revolutionary movements on the left, then, and more dangerously, on the right. At the very time when liberals had

3 *Ibid.*, pp. 12-13.

their greatest chance, popular will deserted them in certain states. Nor was liberalism a guarantee against nationalist extremism. If British and French nationalism had been to some degree appeased by the war, German and Italian nationalism had not. All reactions to World War I were not the same; while the British and French acted to prevent its recurrence, in a real sense Germans seemed to act to repeat it. Probably at no time before the Great War had nationalist aspirations been so high, and yet never before Versailles had they been so completely shattered. Versailles was a far greater humiliation for Germany than Vienna had been for France. Even for the quasi-victor, Italy, Versailles was viewed as a national disgrace. In both countries the motivation behind war had been patriotic sacrifice, but the end of war did not afford sufficient patriotic fulfillment. Even Napoleon I had not demanded such sacrifices of his people at the altar of nationalism, and in 1815 the French could accept their reduced status with a degree of equanimity. The Napoleonic wars were popular compared to those in the eighteenth century, but they did not demand or receive the totality of popular support exacted during World War I. Thus the negotiators at Vienna never really had to come to grips with an unfulfilled French nationalism demanding vengeance. At Versailles, however, the peoples demanded national recompense and if the nationalist ambitions of the French and British publics were largely gratified, the aspirations of the Germans and Italians, partly as a consequence, went unsatisfied.

The difference between peace-making at Vienna and Versailles was partly to be explained by the growth of popular influence upon government and popular nationalism in the intervening period. In 1814 many Frenchmen were as eager as the Germans or Austrians to restrain Napoleon. France as a nation did not identify itself with the Napoleonic regime. In 1871 the losses of the Second Empire were deemed losses of France, despite the widespread opposition to Napoleon III. The transfer of two provinces to the new Germany was viewed as a blot on the national escutcheon. By 1914 popular identification with the nation had reached a new peak. The German Empire had as much support as Louis Napoleon enjoyed, and the German loss was far greater than Alsace-Lorraine. If the latter could evoke mutterings of *revanche* in France, the former would make even more certain a war of revenge. In a sense the real problem of

Versailles was that all peoples could not be satisfied simultaneously; the British "khaki" election and the French installation of the *"Chambre Bleu Horizon"* were indications that allied peoples could not be satisfied except at the expense of the Germans. If nationalism had been appeased in Germany, it would have been further incensed in Britain and France.

Yet, nationalism's failure is not an explanation in and of itself of the special brand of German hostility expressed in World War II. The defeat of nationalist aspirations does not always mean that nationalist fulfillment will be an unending demand. After 1919 German opinion did not renounce nationalism, but sought to fulfill it; after 1917 Russian opinion briefly deserted nationalism altogether. The Bolsheviks attained power in November 1917 on the twin slogans of land to the peasants and an end to the imperialist war. The operation the conservatives in Russia had tried to perform — avoidance of revolution through nationalist expansion — failed completely. Revolution was offered in place of nationalism. The French revolutionaries had successfully used nationalism to protect the revolution, while the Russian conservatives had used nationalism in vain to prevent the revolution. The difference between the Russian and German situations was also marked. The German conservatives had used nationalism to prevent reform; they lost political control in Germany for a time after 1918, but their deposition was not due so much to the failure of their theory as to allied intervention. Although nationalism could be used to prevent revolution in Germany, it could not be used to prevent revolution in Russia.

In the German case class conflict had not gone so far as it had in Russia. The German, unlike the Russian peasant, was not estranged from the regime. The urban working class in Germany had been partly appeased by an extensive program of social legislation, but its Russian counterpart had not. German conservatives, following the Bismarckian example, never opposed all measures of reform; they merely sought to channel and control them. The Russian conservatives were fundamentally reactionary. Since they had never really been forced to compromise, they had not learned the art of compromise. After 1871 in Germany the position of the monarchy and the aristocracy rested partly on popular support. Bismarck tried to make sure that that support would be forthcoming, and his relative success paved the way for a nationalized Germany. On the other hand, the Tsar's disadvantage was his absolutism. When the challenge came, he could not point to popular acceptance of or participation in his regime, and the Duma experiment after 1905 came too late to work a Bismarckian revolution in Russia. As a result World War I had a fundamentally different impact in Russia than in Germany. Turgot's commentary on the *ancien régime* had a certain application in the Russia of 1917: "The nation is an aggregate of different and incompatible social groups whose members have so few links between themselves that everyone thinks solely of his own interests; no trace of any feelings for the public weal is anywhere to be found." [4] With the Russian empire broken into separate castes it could hardly be maintained as a unit without revolution. As the French Republic proved in 1793, when internal chaos is complete, nationalist symbols are abandoned. In the Russia of 1917, likewise, the war not only violated national aspirations, it positively undermined them. And the Russian case portrayed the tragic impact of the war on Germany: if the war had restored Germany to the comity of states, certain national ambitions would have been achieved; if it had cut the bonds of German national society, nationalism might have been destroyed. The actual impact of the war fell disastrously between two stools: German nationalism was exacerbated but not fulfilled.

II But the frustration of militant nationalism was not the only result of the war. The war also brought about in Germany and Italy an economic revolution that had profound consequences. It began the deterioration of economic foundations that was continued in the panic of 1923 and in the Great Depression. Some have argued that the war did little more than carry to a conclusion forces which were already immanent in the economic order.[5] Actually, as we can see now, it transformed economic and social life. Economic planning was first introduced on a large scale; autarchic economic tendencies were carried to a new peak; inflation was allowed to run rampant. The end result was the bifurcation of the middle class in Germany

4 Quoted in Alexis de Tocqueville, *The Old Régime and the French Revolution*, translated by Stuart Gilbert (Garden City, N.Y., 1955), p. 107.

5 See the views cited in G. C. Allen, "The Economic Map of the World: Population, Commerce and Industries" in *The New Cambridge Modern History*, Vol. 12, *The Era of Violence, 1898-1945*, David Thomson (ed.), (Cambridge, 1960), p. 27.

and Italy. Just as the failures of Versailles were fomenting nationalist grievances, the economic supports of liberalism were being progressively undermined. Liberal government and a liberal economic system had been supported initially by entrepreneur and salary-earner. The entrepreneur gained profits as a result of his willingness to take risks; the white-collar worker benefited as expansion of industry furthered administrative development in public and private services.[6] As long as both economic directors and their subsidiary servants could benefit from a liberal economic system, both would be bulwarks of liberal polity. If these benefits had been maintained, a liberal republican regime might have attained greater political support from the liberal economic classes than the Empire had ever been able to procure. The Revolution of 1848 might finally be crowned with success, and Germany might be held together without exhorbitant nationalism.

The problem was, however, that as the political conditions for liberal democracy were ripening, its economic foundations were being undercut. The external conditions for the development of political liberalism were as propitious as they had ever been. No longer was there an international conservative alliance which would prevent liberal fulfillment; on the contrary, there was an international liberal alliance bent on installing liberal governments wherever possible. Wilson was an interventionist although his politics were the opposite of Metternich's. Like Mazzini, Wilson believed that the French Revolution had been truncated by conservative dynastic cliques and had yet to reach its final fruition. The difficulty was that while liberalism now had enormous support internationally, its support was undermined domestically in several states. In Germany particularly, the enforced installation of liberal government occurred when liberalism was losing adherents. The war had been financed by public and private credits in anticipation of the fruits of victory, and when they could not be obtained, the war was financed by the printing press. The inflation which followed liquidated a large fraction of Germany's internal debt. "Individuals and institutions dependent on fixed or relatively inelastic incomes, including large numbers

[6] See Max Weber's remarks on the role of the money economy, the development of communications, and the over-all demand for technical perfection as factors contributory to the growth of bureaucracy. "Bureaucracy," in H. H. Gerth and C. Wright Mills, *From Max Weber: Essays in Sociology* (New York, 1946), especially sections 3-5.

among the middle classes, were virtually beggared. Wage earners also were adversely affected by the failure of wages to rise as rapidly as prices." [7] White collar workers and professional people saw their savings wiped away. In both Italy and Germany the currency unit was but a fraction of its former value at the end of the war.[8] But the lower middle class was not destroyed or forced to amalgamate with the proletariat as Marx had assumed. As Paul Alpert has indicated: "[it] did not feel at all a solidarity with the proletariat, the mass of the manual workers. From them it was distinguished, first, by its political attitude, strongly nationalistic; and secondly, by a feeling of superiority resulting from a better education and higher functions . . . which it fulfilled in economic activity or in the service of the state. The middle class considered proletarianization a degradation. . . ." [9] Communism would not be the result of economic transformations. The working class, in fact, probably fared better than its bourgeois compatriots,[10] and would not be in the van of leftward revolution.

While the white-collar workers, petty tradesmen, members of the officialdom, small investors, and rentiers were being pauperized by the inflation, the upper middle class entrepreneur was making windfall gains. Risk-takers became "profiteers." In the prophetic words of Keynes: "These 'profiteers' are, broadly speaking, the entrepreneur class of capitalists, that is to say, the active and constructive element in the whole capitalist society, who in a period of rapidly rising prices cannot help but get rich quick whether they wish it or . . . not. ·. . . By directing hatred against this class, therefore, the European Governments are carrying a step further the fatal process which the subtle mind of Lenin had consciously conceived. The profiteers are a consequence and not a cause of rising prices. By combining a popular hatred of the class of entrepreneurs with the blow already given to social security by the violent and arbitrary disturbance of contract and of the established equilibrium of wealth

[7] W. Bowden, M. Karpovich, and A. Usher, *Economic History of Europe Since 1750* (New York, 1937), p. 835.

[8] J. M. Keynes, *The Economic Consequences of the Peace* (New York, 1920), p. 239.

[9] Paul Alpert, *Twentieth Century Economic History of Europe* (New York, 1951), p. 86.

[10] *Ibid.*, p. 86.

which is the inevitable result of inflation, these Governments are fast rendering impossible a continuance of the social and economic order of the nineteenth century." [11] The bifurcation of the bourgeoisie weakened it at a crucial moment, and turned it upon itself. While one fraction benefited enormously from the war and inflation, the other was grievously wounded by it. The entrepreneurial "profiteer" feared social revolution as a consequence of his windfall gains and began to distrust his previous white-collar allies. The salary-earner denounced the capitalist as an internationalist and rapacious force. But the lower middle class did not think of revolution in proletarian terms: Communism was not believed to be the answer to "bourgeois internationalism." While the gains of the "munitions makers" and others made the lower middle class doubtful of a liberal economic system and liberal government to go with it, the deduction was not Marxian. It was not the special economic position of the entrepreneur which was the primary object of hatred, it was his "internationalism." The capitalist profited while Germans suffered, and in so doing he had really placed himself outside the boundaries of nation. This ranking of priorities was the measure of the salary-earner's unwillingness to be proletarianized — the economic issue was viewed as a compounding of the profiteer's internationalism, and his internationalism was not viewed as merely contributory to overriding economic oppression. Marx was proved wrong after 1919: nationalism was a more fundamental *desideratum* than economic reward. Thus, the higher bourgeois worried needlessly since socialist revolution was not the primary objective of his erstwhile lower middle class partner. And in one of the strange outcomes of history, the middle class which was supposed to be divided against itself came finally together in yielding to National Socialism.[12] Nationalism was the means of expunging the humiliation of the war gains for the entrepreneur; he could prove his national fidelity by supporting national extremism. He would win back his patriotism by ultranationalism and militarism. At the same time National Socialism could be tolerated because it was the only virile alternative to complete social revolution and Communism. Krupp

---

[11] Keynes, *op. cit.*, pp. 236-237.

[12] A conclusive demonstration that National Socialist support in Germany stemmed mainly from the middle class is given in S. M. Lipset, *Political Man* (London, 1960), pp. 140-149.

and Thyssen knew that the "social" part of Nazism was bankrupt. The lower middle class knew it too, and did not want social revolution so much as national revolution. Hitler was tolerable because he was not a proletarian. The only followers of Nazism who were deluded were the members of the urban working class. After 1929 they gave Hitler his final push toward power, and they probably believed his socialist program. But even they did not turn a ready ear to Communism. The German proletarian was not like his Russian counterpart; he had been treated too well. And after 1914, he had been made a member of the German nation come what might. Nationalism catered to his sentiments.

Thus in certain countries after 1919 nationalism took precedence over liberalism. The catchword "National Socialism" was a hallmark of the times. During the nineteenth century it had been assumed that nationalism and liberalism went hand in hand.[13] Liberalism could best be advanced under a nation-state free from the oppressive restraints of dynastic conservative control. The conservative dynasts could never become real liberals. In the event Mazzini was right: it was not until after the national unifications of Germany and Italy had occurred that even a semblance of liberalism could be pursued economically. Economic liberalism's great flowering was in the seventies; nationalism's initial bloom in the sixties. In the late nineteenth century conservatives seemed to be doing better: they could allow certain liberal economic policies because their national position prevented full-scale capitulation. Liberalism and nationalism still went together.

From the opposite point of view the result was almost the same. Nationalism could reach fruition only under liberal rule. Mazzini could not believe that conservatives would be nationalists. And even after the Bismarckian synthesis had partially proved him wrong, liberals still believed that full national development would wait upon liberal control of government. Conservatives had "dynastic reasons"; they manipulated, and they had to overlook the national, popular will. Liberal government would make popular will effective, and in this sense it would respond most completely to national impulsions. The interests of a narrow clique would no longer govern. This was the liberal-nationalist creed at the turn of the century.

---

[13] See Guido de Ruggiero, *The History of European Liberalism*, translated by R. G. Collingwood (Boston, 1959), p. 407.

But the war and the inflation which followed seemed to deny this
hypothesis. For the first time it was questioned whether liberal government would really be popular government. Government in the interests of the middle class might no longer be government in the interests of the whole nation. This was true not because the entire
middle class was read out of the "Volk"; it was because there no
longer was *a middle class* in the old sense.[14] Government in the interest of the entrepreneurs would not be government in the interest of
the people. And this was precisely what liberal government was held
to signify. Now economic liberalism and liberal government were
regarded to be government in the interests of a narrow clique just as
much as conservative legitimacy had been during the nineteenth
century. Liberal government would not be conducive to the interests
of the lower middle class, who wanted sterner stuff. Middle-class
ethos in the past had always been set by its leading elements; now
the bulwark of liberal stability, the lower middle class, was deserting
that ethos. Government on behalf of the old ethos would no longer
be popular government.

In this odd way both sections of the middle class misunderstood
each other. The lower middle classes were afraid of government by
the higher bourgeoisie. They believed that the entrepreneur wanted
nothing more than to reap profits at the expense of the people and
that he would use liberal government to this end. The *haute bourgeoisie* thought that the salary-earners were supporting social revolution of the Communist variety. Actually, neither was the case. If
both had realized that neither was extremist — the entrepreneur in
money-grubbing, the salaried classes in economic transformation —
they might have got on famously. Liberal government could have
achieved what both wanted, yet both distrusted it. The measure of
their final agreement was common acknowledgment of National Socialism. And yet even this agreement was not fully understood.

This oddity is underscored by the transformations of the German
elite. Under the empire a moderate rightist political orientation prevailed among cabinet members,[15] and the nobility and aristocracy

14 William Kornhauser argues persuasively that the old class lines tend to break
down with the onset of "mass society"; and it is the development of "mass society"
which permits a new revolutionary mass movement to mobilize itself. (*The Politics of Mass Society* [Glencoe, Ill., 1959], Chapter Two.)
15 See Maxwell Knight, *The German Executive, 1890-1933* (Stanford, 1952), Table
7, p. 20.

were predominant in the cabinet.[16] With the creation of the Weimar Republic, the social composition of cabinets changed drastically. While 64.5 percent of cabinet members under the empire had aristocratic backgrounds and 35.5 percent middle class backgrounds, under the Republic, only 11.5 percent had aristocratic backgrounds, 77.8 percent had middle class backgrounds, and 10.7 percent had laboring class backgrounds.[17] With this considerable shift in the class composition of cabinets under the Republic one would have anticipated a corresponding change in political affiliation. "The figures show [however] a much smaller representation of the left, and a much higher representation of the right, than one would expect in a democracy: 21.3 percent left, and 23.7 percent right. . . . What is surprising is that these figures suggest a right-center rather than left-center orientation (after an initial period of left preponderance). If we consider that the Republican regime itself emerged from a revolution of left against right, this fact alone would suggest that something went wrong with the German revolution soon after its initial success.

This is, in fact, what happened. The democratic process encouraged the expression of dissatisfaction, of desire for change, rather than the acceptance of the new regime as constituted. In the period following World War I, economic and political difficulties and disasters of all sorts constantly fed disillusionment and protest. The parties totally identified with the democratic Republic (Social Democrats, Democrats, and center) lost their majority very shortly after the revolution; from the early 1920's on, the Republicans consistently polled less than 50 percent of the vote in the Republic. The rest wanted either to go much farther left (Communists); or to return to the prerevolutionary order (the parties of the right); or, later, to remake the revolution along severely regimented lines with emphasis upon supermilitarism (Nazis). It is not surprising that the Republic fell apart under these stresses.[18]

Thus the middle class members of Republican cabinets (primarily drawn from the upper middle class) adopted different political viewpoints. Conservative and nationalist sentiments animated middle-class functionaries desirous of proving their loyalty to the German state and regard for the old empire. Middle-class government was conceded at precisely the time when the middle class was deserting

[16] See *ibid.*, Table 15, p. 33.

[17] *Ibid.*, Table 15, p. 33.

[18] Paul Kecskemeti in *ibid.*, p. iv.

liberalism and opting for conservatism and nationalism. In these circumstances it was little wonder that the liberal Republic did not endure.

III In the erstwhile liberal nations, full liberal-democratic government was installed after World War I. The appeasement of nationalist grievances of the victorious peoples allowed a greater domestic stability than was achieved where nationalism was destroyed or frustrated. A new attention to the question of regulating international relationships emerged, and three different theories found partial embodiment in the peace treaties and in the Covenant of the League of Nations.[19] The French theory, partly shared by the British and Americans at the end of the war, was that the war was Germany's fault.[20] If this were true, a sufficient international policy would simply be restraining Germany, and since that nation was the only probable cause of war, war might be prevented by controlling German behavior. This line of reasoning justified the repressive sanctions of Versailles. By that settlement Germany lost her colonies, her merchant marine, and her foreign properties, besides having to cede some 10 percent of her population and territory. These losses compounded Germany's economic problem.

The European territories which she lost had been the source, in 1913, of four-fifths of her total production of iron ore . . . almost half of her pig iron, a fourth of her coal, three-fifths of her zinc . . . and more than a third of her lead. . . . The loss of arable land was greater than the loss of population. The burden of reparations not only taxed with extreme severity her curtailed productive resources but subjected both her economic and her political life to external controls. These losses and burdens, combined with trade barriers resulting from the general rearrangement of political boundaries made necessary a thoroughgoing reorganization of the national economy. . . . Germany's dependence on foreign markets was increased while her access to them was impeded.[21]

Germany's economic plight was added to political and military burdens. The Rhineland was demilitarized, the Saar temporarily

---

[19] The author is quite aware that the following portrayal of the three theories only roughly characterizes the views of the three nations. Actually, there were elements of each of the theories in all three national views.

[20] See Louis A. R. Yates, *United States and French Security, 1917-1921* (New York, 1957), Chapter One.

[21] Bowden, Karpovich and Usher, *op cit.*, pp. 733-734.

detached, and limits set upon the German military establishment. When the French did not obtain cession of the Rhineland, they concluded with Britain and the United States a Treaty of Guarantee which was to protect against a revival of the German menace.

The British theory, partly accepted by other Allies, was that the breakdown of the Concert of Europe had led to the war. Sir Alfred Zimmern summarizes the reasoning of a British Foreign Office memorandum in the following way:

> And was not the war itself due, at least in large measure, to the absence of a system of regular Conference under the Concert of Europe? Did not the catastrophe become inevitable from the time that the European powers formed themselves into two sharply divided groups, the Triple Alliance and the Triple Entente, each with its own system or, at least, habit of consultation? And was not this division, which hardened so rapidly into opposition, due to the absence of any obligation to come to sit regularly at a common table, under conditions permitting of frank and friendly discussion? Could not arrangements be devised which would make it morally impossible for a state, or a group of states, to remain apart and drift into an attitude of suspicion and bitterness? [22]

If there had been a regular mechanism which made it simple to convene a European conference when a crisis arose, the Great War might not have occurred. Leonard Woolf wrote: "This system, if it had been in existence for, say, ten years before 1914, would have been an additional and a serious obstacle to war in July, 1914. It would have helped those people who wanted peace and would have hindered those people who wanted war. That is the function, and no negligible function, of pacific machinery. . . . And it is almost certain that if a conference had taken place there would have been no war, even though no nation was bound by the decision of the Conference." [23] How would the convening of a conference prevent war? Woolf and his Fabian colleagues had two answers. Firstly, "it prevents excitement by being so intolerably dull. . . . Even a Serbian or a German would lose interest in a question of Serbian and German nationality if he saw it discussed by diplomatists at a Conference, and not one person in a thousand would ever have thought of Sarajevo again if a conference had met in July, 1914." [24] Secondly,

[22] A. E. Zimmern, *The League of Nations and the Rule of Law, 1918-1935* (London, 1936), pp. 190-191.

[23] Leonard Woolf, *International Government* (New York, 1916), pp. 132-133.

[24] *Ibid.*, p. 134.

"the great advantage of Conferences and judicial tribunals is that they bring things out into the light. . . . And as soon as a question is discussed, reasonable men see that there is a reasonable method of settling it. It is darkness, doubt, and ignorance, which breed fear and fear which breeds war." [25]

The cause of World War I, on this reasoning, was misunderstanding. No striking renovation of the international system was, therefore, necessary to prevent conflict. The mere provision of an institutional format for the old international Concert would be sufficient. The British apparently did not believe that others could be malicious; they believed only that they could be misinformed. Effective means of communication, then, would deter war. The League Council was thus to be the permanent Concert. The logical deduction from this argument was the restoration of Germany to the comity of nations without discrimination. Since there were no fundamental issues between Germany and the Allies, German rehabilitation and representation in the League would serve to keep the peace. The Germans could not be blamed for what was essentially the temporary breakdown of the pre-existing system of consultation.

The American interpretation of the origins of the war was different. Woodrow Wilson was an idealist who believed that "the struggle for power among nations was due to ignorance, selfishness and an insufficient development of proper institutions. Conflict was not a necessary or inevitable state of affairs, but only a temporary disruption of a natural harmony of interests among individuals and nations. People and nations were capable of putting aside their selfish interests through appeals to better impulses, to reason and to a common desire for peace and justice." [26] In Wilson's view the war was caused as much by anachronistic political institutions as by any other single factor. Where popular will was frustrated or unheeded, peaceful restraints could not be expected to operate; where nations were partitioned or combined in the heterogenous amalgam of empires, national will could not make itself felt. The war had been a product of the old conservative and dynastic order. If national self-determination and liberal democracy could supplant that order, pacific sentiments would animate all governments, and a natural

[25] *Ibid.,* pp. 134-135.
[26] Alexander George and Juliette George, *Woodrow Wilson and Colonel House* (New York, 1956), p. 159.

harmony of national interests would ensue. The will of peoples and nations was the best assurance against war. Accordingly the Covenant provided for the principle of "the hue and cry." [27] This principle gave democratic publics a role in bringing recalcitrant governments to heel when war seemed in the offing. The specification of a ninety-day waiting period before states could make war would allow world public opinion to become articulate against the war-bent Power. The full and free discussion of League meetings would inform the world, and peoples would become alarmed enough to bring pressure on their governments to renounce an aggressive course or to take action against a potential aggressor. Hence, the origins of World War I lay not in Germany or even in the old international system. The origin lay in the domestic constitution of the old reactionary monarchies. If the old conservative regimes could be done away with, peace would reign. In this sense Wilson did not simply propose to "make the world safe for democracy"; he proposed to "make the world safe by democracy." Such notions did not require repressive strictures on Germany's present and future development. Reparations, territorial losses, restrictions on militarism — none of these were necessary if the German people were not to blame for the war. Mere deposition of the Kaiser and the installation of a democratic regime would be sufficient without other penalties to keep the peace.

The difficulty, of course, was that no one of the three views prevailed in the peace discussions. What emerged was an inconsistent conglomeration of all three notions. In practical terms this outcome was tragic, for unilateral adherence to any of the three theories might have prevented World War II. If the basic French theory had been agreed to by all the Allies, the peace negotiations would have been devoted only to means of repressing Germany. If the United States and Britain, in addition to France, had been convinced that Germany was the villain of the piece neither would have stood by on the sidelines while Germany rearmed, denounced the League and the Disarmament Conference, and began to tear up the Versailles and Locarno pacts. American and British action would have been forthcoming at least by the time of Hitler's reoccupation of the Rhineland. The menace of National Socialism would have been dispatched at an early stage, though the internal causes of Nazism would not have been dealt with.

27 See Zimmern, *op. cit.*, p. 265 ff.

If the British theory, which Lloyd George temporarily deserted at Versailles, had prevailed and had the war been attributed to the system, there would have been no discriminatory clauses fixed against Germany. Germany would have been readmitted to the fraternity of states even more quickly than Louis XVIII's France, and no domestic overturn in Germany would have been made prerequisite to peace talks. The Empire would not have been humbled, nor German nationalism unnecessarily irritated. The war could be explained on both sides as a failure of the communication which the League apparatus had repaired. The reconciliation of Germany would thus have prevented nationalist grievances from accumulating, and National Socialism would probably not have gained power in Germany. Reparations demands would not have aggravated the economic crisis in post-war Germany.

If the American theory which Wilson himself was forced to compromise had won out, liberal-nationalist governments would have been installed in Central Europe. The war would not have been laid at Germany's doorstep, nor would reparations have been exacted as payment for war guilt. Not Germany, but the reactionary dynastic regime which governed it was the arch enemy, and the deposition of the Kaiser with his coterie would be sufficient penalty for the aggressors of 1914. If the German peoples were absolved of all war guilt, if economic and territorial penalties were not levied, if the victors were willing to help the vanquished with the reconstruction of their economic system, the results of World War I might not have been far different from those of World War II. The German liberal government might have been drawn back into international connections with other liberal-democratic states, and Mazzini's dream would have been partially realized.

IV In the result none of the three theories was followed to the nub. The French had their way in blaming Germany for the war, in the colonial and reparations clauses, and largely in the territorial clauses of the Versailles Treaty. The English got their refurbished Concert in the League Council. Wilson helped to seat liberal-democratic governments and tried to redraw the frontiers of Europe along national lines. The "hue and cry" was written into the League Covenant. As a result Germany was not returned to the comity of nations, or perhaps more accurately, she was re-

turned to international relations with unappeased grievances. Nationalism was not stanched by the peace settlement; it was aggravated by it. And the war and economic crises were permitted by the victors to work an internal revolution in German society.[28] National Socialism triumphed in Germany on January 30, 1933.

The success of Fascist polity made for a new ideological cleavage in European and world politics. As the Napoleonic and revolutionary periods gave birth to an ideological struggle which helped to shape European relations during the first half of the nineteenth century, World War I's legacy was a new and more virulent ideological conflict which determined international politics for more than a decade. But there was an important difference between the liberal-conservative conflict during the nineteenth century, and the liberal-Fascist conflict of the twentieth century. As we have seen, the ideological issue did not determine European alignments much after mid-nineteenth century. At least after 1871, the ideological cleavage was bridged without war. In part this was because the position of the conservatives no longer was dependent upon a total rejection of the liberal-nationalist creed. Indeed, after 1848, the position became dependent upon embracing a portion of that creed. Bismarck succeeded because he stole the thunder of the liberals and nationalists. But the fact was that he had to steal their thunder. In other words, domestically the conservatives had to come to terms with the revolution. They were incapable of fighting it without taking over a portion of its program. This was an indication of the way in which liberalism succeeded *domestically* in eroding conservative rule. Conservatives were not totalitarians, and could not insulate their populations from subversive ideas. They had to compromise *domestically;* and the domestic compromise facilitated a compromise *internationally.* Bismarck and Disraeli understood each other as well as Bismarck and Alexander II.

Fascist totalitarianism in the twentieth century, however, was not similarly forced to compromise. Domestically, the erosion of liberal ideas could be prevented by control of mass media of communications. Hence the groundwork for an international *détente* did not exist. In this sense the Fascists enjoyed an internal stability which conservatives of the nineteenth century could never rely on. At the same time and from another point of view National Socialism was

28 See Kornhauser, *op. cit.,* Chapter 8.

unable to provide the bases of domestic and international stability. Conservatism in the nineteenth century was fundamentally internal in its orientations. Conservatism implied a certain domestic mode of political and economic organization, and it sought fundamentally rule by an aristocratic class. There was, in consequence, nothing in the nature of the conservative ethos requiring international adventure. Sometimes bellicose policies were necessary to ensure an internal position as at the end of the nineteenth century. There was, however, nothing doctrinal in the preoccupation with imperialism. Once the conditions of internal stability were met, external expansion could be abandoned. The National socialists, on the other hand, were never able to separate (nor did they wish to separate) internal and external aspects of policy. National Socialism, though it emerged from the revolutionary domestic conditions fomented by the war and successive economic crises, had to operate in both internal and external realms. Domestically, the polity of nationalism depended upon the utmost internal consolidation and *Gleichschaltung;* internationally it depended upon successive nationalist triumphs. Thus, thought control (although it compelled adherence to the ideology of the regime) was not a means of preserving final stability internally in Germany. The ideology of the regime called for a career of national expansion. In this sense the very success of control made the regime insecure, because it made aggrandizement all the more necessary. The rudimentary ideology which the Nazis propounded left little enough room for rationalization of defeat. If given territories were not secured, if given states were not humbled, if given peace settlements were not torn up, ideology would be denied. Communist concepts were more ephemeral and demanded exegesis: the "dictatorship of the proletariat," "socialism," even "Communism" were vague notions which an elite could interpret and reinterpret. The *Anschluss* with Austria was more concrete, and its occurrence less subject to definitional squabbling. *Mein Kampf* plunged the Nazis into a career of foreign conquest, and any failure of conquest could not be concealed despite totalitarian regimentation.

Thus National Socialism was at once more virulent internationally and equally unstable domestically. The Nazis were not forced to compromise with liberalism because of internal weakness — they were sometimes weak internally because of their ability to project their own doctrine and avoid liberal compromise. As a result there was never any real possibility for a *détente* with Nazi dictatorship. They could not be brought to compromise through domestic avenues; their domestic strength in propagating Nazism meant that the ideological issue could not be resolved. At the same time the virulence of their doctrine and their need for repeated and concrete victories in the international realm made them irreconcilable antagonists. Internal security for Nazism entailed insecurity for neighboring states. Thus National Socialists did not present a challenge like that of a reformulated and militant conservatism. They could not compromise with their international opponents; they could only defeat them.

In these circumstances it was not surprising that the League of Nations failed to keep the peace. The League was the most ambitious attempt institutionally to provide for the governance of international relations. Like the Concert of Europe before it, it weakened when the ideological struggle developed. At the same time the League, as it emerged, largely a British and American creation, was superseded by events even more quickly than the Concert. The negotiators of the Quadruple Alliance of 1815 probably assumed that revolutionary liberal forces could be contained and that the Concert would function effectively only if they were stanched. Yet, as we have seen the Concert managed to function between 1822 and 1848 even when the ideological issue was developing. In the same fashion the negotiators at Versailles probably believed that ideological disagreements would no longer characterize international politics, or that if they did, they would be no more serious than the liberal-conservative disputes of the mid-nineteenth century. Like the Concert of Europe, before it, the League would probably have helped to govern relations among states of a prior period. The Concert would have done an effective job of producing even greater international harmony during the eighteenth century. The League would perhaps have avoided the difficulties of competing alliance systems at the end of the nineteenth century, though it would have had greater difficulty managing the outpouring of imperialism. In any case the League was simply not equipped to handle a dispute of the proportions of Democracy against Fascism. Following the British theory, it assumed the good will of nation-state actors, and provided a forum in which their differences might be aired. Following the American theory, it relied upon public opinion to restrain the aggressive ambitions of governments. Both premises were discredited. Negotiators were not always seeking to reach agreements in good faith; they were often deliberately unco-opera-tive. Public opinion did not play the role assigned to it. While certain publics had learned the lesson of the Great War, certain others had learned something quite the opposite. While French and British opinion was willing to resign aggressive war, Italian and German opinion was willing to opt for it. Kant and Mazzini were right in certain countries, but wrong in others.

V The conflict between Democracy and Fascism was a long time in materializing as a result of the widespread acceptance of the British theory among numbers of liberal-democratic states. Particularly as the passions of war and desires for revenge waned, the conviction grew that the Germans had been wronged and that the real causes of war had been a technical breakdown in the international system. If this were true, there was reason for making reparation to Germany and for trusting its protestations of international good will. German injuries of 1919 could be re-dressed in 1935. In this regard, the public opinion of various countries was behind events. Certainly liberal-democratic opinion had been tutored by the Great War, but it had not yet learned to remain abreast of all international developments. An ex-cellent case could be made that in the interwar era, democratic publics reversed the proper sequence of policy.[29] Stimulated by the ravages of war, Allied publics were inclined at its end to regard the Germans as devils incarnate; and consequently insisted that Ger-many be made to "pay" for the sufferings she had caused others. This policy found expression in the harsh reparations and territorial clauses of Versailles and later in 1923 in the French occupation of the Ruhr. After national ardors had cooled, however, a more dispassionate view of the origins of the war could be entertained, and thus, by 1935, publics were becoming ready to conclude a peace of reconciliation and to restore German status and prestige. The problem was, of course, that the policies appropriate for 1919 were only applied in 1935; those appropriate for 1935 were tried in

29 See Walter Lippmann, *Essays in the Public Philosophy* (New York, 1955), Chapter Two.

1919. The peoples should have succored the German liberal government and turned a stern visage to the Nazis, but they did the reverse. At the time of the greatest challenge, then, publics were in an over-conciliatory mood. They could not believe that national leaders would be insane enough to want to repeat the follies of World War I. In this sense one could hardly imagine a more serious situation than that which emerged from the Great War. If the conviction was everywhere inculcated that peace should be sought, the outcome would have been ideal. If the conviction had been general that antagonism was the ruling principle among states, that would not have been ideal, but at least all the European nations would have known where they stood. They would have been prepared for hostility and would have known how to deal with it. What happened, however, was the worst of both worlds. While one group of states tended to believe in universal pacifism, another group tended to believe in universal antagonism. The first group, therefore, could not grasp the intentions of the second until almost too late. The results of such a confrontation were obvious: the Fascist dictators, believing in conflict, would advance and advance, and the liberal leaders, believing in harmony, would appease and appease. Chamberlain believed that Hitler's interests and those of his own country could be made harmonious. It was not until March, 1939 that the liberal nations realized that they had been operating on totally false premises regarding the international order and girded for the coming conflict. Thus the true nature of the ideological conflict between Fascism and Democracy was not understood until very late in the day.

VI World War I introduced into European and world relations a conflict somewhat similar to that induced by the Napoleonic wars. In both instances conflict had self-repeating and self-negating impacts. The Concert of Europe and the League were factors seeking to restrain conflict and to prevent great wars from occurring again. The ideological cleavage, on the other hand, was a factor militating on behalf of continued conflict and war. In the nineteenth century the ideological gulf made for competition between two groups of states, but the cleavage was eventually bridged without recourse to major war. When World War I occurred, it was fought over issues which had little if anything to do with the struggles of the French Revolution. World War II was different in this respect; it was the direct result of issues generated in World War I. And if the liberal issue could be partly compromised without major war, the National Socialist issue could only be settled by major war. The combination of totalitarianism in a single political organization made for endemic conflict with other organizations. And the appeasement of Nazism did not aid the cause of moderation. While the liberals in the nineteenth century always had to contend with canny and powerful foes, as the Revolutions of 1848 amply proved, the Fascists of the twentieth century were virtually presented with victories by an alliance of pacific states. The opponents of liberal revolution in the nineteenth century were strong; the opponents of Fascist revolution in the twentieth century were weak until the Fascist challenge reached its height. These were not circumstances conducive to compromise of the ideological struggle.

The interwar system of international relations was highly unstable. Regulative and disruptive tendencies did not join issue with one another: the regulative force of the League was effective on those states who portended no real threat to the system; it had no impact at all on the real disturbers. The mechanisms of regulation, even, were used by the disrupters for their own purposes. The conflict was postponed, but not averted by the failure of the liberal-democratic group of states to understand the real objectives of the Fascists. When the war finally came, it occurred on deteriorating conditions, and the task of final regulation became only more difficult. The international system could not produce outcomes acceptable to major national actors.

Once again, objectives and techniques were transformed in a new international synthesis. The unlimited objectives of Nazism harked back to the grandiose claims of Napoleon more than a century previously, and the defensive concerns of the rest of the world were not completely unlike the conservative response to the French Emperor. At the same time the conservatives understood the revolutionaries far better than liberal democrats comprehended Hitler. And the techniques of aggrandizement had undergone a profound alteration in the interim period. Not only were the military arts drastically changed, the growing role of popular opinion in the conduct of foreign policy presented a new instrument for diplomatic manipulation. For five years Hitler played almost faultlessly upon the inward hopes and fears of Europe and the world. He made startling gains without primary recourse to diplomacy or militarism, and cut many fibers of domestic strength with propaganda utterances alone. Unlimited objectives had been seen before in modern history, but the sinuous interplay of means had never been more subtly displayed.

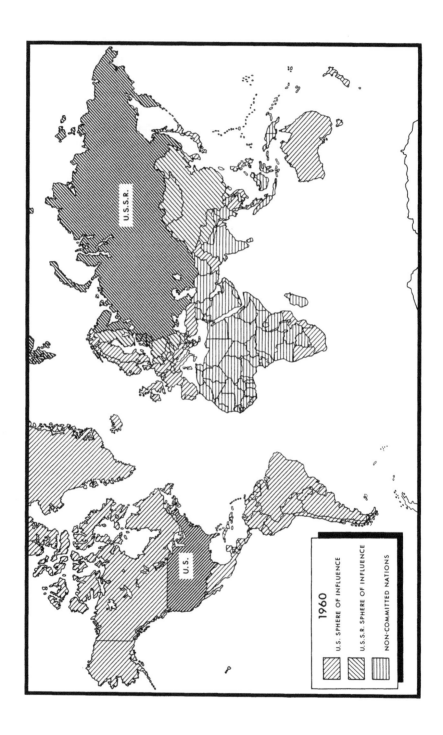

1960

U.S. SPHERE OF INFLUENCE

U.S.S.R. SPHERE OF INFLUENCE

NON-COMMITTED NATIONS

U.S.S.R.

U.S.

# chapter ten
# EPILOGUE TO WORLD WAR II

I The Second World War, like World War I, gave rise to new
fundamental conflicts among nations and introduced a new
diplomatic period. The conflicts, though not directly created by the
war, were, however, greatly aggravated by it. In this respect World
War II had a different impact from the Napoleonic Wars and
from World War I. The two previous war periods had themselves
brought an ideological division among nations. Liberalism and revolution became issues in external affairs as a result of the French
republic and Napoleonic empire. Fascism and National Socialism
had causes which could be traced to World War I.[1] In the two instances war was the agency of ideological cleavage internationally.
In the case of World War II, war did not mark a new division
among nations. Nationalism and Communism had been divisive
strands previously — nationalism had been a phenomenon of the
nineteenth century, Communism had emerged out of the first not
the second war. But both doctrines were given a new lease on life,
at least in certain countries, as a result of the developments of
World War II. While rabid nationalism seemed to have been ex-
punged in Germany as a result of policies which were rejected at
Versailles in 1919, the nationalist cause in the colonial areas outside Europe was given a tremendous impetus by the Second World
War. Indeed, as the Central European states were learning the
maxims that Western Europe had gleaned from World War I concerning the dangers of unfettered nationalism and national expan-

[1] This is not to say that World World I was the sole cause of Fascism, merely that
it was an important contributory factor.

sion, extra-European territories were learning to ignore them. These territories in many cases wished to repeat the career of nationalism and national unification followed by European countries during the nineteenth century.

The war contributed to national resurgence in the ex-colonial areas in two ways: first, it weakened the European colonial Powers and so permitted greater freedom to local nationalist movements; second, it often directly strengthened nationalist forces through Axis intervention. While the second phenomenon could be witnessed in some measure in the German impact on the Middle East, it was clearly portrayed in the Japanese activities in Southeast Asia. As the Japanese were forced to relinquish their hold on Asian territories, they deliberately fostered nationalist groups as a thorn in the side of the victorious colonial Powers. As a result in several countries nationalist developments were accelerated by almost a generation.[2]

The re-creation of nationalism in the former colonial areas of Asia and Africa posed a question for the ultimate stability of the international system. There seemed to be grounds for belief that nationalism was a self-generating movement, past nationalism serving as the cause of future nationalism. The connection between the European nationalism of the nineteenth and the Asian nationalism of the twentieth century was intimate. The success of coalescent or unificatory nationalism in Europe paved the way for integral and expansionist nationalism. Once a political bond was formed around a single nation, it seemed natural to attempt to extend it to include other nations. But the transformation of national determination into national aggrandizement meant that the nationalist process would repeat itself, imperialism provoking nationalist revolt at a later stage, as the successful imperialism of the nineteenth century has led directly to the present nationalist tendency in the extra-European territories. If this process were to be unending, national conflicts would be a continuing feature of international politics, and an obvious threat in an era of thermonuclear war. Thus, the period after World War II could be more dangerous than the period of imperialist nationalism.

Communism was given a great fillip by World War II, and the

2 See Rupert Emerson, *From Empire to Nation* (Cambridge, Massachusetts, 1959), pp. 31-36.

struggle between Communist and liberal democratic nations was thus intensified. The reasons for new Communist strength were three in number: the Soviet Union, the citadel of world Communism, emerged from World War II with a greatly enhanced relative power position; the economic and political disorganization resulting from the war provided the revolutionary ferment on which Communist movements might thrive; the anti-imperialist sentiment in the extra-European areas proved a susceptible target for the anti-imperialist doctrines of Communist thought. In 1815 five great Powers dominated world relationships; in 1919 the United States, Japan and Italy were added and the Habsburg Empire subtracted from their number. In 1945 the United States and the Soviet Union stood pre-eminent — no other Powers were of equal rank. While in 1919 the U.S.S.R. was perhaps the least of the great Powers, twenty-five years later she was near to being the first of them. The change in the Soviet Union's power position brought about a new role for Communism. "Socialism in one country" had been the reaction to the weakness of the U.S.S.R. internationally in the "twenties"; after 1945 the Russian Communists had a superior power base from which to operate. World revolution was now a much more practicable possibility. The Russian position seemed to have parallels with that of the French of a century previous. After 1815 a weakened France had not been able to pursue the revolutionary course in external relations. By 1830 with the aid of England the French could resume support of liberal governments, and the antagonism between liberals and conservatives was revived. After 1917 a weakened Russia was in no position to advance the revolution, but after 1945 it might do precisely that.

The war period also benefited the Communist cause by providing the social and economic conditions for revolution. In both France and Italy after World War II the conditions seemed ripe for a Communist take-over. In China the toll of the war aided the Communists against the Kuomintang. Even more important, perhaps, the anti-imperialist doctrines of Lenin were twisted to suit the conditions of the underdeveloped and former colonial territories. In this manner Communism and nationalism were made to appear as partners in the struggle against the European imperialist. After 1945 the Soviet cultivator of revolution was tireless and strong, and the soil with which he worked was fertile. It was not surprising in these circumstances that the Second World War intensified the ideological conflict between Communists and the West.

**II** *Prima facie,* then, it seemed that the ideological conflicts of liberalism and conservatism, liberal democracy and Fascism might be overshadowed by twin antinomies of nationalism and colonialism on the one hand and Democracy and Communism on the other. Two conflicts, it seemed, would be even harder to manage than one. If previous ideological conflicts had led to international instability, the ideological conflicts of the post-war generation would be even more likely to lead to breakdown and war. Yet, a third war did not occur immediately after the close of the second. And if the two ideological issues partially reinforced one another and made for conflict, they also partially nullified one another and militated in favor of stability.[3] The world was not divided into just two camps but into three or more, and greater room for maneuver followed as a result. Nor was it certain that the conflict between the Communists and the Western Powers was precisely analogous to the conflict with the Fascist totalitarians. For a period of time at least, there were some reasons for thinking that the two worlds, Communist and Western, might exist simultaneously without coming to blows. War was not the necessary concomitant of ideological friction in the immediate post-war world.

In one sense there was a partial analogy with the instance of revolutionary France. As time passed and the earlier aggressively ideological phase of the revolutionary experience was outgrown, France came to coexist with the conservative states. No measure of limitation could be placed upon the French emperor when he was convinced that French institutions had to be extended in Europe at all cost. In this sense Napoleon and Hitler shared a similar brand of fanaticism. At the same time, as revolutionary liberalism attained a measure of respectability internationally and as its domestic foundation became more secure, French policy in Europe lost its air of desperation. In the eighteen thirties and forties England and France together might have been able to force liberal

---

[3] The broader question of the continuation of peace remained unanswered. Central war did not occur in fifteen years after World War II, but destabilizing tendencies appeared thereafter. See Chapter Twelve, Section III.

institutions down conservative throats, but they did not attempt to do so. After 1830 with liberal revolutions shaking the conservative edifices of Europe and with a new liberal attitude in England, the prospects of liberalism were bright. France would no longer be held down by the conservatives, nor would England hold her down. Yet, the improvement in the liberal position did not bring a new war against the conservatives. Paradoxically, capabilities and desires did not coincide. When liberal forces were most powerful, they did not seek world war to advance their doctrines. When their desires were unlimited, on the other hand, they did not have enough strength to remake the world.

Actually, success had two possible results: ambitions might grow with achievement, or they might be appeased by it. Neither Hitler nor Napoleon could accept doctrines of auto-limitation. In both instances gains merely whetted territorial appetites. But also in either case the domestic position was believed to depend upon international success. Bonapartism meant adventure abroad, while National Socialism entailed an overthrow of Versailles and the map of Europe. Neither revolutionary liberalism nor National Socialism attained complete domestic respectability. After the installation of the July Monarchy, however, a liberal constitution seemed to rest on a firmer footing; international adventure was no longer necessary to sustain it. More than a generation of Frenchmen had familiarity with the liberal creed.

But this was not the only difference between the two situations. In 1805 the sanctions levied against foreign conquest were not in evidence. After 1814 it became clear that the sacrifice of certain liberal institutions domestically might be the result of unlimited ambitions internationally. Even Hitler never squarely faced the possibility that an overthrow of the Third Reich might result from his foreign schemes. He never conceived defeat, did not expect the allies to enter the lists against him, and assumed that providence would protect him if they did.[4] The reversal of domestic constitutions was not entertained as a real threat in the Napoleonic or Hitlerian cases. After 1830, on the other hand, the sanctions on militarism were more apparent. Thus, even though the liberal alliance was perhaps stronger in 1830 than in 1805, the consequences

4 See Alan Bullock, *Hitler: A Study in Tyranny* (London, 1952), p. 352.

of unlimited militarism were held in clearer view. As liberalism advanced domestically, there was a greater stake in the existing order and a consequent hesitancy to risk it in a policy of aggrandizement. And for similar reasons there was less need to instil liberalism through military means. Canning and Palmerston repudiated militarism and reduced the military establishment partly because they did not think it would be necessary. Liberal seeds would germinate and sprout autonomously in the soils of conservative countries, without a liberal gardener to oversee their growth. After 1830 England and France merely tried to make sure that the liberal plants taking root in Europe were given a chance to thrive and bear fruit.

In Russia aspects of the same development were evident. The insecure Soviet regime was most inclined toward spreading the revolution by military means in the early stages of its existence. The militancy of "war communism" reached its peak as Red armies neared the gates of Warsaw in the summer of 1920. Many Bolsheviks considered defeat of the capitalist adversary prerequisite to the maintenance of a revolutionary regime in Russia, but both Lenin and Stalin denied this proposition. Lenin knew that a weakened and divided Russia could not take on the European capitalists; Stalin went so far as to proclaim the possibility of "socialism in one country." By 1945, however, a revolutionary war against the capitalists was more feasible, relatively speaking. At the same time the sanctions imposed by such a war were more clearly evident. The Bolshevik industrial and social mechanism which had been painfully constructed in Russia during the intervening generation would be hazarded by an attack on Europe or the United States. When, as in 1917, a regime's hold on power was uncertain, war did not risk so much. But when, as in 1945, the domestic position had been consolidated, war might sacrifice three decades of internal construction. "War communism" might be tolerated after 1917, but perhaps it could not be tolerated after 1945. Nations fully aware of the tremendous losses they may well incur as a result of war do not ordinarily start it.[5]

5 It does not follow, of course, that they *never* initiate war. The possibility of war, moreover, poses additional hazards. See Herman Kahn, "The Arms Race and Some of its Hazards" in Donald G. Brennan (ed.) *Arms Control, Disarmament and National Security* (New York, 1961), pp. 90-92.

War usually occurs under two conditions: first, it may occur when a nation cannot believe that it will lose any of its already considerable resources, territories, or gratifications as a result; second, it may occur when a nation knows that it may lose all it has, but has very little to lose.[6] The first explanation helped to account for the German decision of 1939; the second helped to account for Trotsky after 1917. It would of course be wrong to insist upon an identity of France in 1830 with the Soviet Union in 1945. The two cases were very different. In 1830 France relative to the rest of Europe did not enjoy the power of Russia relative to the rest of the world in 1945. The Communist ideology was propagated and sustained by all the instruments of modern totalitarianism and hence was a more virulent force than the liberal ideology of the previous century. At the same time there were reasons for certain similarities of behavior in the two cases. Despite her relatively inferior power, France did not confront as severe a sanction as Russia faced. Overthrow of France's tempered liberalism was the worst eventuality facing the French rulers; destruction of Russian society itself in a thermonuclear war was a possibility for the Soviets. The techniques of warfare had made all-out war dangerous for even a twentieth-century superpower. Nor was this all. The opportunities for revolutionary advance without recourse to war were just as great and possibly greater in 1945 than in 1830. The Soviets could believe that the economic and social conditions resulting from World War II would themselves induce Communism in Europe; they could also believe that economic and political tactics would help to win victory in the uncommitted and underdeveloped states without warfare. The seeds of Communism did not have to be forcibly planted in alien soil — they merely needed political cultivation.

Ideological fervor seems to be most militant in the early stages of a revolutionary movement. At the outset of revolution the consequences of pursuing a revolutionary war are less apparent, and the behavior of other states is still in doubt. At the outset of revolution the risks are less for there is not yet a full-blown revolutionary society to protect. Nations which are positively dissatisfied with the existing state of affairs may conceivably precipitate war when the

6 These two categories, of course, do not exhaust the field.

predictable outcome is oblivion.[7] Principles can be more important than peace when there is no constituted national society to preserve. External and internal gains may have an inverse impact. External acquisition shows the ease of aggrandizement and is a constant invitation to conquest. Internal consolidation raises the ante and throws a developed domestic order into the international balance-pan, and it is consequently an incentive to conservative behavior. In the National Socialist example fulfillment of ideological goals depended upon constant advance in Europe and the world. Hitler believed that aggrandizement was necessary to fulfill stated Nazi goals. If a nation did not expand, it could not live. Thus the conservative impact of internal construction could not really be felt. Internal construction and external war were believed to be identical. Auto-limitation was impossible. In the Soviet instance, on the other hand, internal and external spheres were separated. Lenin and Stalin started the revolution on the path of separation, and Bolshevik doctrine has reaffirmed the distinction. War and expansion are not necessarily required for the victory of socialism over the capitalism world. The capitalists may destroy themselves while Communists sit by on the sidelines.[8] And even if there is a direct confrontation of Communist and capitalist worlds, war is neither the only, nor necessarily the most expedient way of winning the struggle. Peaceful competition of separate economic systems may help to ensure Communist victory without military conquest.[9]

In 1945, then, the factors making for military conflict with the capitalist world were balanced and perhaps overbalanced by those calling for restraint. The first thirty years of Soviet rule in Russia had been preoccupied with internal consolidation and industrialization. The windfall gains of 1945 resulting from the end of the war were grist for the Communist mill, and they undoubtedly operated to reinforce further expansion. But expansion would not be allowed to jeopardize the political and industrial strength of the

[7] It is this factor which holds ominous portents in the third or nationalist-neutralist area of the world.

[8] Stalin's statements in "Economic Problems of Socialism in the U.S.S.R." are instructive in this connection. See Merle Fainsod, *How Russia Is Ruled* (Cambridge, Massachusetts, 1953), p. 287.

[9] See N. S. Khrushchev's remarks, reported in the *New York Times*, June 23, 1960.

Communist heartland. Risks which were not tolerated in 1917 were even less acceptable thirty years later. Ideological fervor seemed to decline with internal success.[10]

Thus the challenge of French liberalism after 1830 had certain similarities with the challenge of Soviet Communism after 1945. Ideological conflict with an opposing group of states continued in both instances. In both instances there was fear of total war as a means of advancing revolutionary principles. In both instances there were areas of territorial or political expansion which failed to bring ideological antagonists squarely up against one another. In the 1830's territorial outlets in the Near East existed as a kind of safety-valve. In the 1950's political concentration on the under-developed nations prevented the direct conflict of a world divided completely into Soviet and Western camps. Under the circumstances ideological hostility did not provoke conflict of the Napoleonic or Hitlerian type.

III In contrast to the conflict between Communists and the Western nations the nationalist-colonialist struggle gave rise to a series of prolonged military contests after World War II. This ideological struggle between colonialism and nationalism was perhaps of equal if not of greater long-term importance. While the metropolitan Powers of Europe were perhaps more disposed to yield gracefully to the nationalist movements than the Western Powers were to the Soviet Union, the nationalist groups were even more violent in their attacks on Western colonialism than were the Communists. Again the difference in ideological friction partly explained the difference between the two situations. Communists were not willing to risk an unlimited war; nationalists were willing to resort to almost any means to rid their territories of imperial Powers. The nationalists' condition was, by their standards, desperate, and they would not countenance a continuance of the existing state of affairs in Asia, Africa and the Middle East. Having no entrenched and reasonably satisfactory position to defend, they might be willing to risk all to attain independence. The Soviets, protecting an established national society, were reluctant to plunge into unlimited war. The ideology of nationalism was perhaps even more

[10] The decline of ideological fervor is not to be equated with pacific international behavior.

violent in its initial stages of rejection of the West than Communism after an interval of internal construction.

And yet there was a sense in which nationalism of the coalescent type could be appeased more easily than the revolutionary ideologies of totalitarian Powers. The nationalist program, after all, was rudimentary. In its essence it required the political separation of metropolitan and colonial territory. An entire national society did not have to be reorganized in accordance with a detailed ideological plan requiring separate stages of "dictatorship of the proletariat," "socialism," and "Communism." Industrialization and economic development were part of the nationalist creed of the twentieth century, but they laid down no timetable nor rigid methodological approach. Because of the very vagueness and inconsistency of nationalist programs, then, experimentation was possible. The less articulated ideological objectives and means are, the easier it is to proclaim fulfillment. Nationalism, therefore, was a much easier creed to realize than National Socialism or Communism. After independence had been achieved, a fundamental objective in the revolutionary program had been won, and ideological fervor could abate. Internal renovation, despite stresses and uncertainties, did not require war against the imperialists. Nationalism was also a more parochial doctrine than Communism. Communism demanded world revolution before the attainment of the third stage of socialism. National independence was in some measure separate from universal independence. This is not to underestimate the force of Pan-Africanism or Pan-Arabism or to discount its significance. Nationalists in Asia and Africa have been acutely concerned to foster nationalism elsewhere. At the same time the intimate programmatic connection between successful Communism in one country and its triumph internationally did not exist in the case of nationalism "in one country" and national self-determination for all peoples. Nationalism made a few specific demands which could be satisfied within the determinate period. Beyond this, its program was vague and variable. Unlike Communism it did not specify a single form of social and international order. In this sense nationalism's revolutionary character was tempered by its inchoate ideology. A transition between "emergent" and "mature" nationalism was not impossible. From heedless and reckless partisans of universal attack on imperialists, certain nationalists have adopted a more complaisant attitude toward the Western Powers. A degree of political maturation has occurred, though it may not be irreversible.[11] Unless the nationalist creed had been fragmentary, it could not have achieved even this modicum of moderation.

To say this is to indicate that the dangers of self-generating nationalism have sometimes been overemphasized. In the nineteenth century, as we have seen, the consolidative phase of nationalism ramified into expansive nationalism largely as the result of the insecurity of regimes, both liberal and conservative.[12] National aggrandizement was used as a surrogate for social reform. Domestic insecurity then was the link between consolidative and expansive nationalism. In the underdeveloped countries of Asia and Africa this link has not always been present, and the "humanitarian" stage of nationalism has not always been transmuted into the "Jacobin" stage.[13] Thus the chain of nationalist re-creation was broken for certain states, and the pattern of nationalist development of the nineteenth century was avoided. There is, however, no indication that expansive nationalism has been stanched or extirpated. In some countries domestic insecurity is rife, and appeals to aggrandizement are common.[14] Attempts at political modernization domestically have often engendered insecurity for the regimes in power.[15] This, in turn, has led to a bellicose policy internationally. All indications are that expansive nationalism in Asia and Africa will continue to be a feature of the political environment.

The conflicts of idea issuing from World War II did not initially mean world war. The Western-Soviet cleavage was bridged partially through the moderation induced by Soviet achievements at home and by the threat of nuclear weapons; the nationalist-imperialist rivalry was blunted by the possibility of gratifying the most important nationalist desires. There still remained the possibility, however, that the two conflicts would reinforce each other and raise the level of ideological antagonism. The possibility was acute where emergent

---

[11] The Goan imbroglio gives little confidence on this score.

[12] See Chapter Eight, *passim.*

[13] See C. J. H. Hayes, *The Historical Evolution of Modern Nationalism* (New York, 1931), Chapters Two and Three.

[14] Indonesia would serve as a present case in point.

[15] See Max Millikan and Donald Blackmer (eds.) *The Emerging Nations* (Boston, 1961).

nationalists were grouped against members of the Western camp. The greater the hostility between Asian nationalist and European colonialist, the more likely that force would be used. And the greater the force employed against a metropolitan Power, the more the interests of the entire Western alliance would be affected. If President Nasser's weapon against the British and French on November 5, 1956 had been a thermonuclear bomb, it would have been far more difficult for the United States to take a neutral position. An extremely violent contest between nationalist and colonialist holds the possibility of involving the two major Powers, and the danger from the point of view of the general peace is that they may be involved on opposite sides. As nuclear capability is diffused into more and more hands, the danger increases in proportion. Suez is a benchmark in world relations for it indicates that Europeans will not always gracefully concede to nationalist forces; an extremely impetuous nationalist can provoke a nationalist reaction from Europe rivaling those of the nineteenth century. If future developments range the Soviet Union and the nationalists on one side and the United States and the metropolitans on the other, a true bipolarity would emerge fraught with the dangers of the period immediately preceding World War I.

If the national-colonial division may accentuate the cleavage between the Soviet Union and the West, however, it may also help to moderate it. Where mature nationalism has been achieved, and there is no longer need to place sole reliance on military force against the imperialist, a neutral buffer between East and West has emerged. Indeed, at this juncture, there has been a real equivalence of internal and external interests. The buffer between the Communist bloc and the West has helped to prevent the two from coming to blows, and neutrality has in addition served the interests of internal construction in the nationalist countries. If the first part of the nationalist ideology could be realized only by action against the Western colonialist, the second part of the nationalist creed — internal economic development — often depended upon a linkage with him. Neutralism has permitted the best of both possible worlds for a mature nationalist. Reciprocal concessions have been extracted from both sides and internal economic advancement has been speeded as a result. Sectarian adherence to either camp sacrifices the immense bargaining advantages of a neutral position and affects the total amount of assistance, both technical and economic. A neutral buffer in this way has served both internal and external purposes. Logically, neutralist policy is best advised to avoid two extremes: one, an all-out victory by one bloc or another; and two, an all-out compromise of outstanding differences between the two blocs. Either eventually spells disaster for the neutrals and deprives them of their crucial intermediate position. A part of neutralist policy can be understood in terms of this dual imperative; and yet there does not seem to be a clear grasp in neutral capitals of the dangers of a *rapprochement* between the Soviets and the West. Mediation seems to the neutrals to be the be-all and end-all of policy in regard to the two blocs.[16] Nor does there seem to be a clear conception of the good which the "proper" type of war could do for neutralist policy. A war in which the United States and the Soviet Union merely succeeded in knocking each other out without harm to the extra-European world would not seem to be averse to neutral interests, and yet there is little indication that the neutrals have thought along these lines.

IV While the war aggravated the conflict between Communists and the Western Powers and also heightened the struggle between nationalists and erstwhile imperialists, it helped to reinforce a new sentiment against war. If wars create issues among nations, they also rouse peoples and nations to greater efforts to keep the peace. Increased ideological friction was the first result of the war, a new international organization was the second. The basic difficulty of the new United Nations, however, was that it assumed away the first consequence of war. Big Power unanimity would be required in the Security Council for effective international action, and the ideological struggle seemed to rule this out. In much the same manner as the old League, the United Nations was, in its Security Council aspects, merely a reformulation of the Concert of Europe. Like the League it assumed the good will and good faith of the Great Powers in keeping the peace. Further, because of the distribution of world power at the end of the war, the United Nations could not be used as an instrument to coerce one of the superpowers, Russia or the United States. Each would be able to stand

---

[16] It is this desire for mediation in all situations which inhibits a controlling influence on big Power policy. See Chapter Twelve.

off the rest of the world. On this rock the apparatus of collective security foundered.[17]

While the Security Council did not perform the original function set for it, the U.N. did not lapse into desuetude. Instead for a time at least, the General Assembly took on new *de facto* if not *de jure* powers to fill the gap. The high point of Assembly functioning probably was attained with the passage of the "Uniting for Peace" resolution in November, 1950. This measure authorized the General Assembly to recommend enforcement action to its member states when the Security Council was at an impasse. It seemed as if the political and security functions of the Council might effectively be devolved upon the General Assembly. As time passed, however, and as new independent nations were created from old empires, the Assembly became more hesitant to take stands on political and security issues between East and West. As between the great blocs, the new neutralist and nationalist states came to regard mediation and conciliation as sufficient policy, and with the growth of U.N. membership, there was a proportional increase of abstentions on issues which divided the West from the Soviet Union. While there were overwhelming majority votes with few abstentions on certain issues, these generally represented more or less vacuous statements of principle and obtained the concurrence of the great blocs as well. In fact, the increasing representation of neutralist nations in the United Nations tended to weaken the General Assembly as an international organ in the political-security field.

In this sense, the General Assembly went the way of the Security Council before it. While the unanimity rule prevented Council action on such issues, the device of abstention precluded action by the Assembly. In the circumstances, the Secretariat and the person of the Secretary-General emerged as a possible focus for United Nations activity in the political-security sphere. The Secretary-General had certain unique advantages for the exercise of such powers. Unlike the representative of a national state, he was not the delegate of a single national constituency and hence, he could afford to take an international point of view. Unlike an African or Asian representative, he did not have to confine himself to a neutral role. He could afford personal defeat without imperiling a national

17 See Inis Claude, *Swords into Ploughshares* (New York, 1956), Chapter Twelve.

interest. His national interests were fundamentally "personal interests," and he could resign. And in fact, the Secretary-General did take forthright stands on a variety of political and security matters over the years. Trygve Lie took special initiatives on the Iranian question in 1946-1947 which differed from those of the Western Powers. He advocated the representation of Communist China in the United Nations. He formally invoked Article 99 of the United Nations Charter which empowers the Secretary-General to bring to the attention of the Security Council "any matter which in his opinion may threaten the maintenance of international peace and security" in the Korean episode. Afterwards Lie toured the world bringing to many states his ten-point plan for peace. Dag Hammarskjöld was somewhat less dramatic in his political initiatives, but was probably more effective. He successfully negotiated the release of eleven American airmen held by the Communist Chinese after the Korean War. In 1956-1957 he set up and directed the United Nations' Emergency Force in the Middle East, which enabled the withdrawal of British, French, and Israeli forces and which patrolled the cease-fire line. He created the United Nations Peace Force in the Congo under Security Council directives, and was in large part responsible for the degree of internal pacification which resulted in that troubled area. U Thant, his successor, managed to produce a formal settlement of the Dutch-Indonesian dispute over West New Guinea. These actions of the Secretary-General were of considerable importance and they should not be minimized.

Yet, it does no injustice to the achievements of the Secretary-General to note that his gains did not generally occur where there was a diametric cleavage of the Great Powers. And when the exceptional occurred, the very "success" of the Secretary-General's diplomacy led to Great Power demands for a restriction of his influence. It was not accidental that the Soviet Union's "troika" proposal for a hydra-headed Secretariat emerged after Hammarskjöld failed to heed Soviet demands in the Congo and that Lie began to lose his influence after his strong anti-Soviet stand on the Korean invasion. In the main, the major successes of the Secretaries-General in the political and security field came in the underdeveloped and neutralist sphere. Since neither Soviet nor Western prestige was inextricably tied to a totally pro-Western or completely pro-Soviet outcome, the Secretary-General might operate. However, in the central area of confrontation — in Europe, Laos, or Vietnam — miracles could not be worked. A *détente* between the great nations could not be produced.

This was not really surprising. All along, the constituency which actually had been supporting the Secretary-General was the third group of states — the neutralist, uncommitted nations. In his final days Hammarskjöld had to appeal to the third bloc to renew his support; he could not be effective in dealings with the major nations without neutralist backing. But this propounded the paradox of his position: if the neutralists were themselves unwilling to exercise political and security functions in the General Assembly, they would scarcely be likely to support a major role for the Secretary-General in the same area. The Secretary-General undoubtedly conceived of his responsibilities differently from the neutralists; he had a greater degree of independence than they possessed. But he was equally dependent upon political influence and wherewithal. He did not, to be sure, have to tailor his policies to a particular government; he might take stands which no national representative could risk; but in the final analysis he needed the "votes." The Secretary-General was not important because of his position under the Charter or because of the significance of his office alone (though neither of these factors should be discounted), he was a major protagonist in international relations because of the political power he could wield. Like any other politician, he required constituency support. And if the opinion of his "international" constituency varied, he was in some degree bound to vary with it.

When U Thant took over the Secretary-Generalship of the United Nations in 1961, it was made clear to him that a move to real independence would be likely to alienate the Soviet Union and place obstacles in the way of his confirmation as full Secretary-General. It might even revive the "troika." And the nationalists were quick to insist that the Secretary-General not proceed beyond the mandates of neutralism. Under such circumstances it was doubtful that the Secretary-General could step into the breach left by the Security Council and the General Assembly in the political and security field. It may have been true during Secretary-General Thant's first year that no agency of the United Nations could exert a fully controlling influence upon Great Power policy in the realms of aggression, threat to the peace, or war itself. If this is true, then the promise of San Francisco has remained unfulfilled in most essential respects. The world may have to be policed by the states themselves, not by the United Nations.

There remained yet another vehicle of international regulation. While the uncommitted states adopted abstentionist policies in the United Nations, they were politically cultivated by the Big Powers. In this manner they were drawn into international political complications, and because of their uncertain allegiance, they found themselves in the position of being able to influence the conduct of the larger states within certain limits. They might afford a tentative constituency for the Great Powers. While they would not themselves actively seek a control on bloc policy, they found, at least for a time, check reins proffered as gifts by the major states themselves. But this posed another problem.

The constituency to which the two blocs appealed was not the European nations that had already been disabused of the nationalist case for war — but to a constituency which accepted war for at least certain nationalist purposes. Indeed, the nationalists of the underdeveloped areas seemed ready to repeat in Asia the course of European nationalism. Such a constituency would not necessarily restrain, and it might even aggravate Soviet truculence. If the external constituency were composed of "emergent" nationalists, world war could result; if it were composed of "mature" nationalists, peace remained a possibility. In an important sense a major problem of Western policy was that of facilitating the process of maturation in the underdeveloped states. Only as nationalists became at least partially content with an existing state of internal affairs would they be willing to act as responsible members of an international community. There was an unrevealed inconsistency in the phrase "nationalist-neutralist." Nationalists could not afford to be neutral. In their drive for national independence they could not be "neutral" in attitude toward the imperialist; they had to oppose him. And if help in the nationalist struggle was forthcoming from Communist states and from nowhere else, they could not hold Communists at arm's length. Nationalism from this point of view was prior to neutralism. Neutralism could emerge only after basic national objectives had been achieved. Thus the external constituency providing the basis for international regulation and acting as a restraining influence on Great Power policy could

take shape only after major national goals were attained. The behavior of the two blocs was not of first importance when internal
national goals were unfulfilled.

The modest achievements in regulation were due in large part to
the rapid grant of national freedom by European states and to the
remarkable way in which members of the "Triple A" bloc in the
United Nations were able to acclimatize new nations to neutralist
modes of behavior. There was, however, no homogeneous or monolithic uncommitted bloc in the United Nations or elsewhere —
certainly not at Bandung. Some of the Arab-Asian-African nations sided often with the Western Powers, some with the Soviet
states, the allegiances of others were equivocal. Geographical areas
of concern varied from Africa to East Asia. And even states of a
single region did not act cohesively. The significance of the third
"bloc" was not its uniformity but its independence. If the neutralists had consisted of a unitary grouping, both the Soviets and the
Western states would have found them a less attractive political
target. The lack of organizational discipline and cohesion among
the third group was what seemed to make political appeals worth-
while. As long as a bloc had not yet consolidated itself, there was
always the possibility of winning individual adherents to one of the
major camps. On the other hand, if a firm and viable commitment
to neutralism and the establishment of a single political directorate had developed, the major blocs would have been less inclined
to expect a resolution of the cold war to come from shifts in the
uncommitted camp. If neutralism had been formalized in an Asian-
African NATO, and if domestic developments had permitted a uniformity of international policy, the Western nations could not
have hoped to extract an early commitment to the free world, and
conversely, they would not have expected a sudden trend to Communism. In such circumstances the neutralists would no longer
have been a constituency to be wooed. Literally, however, the third
grouping did contain the "independents"; they were the "floating
vote" of the international community.

The existence of a third, loosely organized group of nations separate from the major blocs prevented the emergence of strict bipolarity. In so doing it obviated the dangers of a pre-World War I
situation. In July 1914 new coalitions could not be formed to deal
with the Sarajevo crisis; existing participants in world diplomacy

were already committed, and the United States was not persuaded to throw its weight into the scales. The bipolarity of 1914, then, helped pave the road to war by removing the "balancer." The Triple Entente and the Triple Alliance were hard up against one another and had no room for maneuver. No states were "uncommitted," and neither group could believe that it would win out in the long run through the eventual pledging of new alliance partners. Neither group believed that time was on its side. The contrast of this bipolar situation with the tripolar world of the post-war period was both marked and instructive. In the post-war system each of the major blocs seemed to believe that time was on its side; each seemed to believe that the commitment of the unorganized and uncommitted group of states would sway the balance irretrievably in its own favor. War was postponed in part, as we have seen, because it was not necessary. The struggle between Communists and the Western Powers could be decided without recourse to it. Victories in the United Nations could be a partial substitute for victories in battle.

The fluidity of world relations with the neutralist countries had certain advantages. If the third bloc had possessed a rigid organizational structure as was sometimes advocated by Nkrumah and others, a uniform noncommitment could have been anticipated. If a cohesive third bloc had refused to play "balancer" and had held aloof from entanglement with East or West, the two great blocs would have been hard up against each other once again. The neutral camp might then have exerted no greater a moderating influence than that of the United States before 1914. The neutrality of the United States did not prevent World War I even though America was strong enough to knock European heads together. The neutrals would have had to be willing to adopt Britain's eighteenth-century role and balance between coalitions in order to prevent conflict. Failing that outcome, disorganization and discohesion in the third group of states served as an invitation to the two major blocs to instill cohesion along sectarian lines.

V  The system of international relations of the immediate post-war period differed from those of the past in numerous ways. Ideological conflicts were notable, but they did not issue in total war. The existence of two partially overlapping conflicts held generally optimistic portents; in most situations one helped to moderate the other. The existence of the extra-European buffer initially directed attention away from a bipolar confrontation in Europe. It was perhaps not accidental that the solution of the ideological issue in Europe during the nineteenth century coincided with the new imperialist urge internationally. Nations tended to forget ideological frictions as they became immersed in a universal quest for colonies. And as long as colonial real estate remained to be partitioned, imperialism itself acted as a safety valve. In the aftermath of World War II the ideological issue was not forgotten in the competition (which had certain imperial analogies) for the affection of the uncommitted states of Asia and Africa. At the same time the projection of ideology into a third area obviated the immediate need for direct conversion of the enemy. The methods which neutralists were willing to tolerate transformed proselytizing tactics into pale replicas of their nineteenth-century counterparts. Technicians and economic aid were not the same as military conquest and political rule. More important perhaps, the tactics of the mature nationalists seemed designed to avoid the danger of complete partition of extra-European areas among the major blocs. Political real estate did not run out.

In this manner, direct conflicts between East and West were moderated. Neither the neutralists nor the United Nations was an active force on behalf of regulation, but the Great Powers afforded the former a control as a result of their concentration on winning influence in the underdeveloped world. It was the major blocs' own decision to lend significance to happenings in the non-European area of the world that placed restraints on bloc policy. Paradoxically, the Great Powers tied their own leading strings. Rather than face thermonuclear war, the major protagonists accepted auto-limitation.

VI  Thus World War II led to a new international system, a system which temporarily checked or controlled major destabilizing tendencies. Later developments suggested, however, that the world was in 1962 on the threshold of a new system and that the characteristics of the post-World War II order were in process of being modified. The international constituency device, in particular, seemed to be losing most of its controlling influence. The neutralist-nationalist constituency was able for a time to exert a limiting impact upon Great Power policy. In the Soviet case this constituency provided external restraints where none existed internally. The operation of these restraints, however, depended upon adherence of the neutralists to a fixed point in the continuum of possible international outcomes. The neutralists had to insist upon certain types of results and to interdict others. They had to mandate reasonably pacific behavior, and they had to inveigh against conflict, the threat of force or force itself. General or sustained acquiescence in these types of international behavior would emancipate the system from effective constraints.

Unfortunately, by 1962 the neutralists seemed unable to hold international outcomes within the necessary limits. This inability did not flow from a sudden change in the factors which produced the post-war system; rather, it followed from a greater understanding of weaknesses in the regulative position of the uncommitted nations. The Great Powers operated upon a model of neutralist conduct which proved to be incorrect. If neutralist policy represented a fixed position in the system, the great blocs would have to range themselves on opposite sides. Attempts of either bloc to press outward or away from the fixed mid-point would be met with failure; neutralists would be able to reprove the extremist camp and to bring it back to a moderate position. Because of the bilateral pursuit of neutralist allegiance, neither bloc would be willing to offend the neutralist by adopting a permanent extremism. This conception of neutralist fixity, however, could not be sustained because it vastly exaggerated the regulative capacities of the uncommitted states. In actuality, neutralist policies were as dependent upon Great Power formulations as the reverse. If the neutralists were to continue to obtain the special advantages of a mid-position, it was necessary that they avoid being linked too closely with the policies of either major bloc. Hence, there seemed, in 1962, to be a tendency for neutralist policies to shift partly as a function of Big Power extremism. As the Soviet bloc resumed nuclear testing in the atmosphere and trumped up new issues on Berlin, the neutralists shifted further in the Soviet direction. If one conceives of a continuum linking Soviet and Western policies and posits that the neutralist position must always remain at mid-point, then attempts to extend the continuum in the Soviet direction must also shift the mid-point. Western attempts to move in the opposite direction might theoretically restore the old mid-point, but in the meantime a much wider range of behavior (the length of the continuum) is sanctioned by the system.

And even such means of restoring the neutralist position probably exaggerated the latitude available to Western policy. The neutralists were far more successful in preventing Western extremism than Soviet extremism. Because Western departures from a moderate internatonal position were interpreted as imperialist atavism, neutralists tended to stand against them. Because Soviet departures were interpreted in a context of anti-imperialism, neutralists were far more hesitant in opposing them. At the limit, the Soviets were able to shift neutralist policy; the West was shifted by it. The neutrals may have remained at mid-point for a time, but the West was bound eventually to become dissatisfied with the leftward train of events. At that juncture the West was destined to pull back, leaving the neutrals to their pro-Soviet sentiments. As neutralist policy took on an *ex parte* flavor, the central regulative mechanism of the post-war system was almost certain to disappear. In reality, of course, the policy of the uncommitted nations was probably not a function of Soviet diplomacy any more than Soviet policies were a function of opinion in New Delhi or Cairo. Influence extended in both directions. But neutralists could no longer be relied upon to hold Soviet policies within strict limits. The Soviets found the central weakness of the neutralist role. Just as the United Nations after 1945 came to express big Power hostilities as much as limit them, so the neutralists came to adjust to Great Power doctrines as well as restrain them. It was by no means certain which influence would prevail in a given case.

The revelation of neutralist weaknesses, however, was not the only destabilizing factor at the end of 1962. Military developments posed independent hazards. Between 1945 and 1960 deliberate all-out war was not a serious possibility, accidental war was equally remote, and catalytic war could be disregarded. In the next twenty years the first two may remain true, but the third may not. Accidental attack may be precluded by greater "hold" capability on both sides; all-out war may even be ruled out in conditions of central war, urban centers being carefully avoided as targets. The spread of nuclear weapons, however, may make it easier for one nuclear power to induce war among others. Anonymous delivery capabilities may make it difficult to discover the source of nuclear aggression and thereby give rise to mistaken retaliation. Two smaller states possessing atomic weapons may find their conflict of interest to the Great Powers as the struggle grows in intensity. If either is the protégé or ally of one of the major nuclear states, a Great Power might be drawn in. And even the procurement of the vaunted "relatively invulnerable" deterrent may not be as simple as it seems. In these circumstances total reliance upon bilateral or multilateral deterrence may not be sufficient to keep the peace in the next generation.[18] The initial impact of World War II was beneficent, and a stable international system issued from it. Regulative forces more than matched disturbant ones. Developments of the early 'sixties muddied the picture, however, and it was no longer certain that a new system would avoid conflict, extremist behavior, or war.

The post-World War II system of international relations represented a new amalgam of objectives and techniques. Expansionist goals were limited by the desire to avoid thermonuclear war on populations. The existence of a third, loosely organized group of nations helped for a time to prevent a direct confrontation of major antagonists. The tactics of political war, subversion, and propaganda were surrogates for the military combats of yesteryear. When force was employed, it was at a different level of violence. The reshaping of the domestic order after the pattern of one sectarian political philosophy then could not be pursued to the nub. Relatively unlimited objectives had to be pursued by straitly limited means.

18 See Chapter Twelve.

# PART II
# systemic
# analysis

## chapter eleven

# NINE INTERNATIONAL SYSTEMS

Basic historical characterizations have now been given of each of the nine systems of international relations treated in this work. These characterizations are not, strictly speaking, history. It is impossible to sum up a diplomatic age in homogeneous formulae, to abstract without violence to the record.[1] The historical characterizations provided in the preceding pages inevitably rest upon exaggeration of certain factors and undervaluation of others. In searching for recurrent themes or regularities that would permit comparative treatment of distinct international systems the writer has doubtless omitted much of importance and erred in what has been included. But if the connections adduced are wrong or superficial, they may yet contain important grains of truth. Many of the problems which the international system faces today have been faced before; the lessons of the past must and can be made relevant to present discontents. The quest for regularities is illusive but it is also imperative. And the author is convinced that the factors discussed in the preceding pages, though they may have been incompletely portrayed, are of vital importance to an understanding of the international system. The historical models outlined above are models in that they cannot hope to take account of all relevant empirical variety, but they were drawn after an inspection of the historical record, and they reflect a number of empirical interrelationships.

In this chapter an attempt will be made to systematize the pres-

---

[1] It is perhaps consoling to note, therefore, that even in the physical sciences specific exceptions to general laws can always be found. See Stephen Toulmin, *The Philosophy of Science* (London, 1953), pp. 78-79.

entation of the historical chapters into regular patterns. In particular, constituents common to all nine international systems will be derived, and the analysis will seek to show how variations in the states of these constituents account for the different international systems. In short, the components of the nine systems will be presented, and it will be shown how changes in these components make for changes in the international system. We will then have a logical conspectus of the systems considered in this study. The derivation of this conspectus involves a further abstraction from atomic diplomatic events. If the summarizing of general diplomatic features of an age in historical terms required a first order abstraction from the facts, the collation of these historical characterizations into systems requires a second order abstraction. In the process, therefore, the variety of international experience has been further sacrificed. The number of empirical characteristics obscured is probably a function of the order of abstraction. If the historical analysis of Part I deals summarily with certain facets of international relations, the systemic analysis of Part II further sacrifices perfect dependence upon all relevant political events for the clarity and rigor of systematic presentation. In the models which follow, then, the aim has been only to outline the general, not the specific, features of the international environment at different times. A systemic analysis is not yet equipped to take account of all the variables of the international situation, and some must temporarily be neglected if even a rudimentary account is to be given of the general features of the situation. The systemic features described below, in addition, fail to do full justice to the variety of the historical characterizations presented earlier; certain threads of the previous analysis have had to be neglected in the building of the nine systems. With these caveats laid down, the general systemic analysis may now be presented.

## INTRODUCTION

Each international system about to be considered is comprised of four mechanistic elements. Following an analogy with formal systems analysis, the general framework posits that a system aiming at stability is comprised of the following elements: (1) a source of disturbance or disruption (an input); (2) a regulator which undergoes certain changes as a result of the disturbing influence; (3) a

Table or list of environmental constraints which translate the state of the disturbance and the state of the regulator into (4) outcomes. If the regulator is effective in producing stability, it must respond in such a way to the input that the environmental Table mandates outcomes within a range regarded as stable or acceptable. If the environmental Table shows the following outcomes with varying states of disturbance (input) and regulator, and *u* is the only acceptable outcome, the regulator is effective in ensuring stability (see Figure 1). If, on the other hand, *t* is the only outcome deemed acceptable,

|  |  | REGULATOR | | |
|---|---|---|---|---|
|  |  | A | B | C |
| I N P U T | 1 | r | t | u |
|  | 2 | u | v | w |
|  | 3 | x | u | y |
|  | 4 | u | t | r |
|  | 5 | t | u | z |

*Figure 1*

the regulator is less effective, producing *t* in only three of the five states of input. In the Table above where repetitions of outcomes are permitted in the columns A, B, and C, the regulator may produce stable outcomes of *u* despite the fact that there are more input options (variations in the states of the input) than there are regulator options (variations in the states of the regulator). However, if no outcome were allowed to be repeated in any column, the only way of producing stable outcomes would be by increasing the number of variations in the states of the regulator. Suppose, for example, the accompanying Table (see Figure 2) were dictated by nature. In this Table (with no repetitions allowed in the column outcomes) the regulator cannot produce $u$ outcomes with all states of the input. *At least* five states of the regulator (A, B, C, and in addition, D, and E) would be required to produce $u$ outcomes with all states of the input (1, 2, 3, 4, 5). In short, only by increasing the *variety* of the regulator states is it possible to reduce the *variety* in the outcomes. "This is the law of Requisite Variety. To put it more picturesquely: *only variety in R can force down the variety due to D* [the Disturbance or Input]; *only variety can destroy variety.*" [2] If we assume the worst possible situation from the point of

|  |  | REGULATOR | | |
|---|---|---|---|---|
|  |  | A | B | C |
| I N P U T | 1 | r | t | u |
| | 2 | u | v | w |
| | 3 | x | u | y |
| | 4 | t | r | v |
| | 5 | w | y | z |

*Figure 2*

view of producing stability (that is, if we assume that no element may be repeated in a single column), the only way of coping with the variety of the disturbance or input is by increasing the variety of the regulator. *"Only variety in R's moves can force down the variety in the outcomes."* [3] If the outcomes in the boxes cannot be foreseen, and it is desirable to regulate stably five possible inputs or disturbances, *at least* five possible moves must be available for the regulator. Five moves *may not be sufficient* to produce the required degree of regulation, but any less than five will only produce the nec-

[2] W. Ross Ashby, *An Introduction to Cybernetics* (New York, 1956), p. 207.
[3] *Ibid.*, p. 206.

essary regulation in the fortuitous event of repetitions in the column outcomes. The designer of the regulator, uncertain of the possible outcomes, will want to provide for the worst possible contingency and therefore will design a regulator with a number of options *at least* equal to the number of possible inputs.

The regulatory process may be described more concretely in the following terms. Suppose that the system in question is a hot water heater with its possible sources of disturbance, and suppose also that the required temperature (outcome) to be maintained is between 150° and 180° F. The regulator works effectively if, no matter what the disturbance, it can always keep the temperature of water in the heater between the required levels. It must, for instance, be able to heat water quickly enough to cope with the disturber who opens the tap and simply lets the water run. It must also be able to cope with sudden changes in the external temperature by either heating or cooling the boiler. From this it may be seen that most hot water heaters are not capable of producing stable outcomes under all conditions, but only under certain ones.

One means of describing diagramatically the process of regulation is as shown in the accompanying diagram (see Figure 3). The ar-

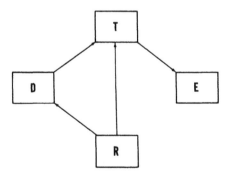

*Figure 3*

rows indicate channels of influence or communication: *D* is the disturbance, *R* the regulator, *T* the table provided by the environment, and *E* the outcome. ". . . the variety in *D* determines the variety in $R$; and that in $T$ is determined by that in both $D$ and $R$." [4] As a response to a given move of the disturbance, $D$, $R$ selects a given move; the two moves are then translated into an outcome, $E$, by the Table, $T$. "If $R$ does nothing, i.e., keeps to one value, then the variety in $D$ threatens to go through $T$ to $E$, contrary to what is wanted. It may happen that $T$, without change by $R$, will block some of the variety . . . and occasionally this blocking may give sufficient constancy at $E$. . . . More commonly, a further suppression at $E$ is necessary; it can be achieved . . . only by further variety at $R$." [5]

An analogy of this formal systems analysis may be applied to the study of international affairs. In this application (and more than analogous application cannot yet be attempted) the actors provide the source of disturbance; regulatory mechanisms are found in formal or informal processes (the alliance system, balance of power mechanisms, a Concert of Europe, etc.); the environment or nature helps to translate disturbances and states of the regulator into outcomes. These elements of the international system may be grouped into two general categories: those seeking to increase the variety in the outcomes and therefore to produce instability; those seeking to decrease the variety in the outcomes and to make for stability. Actor disturbance is a factor for variety and instability; the regulator (reflecting regulative activity of the actors as well as other influences) and the environment are limiting or barrier influences militating against variety and on behalf of stability. Technically speaking the variety of the environment does not change, and therefore changes in the variety of outcomes depend upon the respective varieties of disturbance and regulator. In the pages which follow, however, the variety of the environment will be portrayed as shifting in response to different sorts of actor disturbance. Those who prefer a more formal usage may regard such shifts as changes in the variety of actor disturbance. In the analysis which follows then, the degree of stability in outcomes is assumed to be a function of $D$'s variety, $R$'s variety, and $T$'s variety. $T$'s variety will be said to change when the objective of actor disturbance (ideological, territorial, political, etc.) becomes more or less abundant. If the relevant objective is colonizable territory, and the supply of that territory runs out, environmen-

[4] *Ibid.*, p. 210.
[5] *Ibid.*, p. 210.

tal variety is proportionately reduced. Its barrier impact upon outcomes is consequently lessened. Since environmental factors such as these are usually outside the scope of human ability to influence, however, stable situations can be produced out of unstable ones in most cases only by increasing the variety of the regulator.[6]

The variety of the disturbance ($D$) is in turn dependent upon certain intra-actor variables. The number of options which an elite in control of an actor will exercise in the international system is a function of its particular ethos (that is, of the direction in which control is to be exercised), its control of disposable resources, and the quantity of disposable resources available. Each of these three variables can be further analyzed. The ethos of the elite may be regarded as the product of its attitude toward the internal organization of its own society, toward the internal organization of other actors and toward the outcomes of the international system.[7] Elites may be reformist or reactionary in respect of their own internal institutions and the institutions of other states. In revolutionary times elites are likely to have strong innovative ambitions in regard to their internal polities. If they pass through a stage of Jacobin nationalism, they are likely to want to bring about internal reorganization in other states. If a stage of Napoleonic imperialism is reached, they may become positively dissatisfied with the pattern of international outcomes and seek to overturn the stability of the international system. Conservative elites may also have reasons for wanting to alter the configuration of international outcomes.

The elite's ability to effect such a change will depend upon its control of resources and upon the quantity of resources which it controls. The first is a product of four additional factors. The degree of control will depend upon the nature of allegiance given to the elite by the rest of society, on the latitude of discretionary choice allotted the elite by the rest of society, on the nature of tenure which the elite enjoys at a particular moment, and on the personality dispositions of the elite leadership. The allegiance pattern determines the

---

[6] It is worth noting that this is not the only definition of "environment" used in the application of systems analysis to social affairs. Professor Ernst Haas defines environment as "the socio-economic condition which gives rise to the inputs into the system proper." Here "environment" refers to the physical constraints of the international system which condition the evolution and outcome of policy.

[7] Ethos does not refer to the entire corpus of ideology or to the myth-system of an elite. It has reference only to the three specific aspects mentioned.

type of burdens which the elite can expect the masses to bear. Personal or dynastic allegiance of the sort largely characteristic of the *ancien régime* placed strict limitations on the exactions of the elite; national allegiance of more recent times renders a much more complete support. At the same time the latitude permitted the elite in the formulation of major policy programs has probably been reduced with the increase of democratic control over foreign policy in recent years. Under the old regime elites had considerable discretion in choosing courses of action in world politics, but they could not implement their policies with great force; under democratic conditions today elites have less discretion in the choice of policy, but they are able to rely upon nationalist instruments in its implementation. Patterns of allegiance and discretion are conditioned by the security of tenure enjoyed by a regime at a given time. A very insecure, chronically unstable regime (like those in France during portions of the Third and Fourth Republics) in a nationalist system might not be able to exercise the degree of control attainable by a secure regime under conditions of personal or dynastic allegiance. A moderate anxiety or insecurity, on the other hand, might call for very vigorous exercise of the instruments of power still available and indirectly conduce to greater control of disposable resources. In all cases actual control will depend in part on the personality dispositions of the elite leadership. Personalities of men like Churchill or Palmerston have evoked a firm use of available resources while an almost congenital aggressiveness seems to have formed a part of the personalities of Napoleon and Hitler. By contrast Lord Bute, George III's henchman, was docile to a fault.

The quantity of resources disposed in this manner depends upon three further factors: persuasive skills, the quantity of mobilizable resources, and the speed of mobilization. Where the last two have been present in only modest amounts a state sometimes has still been able to cut an imposing figure in world affairs because of the diplomatic arts of its leadership. Metternich, Talleyrand, and Cavour probably exercised an influence in diplomacy considerably out of proportion to the other resources which their states disposed. Gladstone, because of his inability to project British purposes effectively in the world arena, may well have exerted less than the full influence which Britain otherwise could have commanded. Persuasive talents, however, are inevitably limited by the other factors.

The economic-technological and military resources of a society, as these are brought to bear through a given rate of mobilization, also profoundly affect a nation's role in international relations. A nation without the resources for economic or military warfare will be likely to be at a disadvantage in diplomacy; a nation which cannot mobilize its resources quickly enough in a vital struggle may lose despite an ultimate sufficiency of resources. In the third quarter of the nineteenth century one of Prussia's advantages was its speed of mobilization; in the last quarter one of Russia's weaknesses was its inability to mobilize rapidly. Today victory or defeat in a thermonuclear war is likely to depend in large measure upon continuous mobilization.

These various factors (summarized in Figure 4) provide an exhaustive categorization of influences which determine the variety of actor disturbance in the sense that any other factors which might be listed would either constitute super- or subcases of those already presented. It should also be clear that the variety of actor inputs is actually specified by the variables presented. What different moves an actor-elite can make in the international system depend first of all upon what it thinks of doing; it depends secondly upon how effectively it can manipulate its resources to produce the desired outcome; it depends finally upon the quantity of resources available for manipulation. If new resources are obtained to implement an actor ethos in world affairs, the variety of actor moves is actually increased as a result. If resources are held constant, but actor ethos changes, again the variety of input options is altered. An elite which thinks only of a limited number of strategies and then does not dispose effectively of resources to implement even those has the most limited variety of moves in the international system.

The actor input or disturbance, thus determined, feeds into a system of international relationships, as portrayed in Figure 5. Arrows in this diagram do not indicate the logical sequence of disturbance, regulation and translation into outcomes; rather they depict the balance of forces seeking to increase or to reduce variety in international outcomes. Solid arrows denote variety-increasing influences; dotted arrows denote variety-decreasing influences. In the international system the regulator and the environment act as barriers to ·variety, the actor disturbances as facilitators of variety. Degrees of variety in the disturbance and in the regulator are indicated

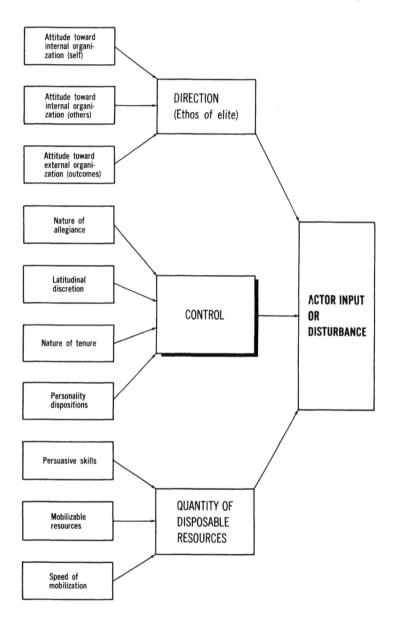

*Figure 4*

by the respective thickness or thinness of the arrows.[8] In Figure 5 variety-inducing and variety-reducing influences are approximately balanced.

Regulative forces in the international system may be institutional or informal. An international organization, or a regular system of international consultation and action (the international Concert) would be examples of an institutional type of regulator. The regulator may also be reflected in the opposition of certain states in the

---

[8] There is no way of giving an *a priori* quantitative account of the thickness or thinness of the arrows. These are historically determined and stem from the moves available to disruptive and regulative forces. Satisfaction with internal and external outcomes, limited (though stable) control patterns, and limited resources would clearly conduce to limited actor disturbance. As these factors change, disruptive and regulative variety must change. The variety stemming from the resource category has secularly increased with technological and military innovation; but it does not follow that variety *in general* has unilinearly increased in progression from one system to another.

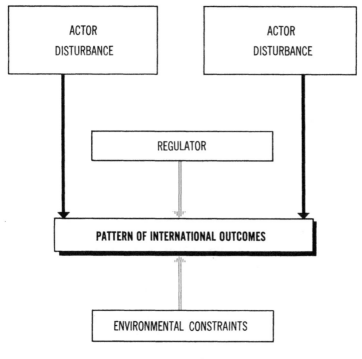

*Figure 5*

system to the disturbing initiatives of another or others. The national actors themselves are in this manner the sources of regulation in an alliance or balance of power system. The regulator then, refers to the actions of institutions and states in the international system.

There will be some who, while accepting actor, environmental, and outcome constituents, will deny that regulative influences always form part of the international system. Some will argue that a regulator requires a separate institutional format and that where such institutionalization is not provided, a regulator can hardly be said to exist. In illustration of such a position some may contend that before the Concert of Europe was created, regulatory influences did not exist. In the present analysis, however, a regulator is assumed to be an analytic component of the international system, and the focus of discussion concerns the magnitude of regulative influence compared to that of disruptive influences. The former may be very small relative to the latter, as, for example, after Austerlitz, Jena, or Friedland, but they are still conceived to be present. And, as a matter of empirical fact after these Napoleonic victories Austria and Russia began another attempt at regulation which culminated finally in Leipzig and Waterloo. One might build a good empirical case for the proposition that national actors have been (and are today) the main sources of regulation of disruptive elements entirely independent of the mediating influence of any regularized international institution. This suggests the obvious truth that actors are not only disturbing but also regulatory forces in world politics. In the analysis which follows the regulative activity of actors is considered in the category of regulation and is indicated by the operation of the regulator. The disruptive or disturbing activity of actors is considered in the category of actor disturbance.

It has been said that the analysis following evinces only the analogous application of systems analysis techniques. Systems analysis, technically conceived, deals with specific outcomes stemming from specific inputs or disturbances. In contrast it is assumed below that a pattern of disturbances and regulative actions leads to a pattern of international outcomes which can be roughly characterized over a period of time. Formal systems analysis also does not deal with the impact of the elements of a system on the varieties of regulator or disturbance; it deals only with the impact on the varieties of outcomes. In the pages following it is presumed that the elements of a system not only call forth responses on the basis of existing armories of moves; they may also, under certain conditions, either augment or diminish the armory of responses itself. Specifically, a regulator may reduce the varieties of actor disturbance in one set of circumstances or, under different conditions, an actor may reduce the options available to a regulator so that it increasingly loses its ability to influence outcomes. Under still different circumstances actors may actually increase the moves of a regulator so that its regulative ability is enhanced.

An international system is conceived to be *stable* if its outcomes fall within limits generally "accepted" by the major participants in the system. All elites do not have to be "satisfied" with all the outcomes. Maria Theresa, for instance, in the eighteenth century was not happy to lose Silesia to Frederick the Great, but this did not cause her to jeopardize the Austrian Empire in order to win back her territories. The Napoleonic conquests, however, caused the conservative monarchs to use every possible means to defeat him. While Maria Theresa was not fundamentally dissatisfied with the outcomes of the system of the eighteenth century, the European monarchs were fundamentally opposed to the course of the revolutionary system. Catastrophic conflict or international chaos are almost certain to be deleterious to some major actor; hence these outcomes are almost always unstable or unacceptable. At the same time it is possible to imagine a rising threshold for the tolerance of violence. The conflicts of the Bismarckian system might have been "unstable" for monarchs in the *ancien régime* and not for the Bismarckians. In the pages which follow, whatever the difficulties of "stability" *in abstracto,* the application of the terms "stability" and "instability" is quite clear. There are major and unacceptable wars in each of the unstable systems indicated.

System-change occurs when the constituents of disruption and regulation undergo major change. In each of the system-changes which follow it will be seen that the different categories composing actor disturbance have been transformed. There have been changes in the patterns of direction, control and resources. In addition, the activity and power of regulative and environmental forces has also been altered. In other words, disruptive and regulative forces have both attained a new state. It would be possible, of course, to regard each

minor alteration in the factors of disruption or regulation as an inauguration of a new system of international relations. That course
has not been adopted here. Only a major change of both disturbing
and regulative forces involving a transformation of most or all of
the components of each, is viewed as system-change. System-change,
moreover, is not necessarily associated with changes from stable to
unstable patterns or the reverse. An alteration of disturbance and
regulation may continue previous patterns of stability or instability
at a new level; it may also, of course, interrupt such configurations.
The system of the functioning Concert terminated in 1822, but reasonably stable and pacific outcomes continued in the next system;
the system of imperialist nationalism ended in 1918, but the new
system which ensued did not find more stable patterns of existence.
System-change, stability, and instability are not interdependent.

## SYSTEM I[9]

**A.** In the eighteenth-century system of international relations (1740-
1789) the variety of actor disturbance was minimal. This made it
possible for a regulator with limited variety to produce a pattern of
reasonably stable outcomes in world politics. The environmental Table as reflected in the quantity of desired international resources unappropriated by major actors limited conflict and held the pattern
of outcomes within stable bounds. Even if all of $D$'s variety had
been allowed to go through the system and (without hindrance
from $R$) determine the variety of outcomes, $E$, the result probably
would still have been satisfactory from the standpoint of stability.
**B.** The ethos of the respective actor elites was generally one of
satiety from both internal and external viewpoints. Despite the reforms of the period of "enlightened despotism" the basic political,
social, and economic structure of the old regime was regarded as
satisfactory by the elite concerned. Nor was the elite more disposed
to change the internal polity of other actors; the quasi-feudalism of
the age was congenial to its leadership. The external outcomes of
the international system did not occasion irremediable grievances
among any of the major actors. Indeed, one of the most remarkable
characteristics of this era is its fidelity to the basic settlement of
Utrecht in 1713. The bilateral agreements comprising the "Prag-

[9] See Chapter Two.

matic Sanction" and the loss of Silesia to Prussia were the only important exceptions to the letter and spirit of the Utrecht framework.[10] Territorial acquisition proceeded apace in Eastern Europe and in the New World, but no permanently dissatisfied political entities emerged from this process save those which had been partitioned.

C. The control of mobilizable resources was moderate in tone and limited in scope. Personal and dynastic loyalties rather than national allegiance characterized the age. While personal ties provided a much more limited allegiance than that involved in national symbolism, the leeway for the choice of policies was not similarly circumscribed. Elites were limited by their own codes more than by popular dictates in the selection of policy programs. Internally until the very eve of the French Revolution conservative elites were secure at the helm of state. They had no need to engage in rash or desperate ventures in external affairs to secure their position; nor, did their security of tenure become so overweening as to tempt them by sheer self-confidence to wholesale assault on the pattern of international outcomes. While Frederick II was probably the boldest leader of the old regime, personality dispositions of eighteenth-century elites were not overly aggressive in their impact on external relations. Compared to the elites of later ages they were often docile.

D. The resources available to the elites of the *ancien régime* were limited in certain ways and adequate in others. Perhaps their greatest assets were high diplomatic skill and persuasiveness. The absence of national loyalties gave great scope to intrigue, bribery, diplomatic tact, and finesse. The fates of whole nations might be settled in this manner and without recourse to military force.[11] In the military-technological field the nascent industrial revolution had scarcely made inroads on old methods of warfare; nor did it permit rapid mobilization of forces to confront a foe. Battles seemed to go on interminably and wars even longer. There was nothing about eighteenth-century economic resources which conduced to decisiveness in the military sphere.

E. The regulator of the eighteenth century managed to maintain a

---

[10] See *The Cambridge Modern History*, Vol. 6, *The Eighteenth Century* (New York, 1909), p. vi.

[11] Between 1764 and 1771 Swedish fates were largely determined by a diplomatic and financial struggle between Russia, England, and France.

rough balance of power on the European continent by manipulating alliance combinations. It was not forced to deal with any fundamental or persistent attempts to destroy the pattern of international outcomes like those which occurred in the first part of the seventeenth and nineteenth centuries. Neither the international system nor the internal constitutions of its various actors was ever at stake. In this fashion the international regulator could save its most far-reaching regulative powers for challenges which did not really materialize. The full panoply of regulative mechanisms would not be called into action until the system showed overt elements of instability, for only when the system produced undesired outcomes would the "error-controlled" regulator be called into full operation. The operations of the regulator, moreover, were evinced more through the processes of the international system than through a particular institutional medium. The regulator took on institutional form only at Vienna.

**F.** The environmental limitations of the system of the *ancien régime* eased conflicts among actors and militated in favor of stability. Territorial resources were abundant, and the imperial movement could proceed without disastrous conflict. The existence of large expanses still available for major actor appropriation helped to make extra-European expansion a safety value for European conflict. Environmental variety, thus, helped to hold outcomes within a stable range.

**G.** The outcomes flowing from the interaction of regulative and disruptive elements assumed the form of a multipolar international system.[12] No single state or bloc dominated international relationships, and a bipolar division of the world was not seen. Combinations changed relatively frequently. Actors contended for the fruits of the system, largely defined in this period in terms of territory. Because of the general availability of this resource, the outcomes of the system could be characterized as evincing a pattern of *compensation:* nations could usually compensate themselves for the gains made by another state.[13] If international resources constituted a fixed

[12] Multipolar, bipolar, and unipolar international systems may be distinguished as follows: multipolarity is a multi-bloc or actor system; bipolarity is a two-bloc or actor system; unipolarity is a one-bloc or actor system. Unipolarity requires in addition a single directorate of the preponderant bloc.

[13] Differing resource patterns may be characterized as follows: (1) *complementarity* indicates a system in which the improvement of one state's position is the

pie, slices of the pie had not all been appropriated. The process of mutual compensation, moreover, was a moderate one, occasioned by the limited means and control of patterns of national actors.

**H.** The interaction of the system is illustrated in Figure 6. It should be noted that regulative and disruptive influences (each indicated

**SYSTEM I**

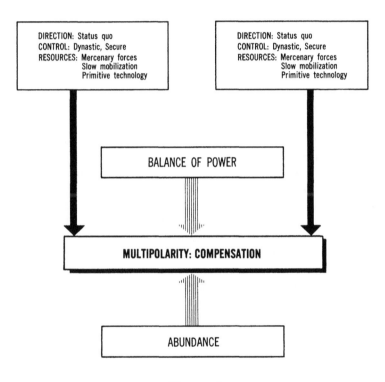

*Figure 6*

simultaneous improvement of the positions of other states: (2) *compensation* indicates a system where physical resources are fixed (hence the improvement in the position of one state does not entail an improvement in the position of others) but where resources have not been fully appropriated; (3) *dissension* indicates a system where *compensation* is conjoined with ideological hostility; (4) *disharmony* indicates a system where physical resources are fixed and also fully appropriated (hence the improvement in the position of one state entails a deterioration in the position of at least *one* other state); (5) *diametric opposition* indicates a system where *disharmony* is conjoined with ideological conflict.

by the width of the arrows) are approximately balanced and that both are at a low level: neither regulative nor disruptive factors assumed great magnitude in this system. Environmental influences also exert a comparable influence on the side of regulation. $\frac{D's \text{ variety}}{R's \text{ variety}}$ is such as to produce outcomes within the range of stability.[14]

## SYSTEM II [15]

**A.** In the system of international relations of the revolutionary imperium (1789-1814) the variety of actor disturbance was very great relative to the variety of regulator options. As a result the outcomes of this system fell largely outside recognized limits of stability. Environmental constraints sanctioned conflict and failed to hold the pattern of outcomes within acceptable bounds. Disruptive forces prevailed over regulative ones.

**B.** The ethos of actor elites differed. The elites of one bloc sought the internal reorganization of other states while either extending or preserving a revolutionary order at home. The elites of the other bloc sought to maintain their own internal systems without change while endeavoring to reform the internal polities of other states. The first group aimed to upset the pre-existing pattern of international outcomes and to transform the international system; the second group aimed to maintain and conserve the previous system of international relationships. In terms of fundamental objectives the elites of the two distinct blocs could scarcely have been more completely opposed. Many of the external outcomes of the new system were disastrous for various of the elite groups involved. Napoleonic and Revolutionary conquests of Central European areas were of vital and terrible significance for the elites of those regions; eventual coalition defeat of France was of decisive importance for the French Emperor and his coterie. International relations now directly impinged upon domestic affairs.

**C.** Vast changes occurred in the control of resources by national elites. The first great transformation was the substitution of national for personal loyalty in a number of actors. In France the change

14 See Ashby, *op. cit.*, pp. 205-207.
15 See Chapter Three.

took place as early as 1792, but in the conservative monarchies it was longer in coming and of shorter duration. However, the Austrian Emperor did rely upon nationalist support in his campaign against Napoleon in 1809. At the same time, the development of national loyalties in a revolutionary-liberal context first began to fix popular limits to the choice of policies. These limitations did not apply in the conservative actors, and they were partly transcended by the Bonapartistic technique of combining nationalist support with a mere façade of democratic control. The previous security of tenure was replaced at various times by insecurity on the part of both revolutionary and conservative camps. As long as insecurity did not go to the ultimate extreme (as it did in France in the spring of 1793), instead of weakening a nation's strategies in external affairs, it actually made for greater actor disturbance. Elites sometimes had to engage in rash actions in foreign relations to cement their internal position. The stresses of the times tended to draw forth leaders with more aggressive personality dispositions in the international field. Compared to the relative docility of the previous period, elites were firm or aggressive in the control of resources in the external arena.

D. The resources available to elites of the revolutionary system, largely as a result of political innovations, were more potent than those of the previous system. Through the *levée en masse*, the national mobilization of production for war and the greater discipline of mass citizen armies, military resources were increased. Mass and enthusiasm, together with new uses of the column and artillery represented the major innovations in military tactics. As the quantity of resources grew, speeds of mobilization also increased. As a result of developing nationalist sentiment, however, persuasive techniques were not as effective as they had been under the old regime. The revolutionaries in particular were not susceptible to the blandishments of traditional diplomacy, and after Napoleonic promises proved worthless, the French Emperor could not rely on his persuasive abilities. Military force as much or more than negotiation was the characteristic means of exerting influence in the international system.

E. The regulator of the revolutionary system did not succeed in holding the outcomes of international politics within acceptable limits. Essentially, the eighteenth-century regulator was carried over into the revolutionary-imperial period, and it was incapable of coping with the enormous increase in actor disturbance. The regulator did not possess sufficient flexibility to protect the internal constitutions of actors against external attack; nor was it prepared to counter wholesale attacks on the international system itself. Only after this "error-controlled" regulator had permitted vast divergences from the accepted norm did its regulatory mechanism come into full operation, and the process of regulation was itself marred by variations from acceptable outcomes. The previous assumption had been that regulation would take place before challenges to the international system could destroy it and before assaults on the domestic order could succeed; in fact, regulation only succeeded

**SYSTEM II**

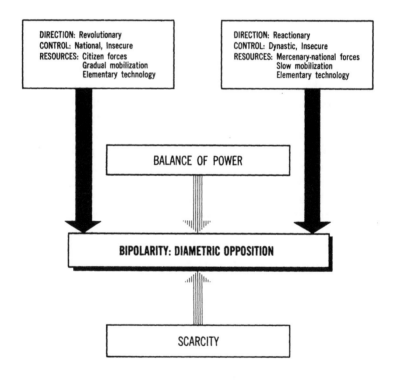

DIRECTION: Revolutionary
CONTROL: National, Insecure
RESOURCES: Citizen forces
              Gradual mobilization
              Elementary technology

DIRECTION: Reactionary
CONTROL: Dynastic, Insecure
RESOURCES: Mercenary-national forces
              Slow mobilization
              Elementary technology

BALANCE OF POWER

BIPOLARITY: DIAMETRIC OPPOSITION

SCARCITY

*Figure 7*

after both international and domestic outcomes had been transformed. In this system the regulator did not possess "requisite variety" to deal effectively with all actor disturbances. Nor did the regulator have an institutional basis.

**F.** The environmental constraints of the revolutionary system were not able to afford a real barrier to the variety of outcomes. Territorial expansion was directed not on the fringes of Europe or overseas, but in the heart of Europe where there were no large expanses available for major actor appropriation. In these circumstances expansion took place in terms of rivalry over already appropriated blocks of land. Moreover, insofar as objectives involved the internal reform of other states, the attainment of objectives by one actor involved the simultaneous failure of the objectives of another. Direct conflict ensued and environmental variety was too slight to hold down variety in international outcomes.

**G.** The outcomes which emerged from the interaction of regulative and disruptive elements assumed the form of a bipolar international system. *Diametric opposition* characterized the system: there was a fixed international pie with all slices appropriated in advance. In both territorial and ideological terms the improvement in the position of one bloc would automatically involve the worsening in the position of the other. The virulence of the bipolar antagonism was heightened by the fact that survival of an internal regime was at stake on both sides.

**H.** The interaction of the system is diagrammed in Figure 7. Here regulative and disruptive influences are not balanced. The regulator's variety has remained the same while the variety of actor disturbance has markedly increased. The variety of the environment has actually decreased. $\frac{D\text{'s variety}}{R\text{'s variety}}$ is such as to produce outcomes outside the stable range.

## SYSTEM III [16]

**A.** In the system of international relations of the functioning Concert (1814-1822) the variety of actor disturbances was minimal compared to the variety of regulator moves. As a result the outcomes of this system fell within the recognized limits of stability. The en-

[16] See Chapter Four.

vironmental Table also served to limit conflict and to hold the pattern of outcomes within acceptable bounds.

**B.** The ethos of actor elites was largely harmonious from both internal and external viewpoints. In contrast to System I, however, elites were not merely content with the existing patterns of internal and external organization; they were positively bent on protecting the internal systems even of minor actors from domestic revolution, and they were intent on maintaining the international system even at the sacrifice of some traditional interests. The new insistence on "legitimacy" in both its domestic and international phases was reinforced by the remembered instabilities of the Napoleonic period. After 1814 elites tried harder to maintain the internal and external order than they had done previously.

**C.** There was a partial reversion in the control of resources to the patterns of the eighteenth century. With the return of legitimist monarchs national symbols were diluted, even in France. The conservative monarchies of Central and Eastern Europe could not expect to rely upon the national support of their peoples except in the face of very great challenge. Partly as a result a new latitude of action was returned to elites, and the diplomatic virtuosity of the period was partly to be explained in these terms. At the same time a modest security of tenure was restored in almost all major European capitals. The resurgent conservatives, protected by the legitimist creed, did not need to consider desperate ventures in diplomacy to protect their positions. The psychological dispositions of the leadership of major actors were firm compared to the relative docility of System I but they were not nearly as aggressive or bellicose as the personalities of System II.

**D.** The resources available to the elites of System III harked back to the eighteenth century in several respects. The mobilization of political resources which had permitted a new militarism during Napoleonic hegemony did not persist for long after the French Emperor's defeat. The basic patterns of French militarism were not extensively imitated either on the Continent or in England and the French themselves partially reverted to a more traditional force. Owing to shifts in the political winds neither quantity of mobilizable resources nor speeds of mobilization approached their counterparts in the revolutionary system. Persuasive skills, however, were at an apogee. Metternich and Castlereagh shone brilliantly in the duels with Alexander and Capo d'Istria, Metternich's success in preventing the Russian Tsar from aiding the Greek revolutionists representing perhaps the signal achievement in diplomatic persuasion of the period. As personal and European loyalties partly supplanted national ones diplomatic subtlety could once again assume a large role.

**E.** The regulator of the Concert system was admirably successful in holding international outcomes within stable limits. The system of periodic consultation established under Article VI of the Quadruple Alliance and the new pattern of domestic intervention to uphold legitimist regimes provided a whole new armory of moves for the international regulator. Indeed, in this period the actors contributed as much to regulator variety as they did to international disturbance. The regulator's internal structure was changed in two major respects. First, the regulator was institutionalized in the Concert; it now might function formally as well as informally in the state system. Secondly, though the regulator was still "error-controlled," it was adjusted to bring regulative activity at the first signs of domestic insurrection; it did not have to wait for a wholesale assault on the European order. The regulator was quite capable of more than matching the variety of actor disturbance; it was even, through domestic intervention, able to exert a modest pressure on actor disturbance in the first instance.

**F.** Environmental factors during the functioning Concert system exercised an equally regulative influence on international outcomes. With the exception of the Polish-Saxon question territorial ambitions were at a nadir, and the environment provided more than a sufficient quantity of territorial resources. In addition, desired international resources were defined mainly in terms of the protection of conservative regimes, an objective which could be most nearly approximated through united action of the major actors. In the Concert system, far from regimes being able to protect their internal systems by unilateral measures, joint or common action seemed necessary against revolutionary outbursts. In this sense the functioning Concert system was different even from that of the eighteenth century: the attainment of one actor's objectives were not indifferent to similar attainment of those of others, it was directly material to such attainment. The attainment of objectives by one actor was the vindication of the objectives of another. Environmental influences, then, displayed considerable variety and militated in favor of stable international outcomes.

G. The outcomes of the functioning Concert assumed the form of a multipolar international system. No single state or bloc dominated, and a bipolar division of the world did not take place. *Complementarity* characterized the system in the sense that the essential objectives of major actors were best achieved in common. In terms of the definition of desired international resources at the time there was neither a potential nor an immediate conflict of interests. Thus resources did not constitute a fixed pie. The Concert's operation, rather, was marked by an expanding pie of desired resources in which the achievement of objectives by one actor aided

**SYSTEM III**

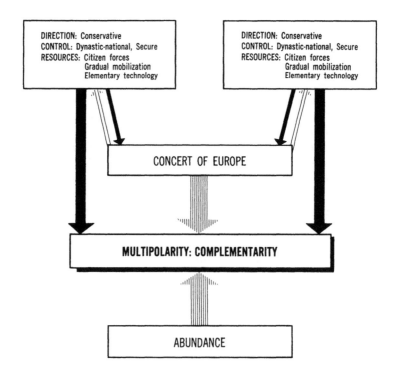

*Figure 8*

the attainment of objectives by other actors. At the same time major actors did not merge themselves into a single bloc under a single leadership: the action of the Concert was not dominated by a single intellect or a single actor; it was influenced by the separate and independent national wills of England, Russia, and above all, Austria.

**H.** The interaction of the system is diagrammed in Figure 8. Here regulative influences are fully competent to handle disruptive factors. The regulator not only exerts a powerful impact on international outcomes, but also a limited influence upon actor variety itself. Environmental constraints are now a much greater inhibition of the variety of outcomes than in the Revolutionary system. The actors' variety-producing influence is much weaker than previously; at the same time, the actors, through the creation of the Concert, actually add variety to the regulator and make it more capable of fulfilling its regulatory function. $\frac{D's \text{ variety}}{R's \text{ variety}}$ is such as to produce outcomes well within the stable range.

## SYSTEM IV [17]

**A.** In the system of international relations of the truncated Concert (1822-1848) the variety of the regulator was barely large enough to produce stable outcomes from actor disturbances. The environmental Table served also to limit conflict, though it did not exhibit as powerful a regulative influence as in System III.

**B.** The ethos of major actor elites showed a partial return to the ideological animosities of the Napoleonic period. While major elites were content with their own form of internal organization, there was a movement for the reform of other states in accordance with accepted ideological principles. As a result there was a partial re-emergence of a bipolar split along the lines drawn during the revolution. England and France worked together for certain ideological purposes; Russia, Prussia, and Austria opposed them on behalf of an opposing ideology. At the same time bipolarity was not permitted to issue in the antagonism of revolution and war. If elites were often discontent with their opponent's internal constitution, they were not willing to upset the pattern of international outcomes on behalf of ideological principle. Territorial ambitions

[17] See Chapter Five.

re-emerged, but they did not issue in fundamental antagonism. C. The pattern of control of resources differed from one bloc to the other. In the conservative camp national loyalties could not be maintained and reversion to dynastic ties had to be acknowledged. Popular influences, however, did not effectively circumscribe the choice of policy. At the same time with the partial containment of revolutionary tendencies conservative elites were safe at the helm of state: security of tenure was not a great worry until 1848. The personality dispositions of the conservative leadership were neither docile nor aggressive; firmness without bellicosity was the order of the day. In the more liberal states of England and France national loyalties came to be the accepted mode of allegiance after reforms were initiated. Popular influences, of growing importance in Castlereagh's time, came to have an important impact on the course of policy. Canning and Palmerston could not neglect public opinion. The leadership in these countries was quite secure for most of the period in question (with certain outstanding exceptions in the French case), and their personality structure approximated and perhaps even exceeded the firmness of conservatives in Central and Eastern Europe.

D. The resources of the actors of System IV differed in basic pattern. The conservative states probably made more of the military-technological resources available to them than did the liberals. They maintained large armies, and in Prussia the Napoleonic model was employed to a degree. In France and England the burgeoning industrial revolution was not made applicable to military purposes — militarism was largely neglected, recruiting followed traditional lines, and armies were decimated by the drive for governmental economy. Conservative armies probably could be mobilized more quickly than liberal ones, but rapid mobilization was out of the question. There was an important difference between conservative and liberal devices in the realm of persuasion. Neither Palmerston nor Canning could summon a powerful British force against the continent; but both could evoke the spectre of revolution and even help to create it. The liberals could use ideas as a force in themselves; the conservatives had to concentrate on the more traditional tools of militarism. In their different ways both conservatives and liberals were able to dispose sufficient resources to maintain their positions.

**E.** The regulator of the truncated Concert was a much more fragile instrument than its counterpart of System III. It no longer maintained a firm grip on internal as well as external developments. It might operate to prevent war among major actors, but it could not determine the domestic evolution of European countries. In fact it so lost variety as to be used to advance individual actor or bloc purposes rather than to regulate or to channel those purposes. The regulator did manage to control the great questions of war and peace, but in the domestic realm it often became the handmaiden of actor policy. Much of the competition between Palmerston and Metternich during this period was concerned with "capturing" the regulator for parochial viewpoints. The institutional format of the regulator remained, and where ideological issues were not involved, it was often able to produce a multilateral settlement of territorial questions.

**F.** The environmental constraints of the truncated Concert were such as to hold outcomes in check. This was a period of major actor expansion in North African and Middle Eastern areas. The English had not yet fully perceived the threat to their positions stemming from Russian or French expansion in these regions; they were not yet fully committed to propping up the "Sick Man of Europe." The availability of lands fringing the European continent where outcomes were not deemed to be decisive made for environmental variety and indirectly facilitated the control of international events. In the ideological realm, however, environmental variety was reduced. The system of the functioning Concert had helped to maintain stability through the assumption of ideological complementarity. This measure of harmony in the ideological arena vanished in System IV, and now the achievement of ideological objectives by one bloc would simultaneously lead to the failure of objectives of the other bloc. In this degree environmental constraints failed to exert the limiting influence on outcomes witnessed during the previous system.

**G.** The outcomes of the truncated Concert took the form of a quasi-bipolar international system. Insofar as ideological divisions were concerned, there was a bipolar split; insofar as territorial expansions was concerned, bipolar coalitions were shattered and a species of multipolarity prevailed. Bipolar antagonism was focussed mainly on the internal sphere where the two blocs clearly disagreed. Similar conflicts did not ensue over the pattern of international outcomes for neither bloc desired a major war. Desired international resources constituted a fixed pie, with the slices incompletely apportioned. *Dissension* characterized the system: the compensatory features of the old regime were conjoined with a considerable hostility over the mode of internal organization. The fear of major war, however, did not permit these antagonisms to find full expression.

**H.** The interaction of the system is diagrammed in Figure 9. In System IV regulative variety declines while actor disturbance increases. The actors themselves have a direct influence in reducing the variety of the regulator and frequently successfully use the regulator for their own purposes. Environmental constraints also

**SYSTEM IV**

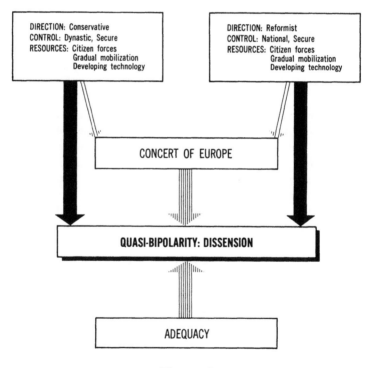

DIRECTION: Conservative
CONTROL: Dynastic, Secure
RESOURCES: Citizen forces
          Gradual mobilization
          Developing technology

DIRECTION: Reformist
CONTROL: National, Secure
RESOURCES: Citizen forces
          Gradual mobilization
          Developing technology

CONCERT OF EUROPE

QUASI-BIPOLARITY: DISSENSION

ADEQUACY

*Figure 9*

lose variety. Despite the reduction of regulator variety, however, $\dfrac{D's\ variety}{R's\ variety}$ is such as to produce outcomes that are barely within the stable range.

## SYSTEM V [18]

**A.** In the system of international relations of the shattered Concert (1848-1871) disruptive influences far outbalanced regulatory ones. Regulator variety was sharply curtailed as the variety of actor disturbances increased. The environmental Table also lost variety and was unable to contain destabilizing influences. The Concert failed as an institution, and the regulator was even more ineffective than in the Napoleonic system.

**B.** Fundamental changes occurred in the ethos of actor elites. While each major actor sought to maintain his own internal system, there was not the same antagonism to the internal regimes of other actors. Indeed, the internal constitution of other states was not of primary concern to actors in System V. They were concerned much more with maintaining their own regimes and with producing changes in the pattern of international outcomes to secure those regimes. The bipolar split of the previous period evaporated; Russia, Prussia, and Austria did not work together effectively, and neither did England and France. Each major actor was out to preserve its own institutions at the expense of its previous accomplices and the international system.

**C.** The control of resources now seemed to be assuming new forms. In those actors where conservative elites governed, personal or dynastic ties were the dominant mode of allegiance; in lands governed by liberal elites, nationalist symbols prevailed. But elites in both types of states were insecure. Both had been challenged by the revolutionary developments of 1848-1849; the conservatives by the revolution of 1848; the liberals by the counterrevolution of 1849. The personal loyalties of Prussia and Austria did not seem to be sufficient to hold conservatives in power; the national loyalties of France did not seem to be sufficient to hold liberals in power. Only a partial embodiment of alien ideological

[18] See Chapter Six.

appeals would allow the ideologues of one camp to maintain their hold on authority. The latitude of discretionary choice allotted the elite in both types of actors also declined. Conservatives had to pay lip service to a liberal façade, and liberals to a traditional façade. Popular influences in both liberal and conservative states forced "general" appeals on the elite leadership. The uncertainty of the situation in both groups of actors helped to recruit the most aggressive personalities for the tasks ahead. The aggressiveness of both Napoleon III and Bismarck was the result.

**D.** The resources of the new system of *Realpolitik* reflected the first application of major technological advancements since the French Revolution. New weapons such as the Prussian "needle gun" and the French "chassepot" increased infantry firepower. At the same time the successful Prussian utilization of conscript troops made for a more powerful force than the professional armies of the rest of Europe. Moltke's employment of railways for mobilization and rapid transport of armies placed a premium upon speed and mobility. It also permitted the development of mass armies. While physical military resources were both more formidable and more rapidly mobilized, sheer political persuasion was not effective as previously. In the context of desperation and insecurity national elites did not allow themselves to be deflected from their essential tasks by political propaganda. Force partially pre-empted the role of diplomacy.

**E.** The regulator of the shattered Concert lost variety and was unable to hold disturbances to a stable series of international outcomes. Aside from the original disposition of the Duchies in 1852 and the attempted settlement of the grievances which led to the Crimean War, the Concert scarcely managed to control events. At best it was called for the purpose of putting an end to wars which it could not prevent initially; at worst it was used for strictly national purposes or not convened at all. After the Crimean War a conference was held at Paris, but the Concert utterly failed to function after Königgrätz or Sedan. If the regulator of the truncated Concert at least operated to prevent war, the regulator of the shattered Concert could not even do that. By 1870 it seemed to have lost even its institutional foundation. Nor did any informal regulative mechanism limit the outcomes of the state system.

**F.** Environmental limitations of System V failed to confine international outcomes to stable ranges. Territorially, expansion took place in areas of great sensitivity where vital interests were involved. In the Near East, in Italy, and on the Rhine one could not expect to find indifference to the gains of one actor or another; rather, the gain of one actor was likely to be a loss for others. The regimes of all actors could not be made secure simultaneously. Prussian conservatives could not assure their position in a *gross-deutsch Reich;* Austrian conservatives did not believe they could survive outside a *kleindeutsch* empire; the two groups had to contend. Napoleon's internal position seemed to depend upon successful imperial expansion at the expense of the Hohenzollerns or Habs-

**SYSTEM V**

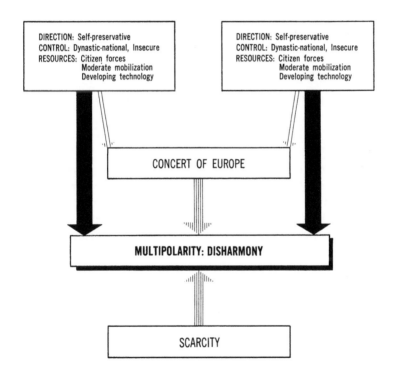

*Figure 10*

burgs. As a result, in neither ideological nor territorial questions could the environment provide sufficient variety to hold outcomes in check.

**G.** The outcomes of the shattered Concert were those of a multipolar international system. Bipolar ideological antagonism was straitly limited, and diplomacy was not organized under a single leadership. Resources desired by the actors constituted a fixed pie with all slices appropriated in advance. If the system did not attain the extreme antagonism of the revolutionary period, it could genuinely be labeled a system of *disharmony*.

**H.** The interaction of the system is diagrammed in Figure 10. In System V regulative variety declines while actor disturbance increases. Again the actors have a direct influence in reducing the variety of the regulator. The regulator is now used for actor purposes in most instances, and loses its controlling influence upon outcomes. Environmental limitations also lose variety. As a result of the further increase in actor disturbance and the general decline of regulative forces, the system is unstable. $\dfrac{D's \text{ variety}}{R's \text{ variety}}$ is such as to produce outcomes outside the accepted range.

## SYSTEM VI [19]

**A.** The system of international relations of the Bismarckian Concert (1871-1890) witnessed the re-establishment of control over actor disturbance by regulatory mechanisms. Outcomes fell within recognized limits of stability. The environmental Table gained new variety and was able to exert a greater regulative influence. The Concert was refurbished as a regulative institution.

**B.** The ethos of major actor elites showed a marked shift away from ideological concerns. No longer was an important source of actor disturbance the desire to reform the internal institutions of other actors: conservatives were willing to live with liberals, and liberals with conservatives. Elites in both camps were intent on preserving their own mode of internal organization, however, and after the uncertainties of the era of *Realpolitik* they sought to hold international outcomes within stable ranges.

**C.** The control of resources in the conservative actors was assuming

[19] See Chapter Seven.

a form not entirely unlike that in the more liberal nations. In the new Germany Bismarck succeeded in obtaining for his largely conservative coterie a nationalist allegiance stemming from the gains of 1866 and 1871. In Eastern Europe Austria tried to gain some nationalist as well as dynastic-personal support and was partially successful. Even Russia made certain gestures in the direction of replacing personal by national ties. In the West the national allegiance pattern was firmly entrenched. The limited shift to national loyalties, however, reduced the latitude of choice available to elites. Even in the conservative actors elites came to lose unlimited discretion in the choosing of policies. A new security of tenure for elites was won by seeking to adhere to popular limits upon policy formulation. Austrian conservatives strengthened their position by conceding equality to the Magyars and by briefly parading a façade of liberalism. German conservatives usurped liberal and socialist devices. Concessions to popular nationalism and a mild dosage of social reform helped the liberals in England and France. No elite had immediate fears for its position. The previous crisis of the shattered Concert had called aggressive personalities to the fore in several states. Bismarck, Disraeli and Gladstone symbolized the forcefulness of post-1871 elites, the former two in interventionism, the latter in intermittent isolationism. As a result, all major actors were now in a position to control resources more firmly than they had done since the revolutionary system.

**D.** The resources of the Bismarckian Concert combined growing technological skills with a rising military expenditure. "The growth of army expenditure in the British empire between 1870 and 1890 was about 350 per cent, in France 250 per cent, in Russia 400 per cent, in Austria-Hungary almost 450 per cent, in Italy almost 350 per cent, in Germany 1,000 per cent." [20] The greater security of elites and the development of the nationalist pattern of allegiance permitted greater exactions from the populace. Speed of deployment was increasing in proportion to the spreading rail network. Despite the enormous mass armies an initial concentration of forces might be changed during a campaign by shuttling forces by rail from one flank to another. If the vast armies of the latter part of the nineteenth century were not themselves as mobile as the forces of Napoleon or the elder Moltke, constituent military units might be moved even more rapidly. Mobilization speeds rose sharply. Persua-

[20] Hajo Holborn, *The Political Collapse of Europe* (New York, 1957), p. 66.

sive skills took an equal place with military posturing in the international system, and Bismarck and Disraeli relied as much on diplomacy and argument as on the threat of force.

**E.** The regulator of the refurbished Concert mechanism gained new complexity and was able to hold international outcomes within acceptable limits. As long as all major actors (with the exception of France) were entangled at one time or another in a single alliance structure, internal combinations might be reformulated to deal with new problems. The alliance network thus facilitated regulatory activity. Regulation was achieved more through changes in the patterns of alliance than through the traditional method of congress diplomacy, for a congress assumed that alignments were open and to be determined. The regulator also did not respond to changes in internal polities as it had done during the system of the functioning Concert; it awaited visible changes in the network of external relationships. When these were altered in some disturbing fashion, however, rapid action followed to prevent instability.

**F.** Environmental constraints operated during the period of the Bismarckian Concert to produce stability in outcomes. No longer were the interests of separate regimes totally disharmonious. The growth of the imperialist movement during System VI did not enhance, it tended to reduce conflict. It did so by focusing ambitions outside the European arena and by opening up enormous vistas of unappropriated colonial real estate. As long as there were vast tracts of land available, European actors would not come into direct collision over ownership. Environmental variety was not unlimited, however. Collisions in Eastern Europe and the Near East would clearly awaken animosities between Austria-Hungary and Russia, and only so long as the regulator was competent to handle disputes in that area could destabilizing conflict be avoided. On the whole, as in the eighteenth century, environmental factors operated to reduce the variety of international outcomes by providing multilateral access to desired resources.

**G.** The outcomes of the Bismarckian Concert were those of a unipolar international system. Bipolar antagonism did not exist, and there was a single directorship of alliance combinations at Berlin. Genuine multipolarity of the period of the functioning Concert (System III) was not to be seen; both in terms of diplomatic subtlety and in terms of physical resources Bismarckian Germany was in a position of leadership of the entire international system. The resource pattern of the system was like that of the eighteenth century (System I): a fixed pie of desired resources existed, but all the slices of that pie had not yet been apportioned. The variety of actor disturbance was much greater than that in the eighteenth century, but the variety of the regulator was correspondingly larger. *Compensation* characterized the operation of the system. Territorial gains by one elite group could be compensated by gains of another regime.

**H.** The interaction of the system is diagrammed in Figure 11. In this system regulative influences increase to cope with a substantial variety of actor disturbance. Actors return to the regulator flexibility and variety not possessed in System V. Environmental con-

**SYSTEM VI**

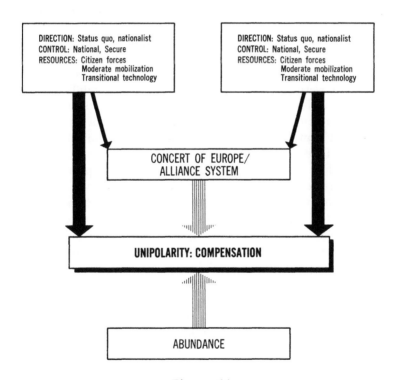

*Figure 11*

straints also gain in variety and are now more capable of dealing with actor variety. It should be noted that regulative and disruptive influences (as indicated by the respective widths of the arrows) are approximately balanced and that both are at a substantial level. $\frac{D's\ variety}{R's\ variety}$ is such as to produce outcomes within the range of stability.

## SYSTEM VII [21]

**A.** In the system of international relations of imperialist nationalism (1890-1918) regulator variety was insufficient to cope with the variety of actor disturbance. Environmental constraints also lost variety and were unable to exercise a stabilizing influence on international outcomes. The Concert failed as a regulatory mechanism and even began to take on an *ex parte* flavor. International instability was the result.

**B.** The ethos of elites marked a return to attitudes prevalent under the system of the shattered Concert. Conservative and liberal elites in various countries were intent on maintaining their own internal system of governance while they were more or less indifferent to the internal constitutions of other states. Most elites sought to change the pattern of international outcomes as a means of securing their position at home. A bipolar split finally emerged, but not as a concomitant of ideological differences.

**C.** Control of resources was assuming a rather desperate and unstable character. In all actors liberal and conservative elites strove to instill national modes of allegiance, greater success being attained in the liberal actors. In all regimes, however, elites were uncertain of their tenure on power. Liberal movements in the conservative actors, and movements for social reform in the liberal actors had produced governmental elites which were out of tune with popular sentiments. Nationalist aggrandizement, as a consequence, was used as a technique of binding national allegiance to a particular political regime. If regimes would not concede social or liberal reform, they had to embrace national-imperial expansion to stay in power. This further constricted their latitude in choosing among

21 See Chapter Eight.

variant policies. A more aggressive leadership was brought to the helm of states. In Austria-Hungary, Germany, and Russia where the position of the ruling elite was in jeopardy, aggressive military and political personalities came to the fore.

D. The generation after 1890 witnessed a basic expansion of the military-technological resources of international actors. While "Europe was reshaped between 1848 and 1914 by the impact of the industrial revolution," [22] the most striking increase in manufacturing production occurred between 1890 and 1913. In 1914 defense expenditure in Germany stood at 384 per cent of what it had been in 1890; in Austria-Hungary the figure was 284 per cent; in France it was 153 per cent; in Britain it was 244 per cent; in Italy it was 190 per cent; in Russia, 304 per cent. [23] Mobilization rates were further increased. In 1905 Count Schlieffen of the German General Staff prepared a plan for victory over France which would have had German troops operating south of Paris short months after mobilization. And as the first days of the war developed in 1914, German forces were deployed beyond the Marne just one month after the outbreak of war. Most military theorists predicted a short war, and mobilization rates had to be speeded to prepare for the decisive battle. In these circumstances diplomacy was at a disadvantage; military *desiderata* would replace diplomatic ones as the crisis drew near. Salisbury, Rosebery, Bülow and Declassé were no match for Bismarck and Metternich. When the challenge emerged on June 28, 1914 there was not enough diplomatic virtuosity to blunt it.

E. The regulator of System VII was unable to hold actor disturbances in check. The regulative mechanism did not keep pace with the variety of actor disturbance, it even lost variety from the preceding system. The system of alliances as it had developed under Bismarck no longer facilitated the work of regulation because combinations were no longer open-ended. After 1894 new combinations could not be formulated to meet new challenges; two alliance systems emerged, neither one of which could be faced down by the other. In these circumstances the regulator was sometimes employed for actor purposes; it could not always employ actors for regulatory

[22] A. J. P. Taylor, *The Struggle for Mastery in Europe: 1848-1918* (Oxford, 1954), p. xxix.
[23] Derived from figures in *ibid.*, p. xxviii.

purposes. In this fashion the regulator itself sometimes exercised a disruptive impact on international outcomes. The Algeciras Conference of 1906 seemed to be an example of this phenomenon.

**F.** Environmental factors failed to operate to produce stable international outcomes in System VII. The further development of the imperialist movement both inside and outside Europe led to the appropriation of all colonizable territory. After 1905 territory outside Europe had largely been divided up, and the imperial drive turned back on Europe itself. In particular it proceeded for the spoils of the Ottoman Empire, and in this competition Austria and Russia could not have common interests. After colonizable lands were partitioned any further attempt to advance the imperial

**SYSTEM VII**

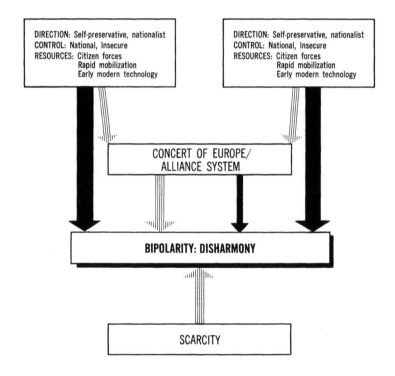

*Figure 12*

claims of one actor would inevitably be at the expense of another. In this situation the interests of two imperial blocs became directly antagonistic. The variety of the environment was reduced to that of the Napoleonic system in the contest for European real estate; in both cases it failed to hold conflicts within the bounds of stability.

**G.** The outcomes of imperialist nationalism took the form of a bipolar international system. Bipolarity was not dictated on ideological grounds; rather it was dictated on grounds of military security, and the combinations which were formed violated previous ideological tenets. If imperialist advance was to bring dangers of war an actor had to be prepared with pledged and ready allies to defend him before the conflict began. Permanent peacetime alliances were the result. The resources of the international system were like those of the shattered Concert (System V). A fixed pie existed with all slices apportioned in advance. The attempt to gain slices was bound to lead to conflict. At the same time the conflict had nothing to do with the character of internal regimes, and initially at least, it did not have an ideological flavor. In this sense System VII was unlike that of the Napoleonic imperium. *Disharmony* characterized the system and the First World War was its direct result.

**H.** The interaction of the system is diagrammed in Figure 12. In this system disruptive influences increase in variety while regulative influences lose variety. Disturbance now greatly overshadows regulation. Indeed, the regulator sometimes exerts a destabilizing impact. Environmental constraints also lose variety. $\dfrac{D's \text{ variety}}{R's \text{ variety}}$ is such as to produce outcomes well outside the accepted range of stability.

## SYSTEM VIII [24]

**A.** In the system of international relations of totalitarian militarism (1918-1945) the variety of the regulator was markedly less than the variety of actor disturbance. In certain areas regulative activity was increased, in certain others the regulator actually contributed to greater variety in international outcomes. Environmental factors could not act as a significant force limiting international outcomes. In these circumstances the international system was highly unstable.

**B.** A sharp bifurcation appeared in the ethos of actor elites. On the

[24] See Chapter Nine.

one hand one group of actors was bent on the transformation of
their own patterns of domestic organization along Fascistic lines, on
the overturn of domestic regimes in non-Fascist countries, and on a
complete revision of international outcomes. International stability
would not be tolerated. On the other hand another group of actors
aimed at maintaining their own internal constitutions, on protecting the international system, and they were largely indifferent to
the mode of internal organization of other actors. This group aimed
at international stability. The result was the eventual consummation of a bipolar system: the Fascist actors recognized the similarity
of their objectives relatively early; the democratic actors (and the
Soviet Union) only became aware of their need to stand together
when the Fascist challenge reached its height. Ideological differences once again were an important factor in world politics.

C. Patterns in the control of resources were also contrasting. In the
Fascist states national allegiance patterns were fully developed. At
the same time national allegiance did not entail democratic control
of policy. Through propaganda manipulation Fascist elites were
able to portray a façade of democratic control while actually tran-
scending its limitations. At the same time Fascist elites were not altogether secure in their grip on power. Dramatic success was necessary to ensure their position. But their insecurity was not of the
sort which paralyzes action. Instead it made for restless activity on
behalf of greater security. Leaders of the Fascist elites were not
merely aggressive, they were at times well-nigh reckless in the international arena. Patterns of control in the democratic actors, on the
other hand, were quite different. National allegiance was largely
accepted, but there was a palpable reduction in the efficacy of national symbols in several democratic actors. At the same time democratic populations placed important limitations on the choice of
policies in international affairs. "Appeasement" was in part a policy
dictated by public opinion in democratic actors. Democratic elites
were generally secure in their positions and did not have to resort
to desperate expedients to maintain it. For the most part democratic leaders were a docile lot.

D. System VIII witnessed a further improvement in the power and
destructiveness of mobilizable resources. The development of large
scale air warfare of both tactical and strategic significance, the increasing mechanization and mobility of armies, and the improve-

ment of firepower made militarism more potent than before. All the political resources of totalitarian states were used to advance the quantity and quality of mobilizable resources, and in the democracies even greater sacrifices were asked than those demanded during World War I. Despite the deductions drawn by military historians from the First World War about the primacy of the defense, aggressive *Blitzkrieg* tactics turned out to be of decisive importance, particularly against France in 1940. Mobilization speeds were at least as rapid as those of World War I. The major difference between the democratic and Fascist camps was not strictly military, it was also political and diplomatic. Hitler was a master of persuasion — in dealing with elites he was nearly the equal of Metternich, and in dealing with publics he had no peer. Political persuasion and the "strategy of terror" [25] were his greatest strengths, and they also revealed the greatest weaknesses of his democratic opponents.

E. The regulator of the system of totalitarian militarism was improved in certain respects over that of the system of imperialist nationalism. It was specifically institutionalized in the League of Nations; it provided forums in the League Council and Assembly for the airing of disputes, and oftentimes it provided vigorous action to dispatch a quarrel among minor actors. If the ethos of all major actors had been in behalf of international stability, the regulator might have coped effectively with the actor disturbance of the period. In fact such an ethos was not universal, and the variety of actor disturbance was greater than it had ever been before. Because the League was formally committed to certain types of regulation and to certain principles, two destabilizing consequences followed: (1) the League was supposed to act against all aggressors whether they were or were not major sources of disturbance;[26] (2) its principles might be used to justify certain actions which were directed against the stability of the international system.[27] It is perhaps significant that Russia was expelled from the League and that Italy was subjected to formal, if innocuous sanctions while Germany

---

[25] See Edmond Taylor, *The Strategy of Terror* (Boston, 1940).

[26] One can only imagine the consequences if the British and French had succeeded in aiding Finland and putting themselves at war with Russia in February, 1940.

[27] Hitler was able to use Wilsonian internationalist and League principles to solemnize his attempts to disrupt Versailles and win German "equality."

was allowed to escape with an occasional reprimand. In its final years the League itself became a disequilibrial force in world politics.

**F.** The environmental constraints of System VIII did not militate in favor of continued stability. Territorially the Nazi elite aimed at continental hegemony in Europe, and this objective could not be conceded either by British or French leaders. Ideologically the Fascist totalitarians aimed to use military force to overthrow the domestic constitutions of European states, another goal which democratic leaders could not abide. The problem, however, was that democratic leaders either were ignorant of or they succumbed to incredible wishful thinking about environmental limitations. For a period of time the policy of "appeasement" managed to keep inter-

**SYSTEM VIII**

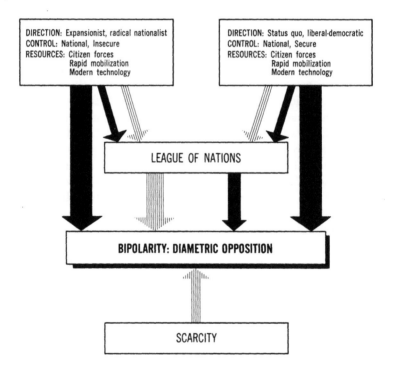

*Figure 13*

national entanglements from producing conflict by obscuring the actual complex of interests. "Appeasement" was fundamentally a policy of giving away slices of a fixed international pie which had already been completely divided. If British and French statesmen had taken the "fixed and divided" pie into their calculations, they would have seen that "appeasement" could only worsen their position. "Appeasement" therefore reduced conflict only by concealing it; in the long run it could not prevent an overt collision of interests. True environmental limitations then could not reduce the variety of international outcomes; only a false perception of those limitations could make them seem able to do so.

**G.** The eventual pattern of outcomes was that of a bipolar international system. Its structure was partially concealed by the assumption of Democratic elites that they might get along with Fascist elites and that there need be no ideological antagonism over internal systems. Only when the fact of internal and external antagonism was revealed did the bipolar system assume overt form. Ideological differences were once again at the heart of the bipolar division; and the antagonism in both internal and external terms assumed an even more virulent form than it had done in the age of Napoleon. *Diametric opposition* characterized the system. The fixed pie of completely divided resources joined with ideological hostility to produce World War II.

**H.** The interaction of the system is diagrammed in Figure 13. In this system both regulative and disruptive influences have increased in variety, but the increase in disruptive influences far outweighs the increase in regulative ones. While actors have contributed variety to the regulator, they have also operated to reduce its variety in certain aspects. The regulator itself exercises a destabilizing as well as a stabilizing influence on international outcomes. Environmental influences have not gained in variety and have not been able satisfactorily to contain the variety of international outcomes. The international system is highly unstable.

## SYSTEM IX [28]

**A.** In the international system of the post-war generation (1945-1960) regulative influences temporarily increased in variety while disruptive influences temporarily lost variety. While in certain areas

[28] See Chapter Ten.

regulative activity increased, in certain others the regulator actually acted as a disturbing force. The environmental Table gained in variety, and it was able to exert a greater regulative impact than previously. A tenuous stability emerged, for a time, but whether it will continue is uncertain.

**B.** In 1945 both American and Soviet elites were bound on establishing a new pattern of international outcomes and a new international system. Fifteen years afterward it seemed as if both actors had put off their programs of revision of international relationships and were more willing to accept the current pattern of outcomes in preference to unlimited war. Statements from the Kremlin rejected war as a desirable outcome of the international system: "We cannot repeat today mechanically what V. I. Lenin said many decades ago about imperialism and always repeat that imperialist wars are inevitable as long as socialism has not triumphed all over the world . . . this entitles us to assert with certainty that under present conditions war is not inevitable. He who does not understand this does not believe in the force and creative possibilities of the working class, underestimates the strength of the Socialist camp and has no confidence in the great attractive force of socialism, which has manifestly demonstrated its superiority over capitalism." [29] These statements did not suggest satisfaction with the existing international system, but they seemed to support pacific outcomes in preference to wholesale violence. If leaders of both Western and Soviet blocs accepted such a ranking of priorities, all members of the Soviet bloc did not do so. Continued tolerance of current international outcomes in the Soviet world, then, tended to depend upon the struggle for leadership between the Russian and Chinese factions. In the domestic field both Soviet and Western leaders looked forward to revolutionary changes in the other's camp, but war was not regarded as a necessary prerequisite to the creation of revolutionary conditions. In certain limited respects there was an analogy of the post-war system with that of the truncated Concert (1822-1948); in both systems unlimited war was avoided while ideological differences continued over the domestic scene. Neither the Western nor the Soviet bloc (with the exception of China) seemed bent on changing fundamentally its own internal system; both were in this sense socially conservative.

[29] Nikita Khrushchev, quoted in the *New York Times,* June 23, 1960.

A third rough bloc or grouping existed in international politics and its ethos was not fully formed. Just as the ethos of the Soviet bloc would be determined by a struggle between emergent and mature wings; the ethos of the nationalist-neutralist camp would be determined by a contest between mature and emergent factions. Emergent nationalists were anxious to revise the pattern of international outcomes as well as to reform their own internal systems, while mature nationalists were reasonably content with existing outcomes in international relations and sought internal change only. The stability of the international system in the future might well depend upon which wing is successful.

C. Resources were controlled in different ways in different blocs. Both Soviet and Western blocs relied upon considerable nationalist support owing to national allegiance patterns, but at the same time leaders of the Soviet bloc enjoyed a discretionary latitude in the choice of policies not available to Western leaders. The totalitarian domestic system permitted enormous scope to the policymaker, simultaneously ensuring full nationalist support. In both blocs elites were neither insecure nor oversecure — elites were not tempted to take drastic or precipitate action as a result of insecurity or overconfidence. The personalities drawn to the reins of power in both blocs were generally firm without being persistently aggressive or reckless.[30] In the third nationalist-neutralist bloc national allegiance patterns were the usual mode, and leaders enjoyed considerable latitude in charting policy though not so much as in totalitarian states. Elites in the third bloc were not always in as secure a position as in both Western and Soviet blocs, for particularly in the emergent nationalist actors the security of the regime was in question from time to time. The personalities of these elites, moreover, tended to cover a wider range. In the most mature of the nationalist actors firm personalities were likely to be found, whereas in the most emergent aggressive or reckless personality dispositions were likely to be characteristic.

D. Patterns in the quantity of resources also differed among major blocs. In strict military terms both the Soviet and Western blocs had developed resources of an annihilative character. With the full development of thermonuclear weapons and intercontinental missiles the destructiveness of resources seemed to have been carried to a

[30] Stalin, Mao Tse-tung, and Liu Shao-chi may constitute exceptions here.

new extreme. At the same time, with instantaneous mobilization for all-out war very nearly achieved, the speed of mobilization had also reached a new peak. The danger of accidental attack materialized,[31] though the attempt to achieve relative invulnerability might lessen the threat in time. In contrast to the enormous military resources, posed for instantaneous deployment, possessed by the two major protagonists, the uncommitted bloc had moderate military resources. Large supplies of manpower were canceled by deficient weaponry, mechanization, and firepower. Mobilization speeds were proportionately slower. In the field of political persuasion, on the other hand, the uncommitted bloc was able to exercise a greater influence. Diplomatic finesse in resolving or blunting Great Power conflicts was evidenced on more than one occasion.

**E.** The regulator of the Post-World War II international scene attained increased variety to cope with international disturbances at the same time as there seemed to be a diminution in the variety of those disturbances. The United Nations, the residuary legatee of the League of Nations, was not notably effective; it often operated as the parochial instrument of one bloc or the other. In political and security matters it did not effectively regulate relations among the Great Power blocs. The political competition for the allegiance or favor of the neutralist states, however, sometimes allotted to the United Nations a successful mediating role. In the face of the thermonuclear threat, national actors themselves directly regulated their own disruptive conduct.

**F.** Environmental variety was increased in System IX and was more effective in confining international outcomes within stable ranges. In the absence of recourse to force the two major blocs aimed to acquire influence and support in the third bloc by political, diplomatic and economic means. The third bloc was the "colonizable territory" of the present age, though the means of imperialism were far different from those of the nineteenth century. The desired resources of System IX were political and territorial; it was the political allegiance of uncommitted regimes that was sought in the first instance. The emergence of a third bloc directed initially by the

[31] Albert Wohlstetter writes: "In a clear sense the great multiplication and spread of nuclear arms throughout the world, the drastic increase in the degree of readiness of these weapons, and the decrease in the time available for the decision on their use must inevitably raise the risk of ancient." "The Delicate Balance of Terror," *Foreign Affairs* (January, 1959), p. 231.

mature nationalists, however, helped to prevent sudden transformations of political allegiance among nationalist actors. The policy of the mature nationalist leadership was to adhere to a tolerably neutralist course, to avoid internal or external commitment to either Great Power bloc, and to extract competing favors from both sides.[32] Unlike the colonizable tracts of the nineteenth century here were potential colonies which were able to reject imperial rule. In the circumstances the process of dividing up the unparceled out territory was much more difficult and much more gradual than that in the previous ages of imperialism. As long as territory was left to be appropriated, the interests of the major blocs were not absolutely and fixedly disharmonious, because gains by one bloc might be canceled by complementary gains by the other. Interests were not in absolute inverse relationship. Within the major blocs themselves, however, transformations of political attitude aroused great antagonism. Defections to one bloc or the other were directly inimical to the opposing bloc. In such case direct antithetical interests governed, and environmental variety was reduced. On the whole, however, environmental factors probably exercised a limiting influence on the variety of international outcomes in System IX.

G. The outcome of System IX may be provisionally designated as that of a tripolar international world. Tripolarity was dictated largely on ideological grounds: Communist and Western attitudes were opposed on grounds of ideology; and the neutralist-nationalists seemed to be framing an ideology of their own separate from those of the two major protagonists. Despite the ideological antagonism all international resources were not appropriated, and access to resources of the two major blocs was opened to the third bloc as well as the other way around. A fixed pie of resources with certain slices still unappropriated characterized the system. Ideological differences were an important feature, but it seemed that they would not be aired deliberately in all-out war. The system could best be described as manifesting *dissension*.

H. The interaction of the system is diagrammed in Figure 14. In System IX the variety of disruptive influences decreased slightly while that of regulative influences increased. Actors contributed increased variety to regulator, but also sought to reduce its variety in certain

[32] The ability of the neutralists to regulate great Power policy was subject to important limitations after 1960.

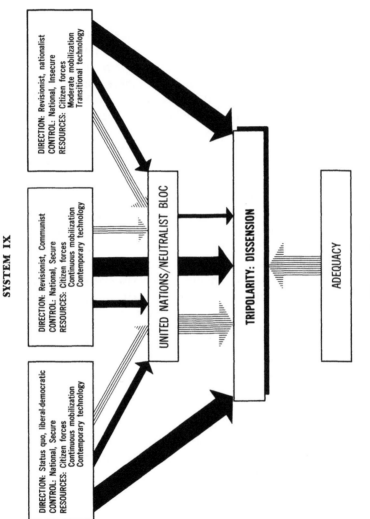

DIRECTION: Revisionist, nationalist
CONTROL: National, Insecure
RESOURCES: Citizen forces
              Moderate mobilization
              Transitional technology

DIRECTION: Revisionist, Communist
CONTROL: National, Secure
RESOURCES: Citizen forces
              Continuous mobilization
              Contemporary technology

DIRECTION: Status quo, liberal-democratic
CONTROL: National, Secure
RESOURCES: Citizen forces
              Continuous mobilization
              Contemporary technology

UNITED NATIONS/NEUTRALIST BLOC

TRIPOLARITY: DISSENSION

ADEQUACY

*Figure 14*

respects. The regulator exerted a variety-reducing and a variety-increasing impact on international outcomes in different circumstances. Environmental influences gained in variety and were more capable of regulating international outcomes. The system was within the range of stability.

## CONCLUSION

The systematic approach to international relations helps to put in perspective prevalent theoretical approaches to the study of international relations. It helps to link the approach of "general organizing concepts" with that of "detailed empirical investigation." While it does not provide for the comprehensive unification of the field under a single theoretical banner nor for the detailed dissection of individual cases, it does constitute a bridge between the two. Systematic empirical analysis permits the incorporation of a considerable fund of factual information in a theoretical approach which aims at a measure of comprehensiveness. Reality is not so neatly encapsulated as to provide full predictive efficacy; neither is a univocal theoretical strand elevated to explanatory preeminence. At the same time the constituents of systems analysis afford accommodation for a variety of theoretical approaches.

**Power.** The *power* theory aimed at minimum to give an account of fundamental changes in the international environment. Changes in international configurations were due, so the theory held, to changes in the amount and distribution of *power*. Where patterns of alliance changed, where economic, diplomatic or military strength grew disproportionately in certain national sectors as against others, where national weakness or instability suddenly created power vacuums — there *power* factors would demand a reorientation of international relationships. Disequilibrium in the power balance would call for redressment. There is no doubt that changes in material power have often underlain changes in international constellations. It was no accident that Triple Alliance helped to provoke Triple Entente. Bismarckian Germany, the pivot of European connections, enjoyed that position in part because of German power. Napoleonic France could not have represented a decisive challenge to the pre-existing European order had it not been for the French population and resource base. Hitlerian Germany would have been a minuscule threat to the European peace if it had been confined to a power position equivalent to that of Spain or Portugal. It would be impossible to understand the system of international relations under the *ancien régime* without reference to power motivations. Where ideological conflicts are absent, quests for power may have unhindered sway. The difficulty of the *power* theory, however, was that it could not be maintained both strictly and universally. Changes in material power, strictly interpreted, did not always account for international transformation, for the drive or motivation for power, strictly interpreted, was not universal. The *power* theory entered the ranks of "general organizing concepts" when it was prepared to sacrifice strict application to logical comprehensiveness. The *power* theory could be maintained universally, but only by constant redefinition of the concept of *power* to accommodate each new real or hypothetical case. In the end, by expanding the notion of *power* beyond its normal or ordinary confines, the *power* theory actually distracted attention from those situations in which it might be applied strictly. In so doing, it made "the struggle for power" an almost definitional postulate and served to allay worries about "real" power factors. If all nations pursue power, then the relative pacificity of U.S.-Canadian or U.S.-British relations is as characteristic as the hostility of America and the Soviet Union. In this sense the *power* "theory" helped to undercut the role of *power* "factors."

The approach of systems analysis helps to re-emphasize the place of neglected power "factors." International disturbance and regulation are a function of the *variety* of moves available to each. The balance of power, like other equilibrial systems, is a situation in which the variety of moves available to regulative forces is sufficient to cope with the variety of moves of perturbant forces. And variety is partly a product of material power. The greater the material power of an actor the greater the number of moves it can make upon the international scene. Its armory of foreign policy choices is simply increased by greater power. Enhanced actor variety, however, does not necessarily mean increased actor disturbance. The greater variety created by material power may be used for regulative or disruptive purposes. Between 1871 and 1890 German power was used largely for regulative ends; between 1933 and 1945 it was used largely for international disruption. Although they are of great importance, power factors, in and of themselves do not determine patterns of stability or instability. Even after the configuration of power has been taken into account much still depends upon whether power-created variety will be used for disturbance or regulation. It is at this juncture that power factors fail to provide a complete answer.

**Ideology or values.** An important gap is filled by *ideological* or *value* theories. While the power theory could not account empirically for all actor motivations, the *ideological* theory helped to explain the residuum. Values and ideological tenets were important factors in determining the possible integration of two or more national societies. International alliances or conflicts were not usually unrelated to ideological belief. Communications patterns which some have held to be determinative of national units depended in part upon the existence of common value frameworks; where those frameworks were absent the flow of communication was truncated. The great revolutionary convulsions of the past two centuries injected ideological issues into the conduct of international relations and thereby contributed to a new genre of international conflicts and combinations.

The ideological approach, however, was subject to the same disabilities as the power approach. "Ideology" or "value" might be construed so broadly as to demean empirical reference. It could be held semantically (but not empirically) that:

(1) All nations seek ends.

(2) All ends are values and a series (more than one) of ends is an ideology.

Therefore,

(3) All nations seek values and ideologies.

Acceptance of such an argument would give formalistic triumph over the exponents of the power theory, but it would do little to facilitate empirical investigation. As with the power theory strict application is sacrificed to universal application. The redefinition of *ideology* and *value* in this manner prejudices the actual contribution which such theories may make. Those who insist on universally interpreting Soviet foreign policy as ideologically motivated make the same mistake as those who see in it an unlimited quest for power. If all Soviet action is "ideological," the term no longer retains a clear or fixed meaning, and it becomes impossible to distinguish ideological and non-ideological phases in the conduct of foreign policy. That nations are often more concerned with ideological objectives than with power may be seen in certain of the revolutionary struggles of the nineteenth century, some of which are partially replicated in the struggles of the new nations today. It is impossible to make legitimate distinctions between the international relations of the eighteenth century and that of the modern period, unless ideological factors are brought into account.

Systematic empirical analysis can accommodate values and ideologies in a framework which does not neglect power factors. As indicated previously, international disturbance and regulation are functions of the *variety* of moves available to each. And if *variety* is partly dependent upon material power, it is also a product of ideologies and values. Actor variety, or the range of moves available to an actor, for either regulative or disruptive purposes, is as dependent upon cognition as it is upon capability. One of the fundamental differences of the revolutionaries from the European dynasts of the old regime was in terms of intellectual conception. Louis XV would simply not have thought of using his capabilities for revolutionary ideological purposes. His intellectual horizons were limited by the prevailing aristocratic ideology of the period. The introduction in this instance of new ideological strands increased actor variety entirely independent of actor power capabilities. Actor variety, in sum, is a product of what a nation seeks to do as well as of what resources it may devote to that purpose; it is a function of both objectives and capabilities. Ideological objectives may increase actor variety by stretching intellectual conceptions beyond a tradition-bound pursuit of power, or they may decrease actor variety by limiting and rigidifying rational power objectives. In either case they affect the configuration of choices which a national actor has before him.

**Equilibrium.** Perhaps the major deficiency of both power and ideological approaches, however, is their tendency to neglect interaction. A universal pursuit of power does not engender conflict if the "power pie" is increasing.[33] Pursuit of ideological goals or values produces antagonism only if there are two or more competing value

33 This statement applies, of course, only to the absolute and not to the relational conception of power.

systems. By focusing upon the objectives and capabilities of individual national actors both power and ideological theories obscure the relationships *among* national actors. Only the traditional theory of "the balance of power" alleviates this deficiency, and it is so largely couched in terms of power that it overlooks ideological and value goals. *Equilibrium* theories have, on this ground, much to commend them. They are neither stated wholly in terms of power, nor neglectful of the interrelation of national policies. Power and morality are seen as different constituents of a "multiple equilibrium" which has many different phases. The equilibrial tendency is posited as basic, but it may manifest itself in "stable, neutral and unstable; long-term; perfect and imperfect" [34] forms. One of the difficulties faced by this approach, however, is its insistence upon "equilibrium" as the central organizing concept. Any recital of past or present international happenings would be as concerned with disequilibrium as with equilibrium as a basic feature of the international environment. And even a tendency toward "the balance or equilibrium of power as the irreducible if changing central dynamics of international relations" [35] would be countered by equally powerful tendencies in an opposed direction. There is no observable net trend toward international equilibrium and away from chaos. The equilibrial theory either makes claims for progress which the evidence does not support or dilutes the notion of "equilibrium" to admit instances of what most of us would regard as "disequilibrium." In this manner it fails to provide a satisfactory summation of international relationships.

Once again systems analysis has something to offer. The constant competition between forces of disruption and regulation provide instances of the "equilibrial tendency" though the outcome of the struggle is very much in doubt. Whether regulative or perturbant forces are successful depends upon the variety of responses available to them both. Until the variety of their moves can be ascertained, no predictions can be made concerning stability or instability. It is perhaps instructive to recall that of the nine systems of international relations considered above, five were deemed stable, and four unstable. A secular tendency toward equilibrium does not

[34] See George Liska, *International Equilibrium* (Cambridge, Massachusetts, 1957), p. 12.
[35] *Ibid.*, p. 193.

emerge from these instances. At the same time, systems theory permits the incorporation of the interactive features of the equilibrium approach. Regulative and disruptive constituents portray the interaction of balance of power or "multiple equilibrium," and the relationships among national actors are a focus of attention.

**Innovation.** The equilibrium theory underscores another important but much neglected feature of the international scene: dynamic change. Forms of equilibria undergo transformation. The multiple equilibrium of today is far different from that of yesteryear. But the dynamic features of international relations are better illuminated in theories of *innovation*. Economic, technological, and military factors have revolutionized the conditions of international diplomacy. In many respects the present international system is fundamentally different from that of past epochs, and economic, technological, and military change has helped to produce the difference. In contrast to previous decades modern technology and economy have given rise to a proliferation of international and interstate contacts through communications, travel, economic relations, and the development of a new network of international organizations. The multiplication of "functional" contact of all sorts helps to differentiate past from contemporary periods. One of the most important aspects of the technological revolution, of course, is the revolution in the conditions of warfare and weaponry to which it it has given rise. The airplane and intercontinental missile together with the thermonuclear bomb have transformed "impermeable" states with "hard shells" into "permeable," "soft shell" units.[36] The central core of a state is now as vulnerable to assault as the periphery. The revolution in weaponry has also helped to effect a transition "from balance to deterrence." [37] The international constellations of the deterrent age are likely to be different from those of the age of balance of power.

The dynamic transformations of the international system engendered by innovation are of enormous significance, and any analysis which is framed in purely static terms does violence to the degree of international change. At the same time, factors of continu-

---

[36] See John Herz, *International Politics in the Atomic Age* (New York, 1958), Chapter Six.

[37] See Arthur Burns, "From Balance to Deterrence: A Theoretical Analysis," *World Politics*, July, 1957.

ity have been at least as important as factors of change in charting the course of the international system. The states of the constituents of the international system have varied considerably over time, but the constituents themselves are a constant. In assessing the outcomes of the international mechanism, one must take into consideration the same factors for the *ancien régime* as for the present generation. In this sense, theories of *innovation* overlook recurrent patterns, and they may even foster notions of discrete and incomparable international systems. In this case the analysis of change overbears the analysis of stability; international relations is seen in constant flux.

Systematic empirical analysis allows elements of dynamism while permitting adherence to a single mode of representation of the international system. Systemic categories are the same for different international systems, though their form and condition undergo alteration. Input, regulator, environment, and output are constant systemic constituents, but their variety may change enormously from system to system. And the constituents of input: direction, control, and resources may also go through a perceptible transformation. Systems analysis, in short, is capable of rendering elements of stability *and* change. All systems may be represented in terms of common categories, but system-change is nonetheless real. It is still possible to speak of a single overarching international system.

**Decision-making.** A probe into the organizational or decisional unit of the national actor is made by decision-making approaches. The general organizational setting, its relation to the organizational unit, the type of decision-maker, and the particular limitations of information, communications, precedent, perception, and scarce resources are all discussed under the decision-making rubric. The decision-maker is placed in a milieu of social forces.[38] The intra-actor determinants of policy making are considered in well-nigh exhaustive fashion. At the same time, the decision-making approach tends to incorporate empirical variety at the expense of generality. A painstaking investigation of individual foreign policy decisions may possibly illuminate the characteristics of a limited range of international behavior, but it can scarcely expect to provide the basis for a general theory of international politics. The

[38] See Richard C. Snyder, H. W. Bruck, and Burton Sapin, *Decision-Making as an Approach to the Study of International Politics* (Princeton, 1954).

sheer attention to the internal mechanisms of decision processes means (1) that the number of foreign policy decisions which can be considered in the framework of a given analysis is strictly limited, and (2) that the external factors shaping policy formation and results must in a degree be slighted.

The approach of systematic empirical analysis seeks to incorporate less empirical variety than that of decision-making, but aims at greater generalization of results. Decision-making processes are not neglected, but they constitute only one of the vectors making up the input into the international system. In particular, systematic empirical analysis considers the relationship of elite and mass and the ethos of actor elites as influenced by domestic determinants; it includes as well the interrelation and interaction of different national inputs; and it considers specifically the resource base upon which decision-making operates. In so doing, it stresses the multidimensional character of the international system.

**Environmental capacity.** All of the theoretical approaches mentioned above tend to minimize the role of *environmental capacity* as a factor in international relations. The ability of the *environment* to channel or mitigate international conflict tends to be affected by changes in national objectives and by their continued pursuit. Because of the availability of colonizable territory between 1880 and 1890, environmental capacity was great enough to accommodate imperialist movements, and because colonizable territory was rapidly being used up after 1890, the environment could no longer contain imperial motivations or restrain conflict. During the old regime environmental capacity was sufficient to hold within acceptable bounds the power ambitions of Europe's princes, limited as they were by convention and aristocratic internationalism. After the French Revolution, however, the international environment could not restrain the direct confrontation of revolutionary liberalism and entrenched conservatism. Environmental capacity simply was not great enough to permit full realization of ideological objectives by both revolutionaries and conservatives. After 1822, on the other hand, though the ideological competition was resumed, it was held within bounds. Territorial ambitions in North Africa and the Near East helped to distract national actors from an unmitigated ideological struggle, and that competition itself was restrained by the fear of war. Environmental limitations once again.

helped to hold disruptive forces in check. Environmental capacity is both an essential and a separate constituent of the international sys- tem. If it is not treated explicitly, it must be assumed.

**Summary.** Systematic empirical analysis of international politics, employing the notions of systems analysis, is capable of rendering the outcomes of the international system in a useful way. It strives to incorporate the essential insights of other approaches, while com- bining them in a novel fashion. It seeks particularly to steer be- tween the extreme of the logically comprehensive single factor on the one hand and detailed empirical dissection on the other. The categories employed force consideration of empirical components, but they do not become immersed in a sea of atomic events.

The analysis presented above seeks on the basis of multiple cate- gories to characterize the phases or states of the international sys- tem; or alternatively, it seeks to portray different international sys- tems. The categories or constituents of the system are empirically derived in that they have been chosen on the basis of an empirical- historical survey of various diplomatic periods. Another writer would no doubt have seen the components of the system in a differ- ent way. The present scheme classifies the phenomena of interna- tional relations in a logically exhaustive manner, but there are any number of logically exhaustive schemes. All usefulness of this scheme depends upon the range of events which it can illuminate.

# PART III
# dynamic
# analysis

## chapter twelve

# STABILITY AND INSTABILITY
# IN THE INTERNATIONAL SYSTEM

There is a dual problem involved in the attempt to depict the international system in terms of an intricate series of conceptual categories. On the one hand, the attempt to describe international reality in terms of a variety of categories is oversimple because national activities are so multifarious that they cannot effectively be summed up even by reference to a large number of central variables. On the other hand, an effort at depiction of international relations in terms of a multiplicity of categories is overcomplex. It is always possible to devise a theoretical scheme which can render the outcomes of world politics, but an intricate scheme often neglects levels of significance. Are all variables of equal importance in determining the outcome of the system? Is it possible to combine variables in such a way as to locate the really influential factors? Most important, perhaps, is it possible to overcome the disadvantage of multiplicity and hence complexity without succumbing to the single factor? Is there a way station between a sterile unity and a baffling diversity?

In this chapter an attempt will be made to find such a theoretical halfway house. Specifically, four major determinants of the international system will be elucidated. These determinants are logically exhaustive. They derive from the historical analysis of Part I and the systemic analysis of Part II, and they provide a clue to an understanding of stability and instability in the international system. The four determinants are *direction, control, resources,* and *capacity. Direction* represents the complex of elite objectives in national and international politics. It refers to elite ambitions in reforming or conserving national or foreign society, and it portrays elite attitudes toward the outcomes of the international system. *Control* relates to the factors which affect an elite's exercise of power. The nature of allegiance given to the regime by its subjects, the scope of decision-making open to the elite, the security of tenure which the elite enjoys, and the personality dispositions of the elite leadership together comprise the elite's *control* position. *Resources* refer to the base upon which control is exercised. Persuasive skills, the quantity of mobilizable resources, and speed of mobilization are the components of *resources*. *Capacity* is a generic term designating the total ability of the international system to contain disruption. It is composed of regulative and environmental forces. For immediate purposes, regulative influences may be viewed as those which seek directly to reduce the variety of disturbance or to prevent disruptive actions from being initiated. Environmental influences are those which seek to render disturbance innocuous. Without directly affecting disturbance, they tend to mitigate or control its impact.

## MAJOR DETERMINANTS

**Direction.**   Elite or directional ethos has had an important relation to international stability. The most violent forms of international conflict have usually been associated with wide divergences in elite ethos. The revolutionary and Napoleonic system and the inter-war system were perhaps the best examples of virulent ideological conflict. Yet, ideological divergence was neither the necessary nor the sufficient condition of instability. The system of *Realpolitik* and that of imperialist nationalism were not predicated on an ideological conflict at the international level. And, the ideological cleavages of the post-World War II system and of the system of the truncated Concert did not conduce to war and instability. Ideological harmony was not necessary for a modicum of stability internationally, but it did apparently facilitate it. The most stable systems of the nine considered in this study were the eighteenth-century system and the system of the functioning Concert, both of which rested upon a solidarity on behalf of conservative internationalism. Direction, therefore, seems to have its greatest impact in the extreme cases: extreme instability is correlated with ideological conflict; extreme stability is associated with ideological concord.

**Control.** The influence of *control* patterns upon the course of international relations has been decisive. It is significant that each of the four disequilibrial systems of international relations were either immediately preceded or accompanied by fundamental changes in the security of tenure of the national elite. The shift from the system of the *ancien régime* to that of the revolutionary generation was correlated with changes in the nature of allegiance and tenure. In France for perhaps the first time, the mass of people became available to large-scale influence and mobilization. The limitations of traditional society which had held masses unavailable and elites inaccessible were breached.[1] No longer could mass and elite be kept in separate compartments, each incapable of affecting the other. The temporary development of a "mass society" in which elite and non-elite became simultaneously vulnerable to influence placed the French monarchy in danger. As it turned out, the old regime could neither effectively control the masses, nor protect itself from their incursions. In the end, a mass revolutionary upheaval over-threw the monarchy and instated a new regime. But the revolutionaries were also vulnerable to mass movements among the populace, and they did not enjoy the legitimacy of their predecessors. They fought a bitter and sometimes losing struggle to maintain their position, striving to avoid dictation by Paris mobs or provincial surrender to rebellion while maintaining a semblance of control over mobilized masses. It was in the fire of internal desperation that external policies were initially forged. External war became the means to internal consolidation. It was the elite's attempt to avoid the instability of mass society which first projected the revolutionaries into a European conflict which transgressed the limitations of the eighteenth-century international system.

After 1848 it was again the threatened emergence of mass society which challenged international stability. The revolutions of 1848 had proved that elites were once again accessible to popular influence and that they might not be able to wield decisive controls over available masses. Not only were existing elite cadres in danger of being replaced, the very structure of regimes was in jeopardy. It was

[1] See William Kornhauser, *The Politics of Mass Society* (Glencoe, 1959), Chapter Two.

this atmosphere of internal instability and uncertainty which gave rise to the age of *Realpolitik*. Unlike the limited autocrats of the eighteenth century, however, the traditional classes of 1848 were able to take action before the chronic instability of mass society provoked a new and irresistible wave of revolution. Without losing their political grip, elites indulged in foreign war, intrigue and national consolidation and thus reinsured their position. The lesson of the French Revolution had now at least been partially learned, and mass society had become a signal for drastic action. But the new age of "blood and iron" which was ushered in was not one of international tranquillity. Instability and war once again characterized the international system.

After 1890 the domestic synthesis which had permitted conservative rule of Central and East European states in an era of general political and economic reform began to come unstuck. Conservative nationalism would not be enough to placate the rising classes or to induce them to accept continued conservative government. By the last decade of the century only a policy of foreign imperialistic expansion would satisfy the discontented factions.[2] External potency of the nation would partly compensate for internal impotence of the classes. The imperialist-nationalist conflict of the period after 1890 finally resulted in World War I. The danger of mass society had been averted, but again only at the price of international instability and conflict.

World War I was not conducive either to domestic or international stability. Instead, the sinews of domestic strength were severed and class alignments revised or overturned. The brief period of international pacification following the First World War was purchased only at an extreme internal cost. The "mass society" which ensued under the Weimar Republic made the democratic regime vulnerable to totalitarian movements. Like the French aristocrats, the Weimar democrats were unable to keep the fragmented masses from heeding apocalyptic appeals. The Republic fell because it could not fashion a political strategy to neutralize mass movements.[3] Unlike the European conservatives of the previous

---

[2] It was particularly effective in satisfying the industrial middle classes. See G. W. F. Hallgarten, *Imperialismus Vor 1914* (Munich, 1951), Vol. 1, p. 198.

[3] See Kornhauser, *op cit.*, Chapter Five and S. M. Lipset, *Political Man* (London, 1960), Chapters Four and Five.

century, the Weimar republicans were not able to turn mass society to their own purposes.

The rise of National Socialism in Germany harked back in certain respects to the triumph of the French revolutionaries. The problem of the French insurgents was to contain and channel the revolution and to remain in power. The Nazis faced a similar problem of creating domestic order out of what had been endemic instability. In embarking upon foreign war the Nazis embraced the solution of the Girondins. The entire course of the nineteenth century seemed to demonstrate that victory abroad was a means of dealing with dissatisfaction at home. But what the Nazis failed to realize was that the arts of control had vastly increased over the same period. Expedients obligatory to nineteenth-century conservatives were optional for the National Socialists. National expansion was a crude means of obtaining an internal security of tenure which might better be obtained by propaganda manipulation. And yet the entire Nazi myth-system was founded on the belief in foreign conquest. An ideology created in the Weimar mass society naturally overplayed the problem of security for the regime. In turn, it gave rise to independent problems of fulfillment. An ideology of rabid, expansionist nationalism, a creed of successive victories imposes its own regimen. Even successful propaganda provokes action. In the end the Nazis fell prisoner to their own dialectics.

But the importance of control as a major determinant of international politics is not confined to unstable systems. International stability has been profoundly influenced by control patterns. A signal characteristic of international relations under the old regime was the security of tenure enjoyed by traditional elites. Unlike the mass society which ensued, the "communal society" [4] of the eighteenth century made elites inaccessible to popular influence and masses unavailable to mobilization by elite or revolutionary movement. The compartmentalization of elite and mass prevented encroachment in either direction. The relatively moderate relationships among European sovereigns and the general cosmopolitanism of the age were due in no small part to the security of individual regimes. Extreme or unlimited measures were not required to safeguard the helm of state.

After the rampages of the revolutionary period, a tolerable se-

[4] See Kornhauser, *op cit.*, p. 40.

curity of tenure returned. Conservative elites, threatened or deposed during the revolutionary and Napoleonic wars, managed to regain their positions, and legitimacy became a temporary credo for the international system. After the ravages of war, masses were eager for stability and willing to accept their previous rulers in order to gain it. And the revolutions which plagued the legitimist order were as much militarist as popularist in inspiration. For a short period at least security of tenure for conservative elites was restored, and with it came a new international stability.

The truncated Concert after 1822, though it saw the resumption of the ideological competition, did not witness a fundamental breakdown of domestic control. In the liberal nations, public demands forced a more progressive and interventionist demeanor in foreign policy, and the conservatives had to take more active measures in response. At the same time, neither conservatives nor liberals were forced by the insecurity of their internal positions to adopt extremist or bellicose attitudes in external affairs. Strangely enough, the Concert of Europe continued to function and a modest rapport among the Powers continued until the revolutions of 1848. The relative security of regimes on both sides conduced to international limitations on action.

The re-establishment of a secure position for elites also had much to do with the termination of *Realpolitik* in the international system. When the spectre of mass society arose in the revolutions of 1848, drastic action had to be taken to exorcize it. But by 1871 conservatives had succeeded in manipulating nationalist symbols in such a way as to protect their power position, and after 1871, even the ideological issue departed the scene. An ideological crusade was no longer the required means of maintaining domestic stability — in fact, stability might even be jeopardized by such a crusade. Once regimes reinsured themselves, the need for desperate action in international relations disappeared, and a refurbished Concert could function once again. For a time at least, even conservative dynasts could find a haven in an intricate network of complementary alliances.

The transition to the tenuous stability of the post-World War II generation also was marked by important changes in the pattern of control. The dislocations of war cut in two directions. In certain states the fear of war and the longing for stability contributed to security of tenure; in others the war provided an opportunity for nationalist revolution. After a period of initial uncertainty most Western democratic states attained basic internal strength; the Soviet dictatorships won internal security through totalitarian control. It was mainly in the uncommitted world that security of tenure could not be guaranteed. Not coincidentally, it was also in this realm that external stability was not assured. In particular, the Soviets seemed to have learned that totalitarian controls over the populace could be more effective than external war in gaining full national allegiance. Military expansion was not the *sine qua non* of domestic security for the regime.

More generally speaking, it seems proper to conclude that signal changes in the international system have been accompanied by changes in the security of tenure of national elites. Destabilizing systems have been introduced concurrent with mass societal tendencies; a greater international stability has been gained coincident with a greater internal stability of ruling elites. Fluctuations in the internal position of elites, then, may often be correlated with decisive changes in the international system. Security of tenure may have profound international implications.

**Resources.** Changes in *resource* patterns have also occurred in conjunction with important shifts in the international system. The very existence of a large pool of mobilizable resources has often proved a well-nigh irresistible temptation to action. Napoleon unquestionably was not blind to the impact of the powerful French army; that formidable force made the decision for battle easier to make. In his own time Hitler's decision for expansion and war was facilitated by the power of the *Wehrmacht*. Even Bismarck could risk national expansion in Germany because of the strength of the Prussian army. Periods of instability in the international system have often been linked with periods of military preponderance of one or more states. Except in the Hitlerian case, aggrandizement and the attendant international instability was risked only when there seemed to be a clear disparity between national forces and those of the enemy.[5] And in the case of Nazi Germany, Hitler's

---

[5] Professor Robert C. North maintains that the German and Japanese empires were also exceptions. In general he believes that the proposition: "A state will not go to war if it perceives its power as 'significantly' smaller than that of the enemy at the time that such a decision has to be made" is false. See Robert C.

propaganda skills in the international orbit seemed partly to compensate for the lack of a preponderant military position. Power was not irrelevant to purpose.

Resource patterns have also influenced the acceptability of war. As long as warfare was confined to the learned stratagem of siege and maneuver, military campaigns were politically tolerable and not infrequent. When war began to involve populations and the entire economic resources of a nation, however, it was not to be risked on mere affront. After the revolutionary wars ended, a general conviction against war temporarily held sway. Neither the conservatives nor the liberal Powers would risk becoming embroiled in a war of peoples which might unsettle all regimes. It was only when overriding considerations in favor of war appeared at mid-century, that this conviction was discarded. And even then, the type of warmaking which took the stage was quite unlike the revolutionary struggles of an earlier period. The Austro-Prussian and Franco-Prussian Wars provided decisive victory in a brief time. They did not carry the lesson that war itself is disastrous. But the contrary lesson was too well learned. World War I could be initiated in part because it was believed that it would be decided in a few short months. One of the adversaries would seize the offensive and carry the war to a successful conclusion by supremacy of the plan or supremacy of the will. Pre-existing resource patterns, as they were understood, were not an effective deterrent to the Great War of 1914.

The appreciation of the conditions of war, however, was not a universal determinant. Despite the horror of World War I, there did not emerge a general consensus that war could not be allowed to occur again. Hitler was prepared to wage aggressive war, even if it meant a repetition of the sacrifices of the First World War. He hoped (vainly), however, that it would involve nothing of the sort. Resource patterns as evinced in military conflict were important considerations in the decision for future war, but they were not always all-determining. Destabilizing actions were sometimes taken, even when the foreseeable result was general disaster.[6] The sheer violence of past war has not, in and of itself, prevented future con-

North, "Report to the Ford Foundation from the Studies in International Conflict and Integration" (Stanford, August 31, 1961), pp. 3-5.
[6] See *ibid.*, pp. 3-4.

flict. Such a conclusion must give pause in the thermonuclear age.

Speed of mobilization of resources has had more than a negligible impact upon the stability of the international system. The wars of the third quarter of the nineteenth century did not deprive political leaders of the initiative or preclude diplomatic settlement of outstanding issues. Even in 1914 the need for early mobilization in a decisive crisis did not provoke a usurpation of diplomatic functions by the military. By and large political questions were still fundamental and military questions derivative. The development of hypersonic delivery systems and thermonuclear bombs, however, has raised the possibility of the "autonomy of weapons." Certain types of weapons-postures may be provocative, independent of political intent, and if this is true, weapons may accelerate political conflict.[7] If history affords any guide on this score, it may suggest that increases in the speed of mobilization have also tended to foreshorten the process of political decision-making, and this could mean that wars may begin before political solutions of the points at issue can be fully explored.[8] Such deductions do not hold optimistic portents for the nuclear epoch.

An analysis of resource patterns of the past tends also to indicate that a not inconsiderable stability has been conferred upon the international system by the clear distinction between Great and Minor Powers. Five Great Powers monopolized the major instruments of violence during most of the eighteenth and nineteenth centuries. Small states could not expect, through exercise of their own armed forces, to interrupt understandings among the great nations where there was no other reason for Great Power discord. In more contemporary terms, the small nations of the past could not precipitate "catalytic war"; they could not portend the danger of anonymous attack. Bipolarity, or an approximation thereof, was often achieved in past international systems, but a wholesale diffusion of Great

---

7 See Thomas C. Schelling, "Reciprocal Measures for Arms Stabilization" in Donald G. Brennan (ed.), *Arms Control, Disarmament and National Security* (New York, 1961), p. 170. Dr. Samuel P. Huntington questions this proposition. See S. P. Huntington, "Political Imperatives and Arms Control," Arrowhead Conference of the National Security Studies Program, University of California (Los Angeles), June 4-6, 1961, p. 7.

8 Whether this eventuates or not will depend on the major nuclear Powers creating truly steady and *stable* deterrents with an approximation to invulnerability.

Power military strength did not take place. There was a limit to the multipolarity of past eras.

Great or World Power monopoly of large-scale violence, existent in the past, is uncertain in the future. Undoubtedly the concern over the dissemination of nuclear weapons among a large number of states in the next generation has been overdone. The "Nth Country Problem" may not turn out to be a major "problem." It is even possible that nuclear diffusion will strengthen bipolarity, new nuclear states being forced into connection with established nuclear Powers in order to maintain and improve their atomic and delivery capability. Present studies indicate that it is more difficult to become an "Nth Country" than it was once believed.[9] At the same time the sheer proliferation of weapons may eventually make possible "anonymous delivery" for certain states either through an extension of Polaris-type capability or through the rather horrendous device of orbital hydrogen bombs. The multiplication of control centers for nuclear missiles may confront the world with a greater problem of co-ordination and enhance the risks of war. It is certainly possible that important controls of weaponry may pass out of the hands of the great nations.

In summary, resource patterns have been influential if not decisive determinants of the international systems. The quantity of mobilizable resources has often had an important role in influencing stabilizing or destabilizing national decisions. The speed of mobilization has increasingly curtailed the time available for political decision-making, and thus has tended to make real political crises harder to overcome. At the same time previous resource patterns, as expressed in war, have had some influence in defining the political acceptability of future war. Especially disastrous wars have often contributed to a conviction against future war, though this has not always been the case. The international cartel of the major Powers on the means of wholesale violence probably restrained conflict in past periods. The ending of that monopoly and the emergence of many "freely competitive" suppliers of weapons of mass destruction is a possible destabilizing feature of the future international environment.

**Capacity.**  With direction, control, and resources, *capacity* patterns

---

[9] The book by Leonard Beaton and John Maddox on *The Spread of Nuclear Weapons* (New York, 1962) underscores this point.

have represented important variables of international relations. How well the international system can control disruptive influence is determined by its capacity. Capacity tends to shift from system to system because disruptive inputs, controlled in one epoch, will not be controlled in another. The kind of regulator devised by national actors in one era will be quite different from that employed in another. The ability of the environment to provide sufficient variety to accommodate diverse claims upon it will vary from time to time. If, at any given period, the demand by national actors for environmental resources such as territorial real estate or political dependencies can be amply fulfilled, conflict among actors can be postponed. If, on the other hand, there is not enough of the environmental resource to go around, and the resources of a constant sum international game are already fully apportioned, the pursuit of further gain will entail conflict among actors.

An investigation of past systems of international relations tends to underline the significance of capacity factors. In the period of the old regime, both regulative and environmental variety helped to contain antagonism within narrow limits. The balance of power mechanism adjudicated differences among states in a rough and ready manner. Perhaps more important, the claims upon the international environment were moderate enough, owing to the archaic social system, that environmental capacity could provide due "compensation" for all major actors. When ambitions were modest, general fulfillment was not out of the question. A limited harmony of interest could function in certain respects. With the growth of revolutionary ferment, however, and with the demand by certain national actors for a wholesale revision of international outcomes, neither the regulator nor the environment could confine policies within stable bounds. The regulator proved incapable of restraining French expansionism, and the environment could not admit the designs of the French while still accommodating the interests of the several coalitions. International conflict and instability was the result.

With the creation of the international Concert after the Napoleonic Wars, both regulative and environmental factors attained a new influence. The Concert, acting through the military force of its members, managed to hold, for a period of time at least, the policies of actors within narrow bounds. And the legitimist aspirations of the conservative victors were easily gained *ensemble*. It was not until England began to modify her solidarity with the conservative allies, that the objectives of major Powers could not all be realized simultaneously. Nonintervention was simply inconsistent with the Protocol of Troppau, and environmental factors were incapable of providing for both at the same time.

The system of the truncated Concert was ushered in by a decline in regulative capacity. The international mechanism was no longer capable of regulating inputs directly at the point of origin. Ideological dissension resumed, and the Concert could no longer maintain conservative dikes against the liberal flood. At the same time the international regulator helped to prevent full-scale war, though it could no longer rule out ideological dispute. The deflection of antagonisms into a pursuit of territory and influence in the Near East and North Africa, however, served to hold international outcomes within acceptable limits. Environmental capacity was sufficient to prevent military conflict over the imperial spoils where it could not have confined an unlimited ideological struggle.

The period of *Realpolitik* made impossible demands upon capacity restraints. The international regulator virtually vanished from the scene, and the desperate conflict of conservatives and certain liberals to win domestic legitimacy through nationalist expansion, made for a practical disharmony of interest in notable instances. Prussia and Austria could not both pose as the champions of the national Germany; the triumph of one meant the temporary discrediting of the other. France could not pursue the course of national grandeur without treading on European toes. Since national supremacy could not be attained by all actors simultaneously, environmental constraints failed to prevent international conflict.

The Bismarckian Concert witnessed an interesting conjunction of regulative and environmental forces. The manipulation of national symbols gave the conservatives a new lease on life and permitted a reformulated Concert; a new regulator functioned. But internal legitimacy could not be obtained forever by internal nationalist expedients. Toward the end of the Bismarckian system, the conservatives' position became more desperate and could be secured only by more desperate measures. National imperialism was the device to win new acquiescence to conservative rule.[10] To a degree, it served initially to moderate intra-European quarrels. The French desire for *revanche* could be distracted by spoils overseas. But if imperial territory had been limited or fully appropriated, imperialism would have led directly to international conflict. Thus it was the availability of colonizable real estate, the adequacy of environmental capacity, which tended to submerge hostility.

After 1890 the Bismarckian synthesis no longer worked. The international concert continued a rather desultory functioning, but environmental variety no longer restrained conflict. The dividing up of imperializable territory forced European states into collision with one another willy-nilly, and overseas expansion turned out to be equally as dangerous as expansion in Europe itself. The modest successes of the Concert, as in the Balkan crisis of 1912-1913,[11] were overshadowed by the overriding limitation of the coveted object of gain — territory.

The Hitlerian period represented the nadir of both regulative and environmental restraints. The international Concert, now in the guise of the League of Nations, was powerless to prevent the aggressions of the nineteen thirties; the Powers could not be directly restrained from pursuing their chosen objectives. At the same time, environmental capacity was utterly unable to discharge national ambitions harmlessly. The goals of the German dictator were directly (if not always obviously) antithetical to those of Western statesmen. Objectives could not be reconciled; they could only (through the policy of appeasement) be abandoned. Ultimately conflict could not be prevented.

The post-World War II world witnessed a different situation. The United Nations did not serve as an effective prophylactic against war; the danger of thermonuclear war itself together with the existence of opposed nuclear Powers helped to preclude deliberate war. At the same time the U.N. mobilized for a time the sentiment of third bloc countries and made them a more effective influence in world politics. Insofar as Soviet or Western policy was

---

[10] See C. J. H. Hayes, *A Generation of Materialism, 1871-1900* (New York, 1941), p. 220.

[11] See Luigi Albertini, *The Origins of the War of 1914* (London, 1952), Vol. 1, Chapters Seven and Eight.

devoted to conciliating the uncommitted group, the United Nations allowed the neutralist-nationalist nations a considerable control on Great Power decision-making. Even the great states initially shaped their policies in some measure to suit the uncommitted constituency in the United Nations. Simultaneously, environmental capacity increased in at least some areas. When the two major blocs directly confronted each other, there was little room for maneuver and little hope that the direct pursuit of aggrandizement would not lead to a clash. It followed that Europe was the most dangerous arena of policy collision. When the two blocs competed for influence in the uncommitted regions, however, neutralist policy could demonstrate a considerable environmental variety. Colonizable territory would not be allowed to run out. And this was not because of unlimited supply, but because neutralists would not pledge themselves irrevocably to one side or the other. Great Power blandishments did not succeed in diminishing the pool of coveted political prizes.

Capacity factors have played a considerable role in the international system. At certain periods, regulative forces have exerted a direct and limiting impact upon national policy formation, preventing disruptive actions. Environmental restraints have also been influential in more than a few situations. The most drastic confinement of international outcomes has occurred when both regulative and environmental restraints have operated vigorously. Regulation has sometimes succeeded in reducing national options while environment has made ample provision for different national objectives to be realized harmoniously. During the eighteenth century modest regulative controls sufficed while the environment exerted a profoundly limiting influence. If, after 1822, the international regulator had allowed the full ideological struggle to be resumed, environmental capacity could hardly have accommodated it and averted conflict. In some instances, the regulator has failed to check national ambitions, but overt antagonism has been avoided through adequacy of environmental limitations. The Bismarckian Concert could not prevent the imperialist drive from burgeoning in the eighteen-eighties, but the sheer availability of overseas territory rendered its consequences innocuous. The worst of all worlds appeared when neither regulative nor environmental restraints functioned. The League regulator could not prevent the collision of objectives; the environment could not render them harmless. When international capacity is not sufficient, instability can rarely be avoided.

## DIAGNOSIS OF THE INTERNATIONAL SYSTEM

The four major determinants of the international system — direction, control, resources, and capacity — may be used to ascertain the state of that system at any given time. A diagnosis and perhaps even a prognosis of the international system is not impossible. Directional factors seem to have some influence in producing stable and unstable systems. Utter ideological hostility tends to be correlated with instability, and ideological harmony with stability. Even virulent ideological hostilities, however, will not necessarily mean an unstable system, since much depends upon the resource base on which the ideological struggle is waged. New nationalist movements have often displayed unlimited antagonism toward metropolitan Powers, but this has not necessarily led to international instability. Nationalist-colonialist frictions have sometimes been held in check by other great Powers. The Soviet revolutionaries expressed unlimited antagonism to capitalist states, but they were not able to unseat the capitalist international system. Ideologues have not always been able to disrupt an overarching stability. The French revolutionaries, conversely, operated from a powerful resource base, and their ideological conflict with the conservatives could not be contained within accepted limits.

Ideologic harmonies, on the other hand, have facilitated agreement among states irrespective of resource positions. Ideological accord facilitated consensus and stability in the eighteenth century and during the period of the functioning international Concert. When that consensus was disrupted, the international system suffered, though it did not in all cases break down in disastrous war. Nor are catastrophic wars apparently ruled out in the absence of ideological conflict. Neither the system of *Realpolitik* nor that of imperialist nationalism was determined by ideological questions, and yet decisive military conflicts emerged within them.

Control patterns seem to be the most reliable and perhaps also the most fundamental indicators of potential international instability. This is most assuredly not to say that there is a one-to-one correspondence between internal and international instability. Problems of internal instability may be dealt with in other ways than by projecting internal uncertainties into the international orbit. The penalties visited upon expansionism in the external world may be such that no elite would risk their imposition, regardless of internal crisis.[12] In certain cases undoubtedly, like that of imperial Russia in 1914, external war is more likely to undermine than to support the position of a native elite. At the same time, an internal system on the verge of chaos is a lodestone for international conflict. If national elites do not seek war as a means of reinsuring their position, foreign elites may be incited to fill a tempting power vacuum. The initial allied response to the French Revolution had elements of this attitude. Chronic arenas of discontent or "mass society," then, are potential trouble spots. There may be other reasons for commencement of hostilities, but internal instability seems to be closely connected with the major destabilizing military transformations of modern times.

Internal chaos, or its threat, however, is not a sufficient cause for the onset of a new international system. The inauguration of war may have only a minor impact on the system if there is an inadequate resource base to sustain it. The period of War Communism was not a turning point in the history of international relations because Soviet resources were very weak. Despite Trotsky, the revolution could not be exported by military means. The Russians could not emulate the French example. Thus, much seems to depend upon the relative resource position *vis à vis* other national actors. But the relative ranking of resources will not be the only factor influencing external stability. Of considerable importance also is the absolute level of the resource base. Even a lesser nuclear Power could cause considerable disruption in the international system; even a first-rank nuclear Power might hesitate to act against a third-rank nuclear state. The absolute level of resource potential is significant even where the disparity among power bases is great. The contemplation of past resource potentials, as demonstrated in war, may also be of some importance. The "folklore" of war, general views of warfare's acceptability or disastrousness, will influence possible disruptors of the international system. If warfare is deemed

---

[12] Professor North's findings cited above seem to indicate that the "perception of injury" is more important than the sanctions upon expansion.

congenial, it will be likely to occur, as was the case in the eighteenth century and at the time of World War I.[13] If it is deemed catastrophic, inhibitions relative to starting it will be greater. Folkway beliefs may have a role, moreover, entirely aside from contemporary and supposedly "objective" military assessments of the situation.

Where there is a conjunction between internal instability and resource potency, however, destabilizing outcomes may still not occur. Much will depend upon the ability of regulative forces to prevent hostile action and upon environmental ones to neutralize them if they take place. A powerful regulator possessing a wide range of possible moves may actually be able to change national policy before it is fully formed. Metternich managed to dissuade Tsar Alexander from aiding the Greek revolutionists before the latter could come to a clear view of the problem. And after national policy is once made, it may sometimes be unmade by regulative pressures. In the Suez adventure Britain and France were probably not fully aware before the fact of the outcry their actions would provoke among their own allies and in the United Nations. Disruptors cannot hope to have anticipated all regulative moves in advance. No matter how careful the calculations of national actors concerning the opposition or antagonism their policies will generate, they cannot actually play the regulative pieces. Suez is a prime example of unintended consequences and limited national vision. A powerful regulator may sometimes alter actor policy that otherwise would lead to international instability.

When regulative forces fail to change disruptive national policy, however, environmental capacity affords another check. A single-minded pursuit of ideological goals does not lead to conflict if goals are common. International relations during the first half of the nineteenth century would have been far different if liberal sentiments had been universal. The quest for colonies might have led to war in the eighteen-eighties if overseas territory had already been fully divided. In the first instance environmental variety was not sufficient to adjust to the new ideological currents; in the second it was great enough temporarily to accommodate the imperial urge.

[13] See Hajo Holborn, "Moltke and Schlieffen: The Prussian-German School," in Edward Mead Earle (ed.), *Makers of Modern Strategy* (Princeton, 1948), pp. 187-188.

A full range of environmental options, then, may bar certain un-
desirable outcomes even when there are no other controls against
them.

Though it is impossible to give a full account of the precondi-
tions of conflict and hostility in general, it seems at least possible to
say that the following factors operate in favor of deliberate actions
against the international system: (1) virulent ideological conflict;
(2) chronic internal instability verging on mass society;[14] (3) adequate relative resource base together with an absolute resource base
which does not involve general, catastrophic risks; (4) regulative
activity inadequate to cope with the planned disturbance; and (5)
environmental capacity insufficient to neutralize the clash of major
inputs.

These are surely not the only causes of international crisis, and
they may not be the only salient ones. They do suggest situations
in which decisions for deliberate disruption of the system might
be taken. Unintended disruption of the system might occur: (1)
where the real consequences of war are not fully apprehended; (2)
where there is no big Power monopoly of the instruments of organized social violence; and (3) where military mobilization and
decision pre-empt the role of political bargaining. In the first
instance minor disequilibrial actions turn out to be major and eighteenth-century wars transform themselves into wars of total involvement. In the second case the diffusion of weapons of mass destruction creates a greater "statistical" probability of major war[15] though
individual parties are no more disposed to commence a nuclear
holocaust. In the third instance, the technology of weaponry acceler-
ates or rigidifies the process of political decision. War is inflicted
as a result of the exigencies of military planning.

## PROSPECTS AND PROGNOSIS

*Directional* factors are not likely to have a benign impact upon
future international systems. Ideological frictions may not be pursued to the nub, but there is little indication that ideological differences will be composed. With the full entrance of Communist

---

[14] If society is in complete chaos, no organized action can be undertaken.
[15] See Fred Iklé, "Nth Countries and Disarmament," *Bulletin of the Atomic
Scientists*, Vol. 16 (1960), pp. 391-394.

China into general international relations, the ideological tone of diplomacy will probably rise. The full development of nationalism in Africa and Asia will probably also heighten the ideological conflict, not mitigate it. It was not accidental that the history of European relations during the nineteenth century was interlinked with the ideological issue. For the first half of the century system-change was denoted by changes in the dispute between liberals and conservatives. Essentially ideological questions were governing. The future may well see a similar phenomenon. Ideological frictions are not the sufficient cause of instability, but they are also not the prelude to international order.

*Control* factors have infrequently been considered to be decisive factors in shaping international outcomes, and when they are considered in this light, uncertain results follow. Classical analyses of international relations, emphasizing the external determinants of national policy, have partly oversimplified the problems of regulating internal relationships. The "balance of power" and other theories, by stressing the implications for one state or group of states of changes in the international position of an opposing group, have tended to suggest that problems of instability could be treated wholly on the international level. Shifts in the "balance of power" would presumably call forth compensating changes in the alliance structure or military preparedness of other states, and the system would attain a new equilibrium. Increasingly, however, it is being recognized that the "balance of power" theory does not give an account of initial disturbance in the international system; instead it helps to explain the reaction of international actors to disturbance. *Control* patterns, conversely, facilitate understanding of initial disturbance.

When these patterns are explicitly considered, the problems of international stability are seen to be complex. Domestic intervention for international purposes is difficult to accomplish; it may easily redound to nationalist objectives and against internationalist ones. The nineteenth century is, in this context, scarcely a propitious example of successful regulation of internal affairs. For the first half of the century, international connections were in large part determined by the issue of domestic reform or revolution; for the second half of the century they depended upon the imperious force of nationalist expansion. In neither period were internal factors generally subject to international regulation. An exception to this rule is provided by the functioning Concert of 1814-1822. Internal politics were temporarily governed according to legitimist principles, but the resumption of movements for reform after 1822 defeated further efforts at internal regulation. Changes in the patterns of *control* in the nineteenth and early twentieth centuries were associated with changes in the stability of the international system. Internal tendencies in the direction of "mass society" were correlated with instability; tendencies in the opposite direction facilitated, though they did not naturally produce, stability.

The problem for the future in this context, then, is the avoidance of destabilizing control patterns in the internal sphere. If the future is to avoid the instabilities of the past, it must somehow escape or neutralize the dialectic of internal revolution and repression which characterized nineteenth century European politics. It must in some way o'erleap or defuse the explosive issues of revolution and reform on the one hand and national consolidation and expansion on the other. It must, in other words, learn to deal with convulsive internal change.

Merely to state the requirements of a stability in these terms, however, is to observe how far they are from realization. If the nineteenth century was not the placid and halcyon era depicted in the textbooks, if the spurs of international conflict were domestic upheaval and transformation in years past — how much more likely does chronic international instability and war seem today. In the nineteenth and early twentieth centuries Europe and North America were in the throes of the reformist energies unleashed by the French Revolution; in the third quarter of the twentieth century Asia, Africa, the Middle East, and Latin America are undergoing an equally dynamic metamorphosis. The instabilities of nineteenth-century Europe seem about to be replicated in other continents.

The tragedy of such a re-enactment lies in the preoccupation of revolutionary regimes with internal control and security. While World War II provoked a new attention to international stability in certain actors, it did not do so in all. In the politically emergent areas, the war enabled nationalists to concentrate upon internal and domestic problems as they had never done before. A society in the agonies of domestic transformation is not likely to regard international determinants as decisive. Revolution rests upon the mobilization of groups of people on behalf of political action. If the mobilization proceeds too rapidly, groups of variant political beliefs are mobilized and the revolution creates its own opposition; if the mobilization proceeds too slowly, support is lacking against the old regime. It is a very fine line which revolutionaries have to toe, and intrinsically their position is an uncertain one. In such circumstances, revolutionary regimes cannot usually afford independent preoccupation with external conditions. Most often, external policies are merely instrumental to internal purposes and rarely are internal programs fashioned in response to the international environment. Only after a measure of internal stability is attained can international influences be expected to work. In the nineteenth century regulative mechanisms could be heeded when the regime was no longer in jeopardy. The Russian Communists could afford to weigh the need for international stability only when the internal regime was well entrenched.

In this sense the emergent nationalist regions of the world present the greatest problem. If international stability is to be achieved, it will have to be given first priority by the nations of the world at some juncture. Yet, the emergent nationalists are neither fully apprehensive of the dangers of Armageddon, nor are they secure enough to attend to them in the immediate future. The establishment of a modicum of domestic stability will be necessary before "emergent" nationalists can be irrevocably transformed into "mature" nationalists. If the nineteenth century holds a lesson on this score, it is that the process of transformation is likely to be accompanied by international conflict.

There is, however, one redeeming feature of anticipated control patterns. Technological developments of the past century have probably added more to the skills and surefootedness of elites than to the agility and flexibility of the masses. Elites now seem to have an advantage over potential mass movements in terms of the mobilization and control of the unorganized populace. This does not mean there will be no more Weimar Republics, although it may mean that they will be a less frequent occurrence. Control of communications is now a more official process; potential mass movements have difficulty utilizing communications media. Indigenous national leaders have resources at their command which were not available a century ago. At the same time, social disparity is probably greater in the underdeveloped societies today than in the developing nation-states of a hundred years ago. In the underdeveloped societies the *ancien régime* in social terms persists into the present, and national revolutions are sometimes inordinately dependent upon preserving the fundaments of an archaic social system. Nationalist leaders, then, are enormously handicapped in domestic politics. They cannot mobilize the peasantry, satisfy its desires, and rely on it as a conservative force. To mobilize it for reform is to sacrifice support by the traditional elements; to fail to mobilize it is to risk mobilization by some anti-regime mass movement. The techniques of control are greater today, but the problems of control are also greater.

*Resource* patterns of the future are not likely to restrain international conflict. It is true, to be sure, that the absolute levels of violence have increased with the dawning of the thermonuclear age. Thus, the risks which are engendered in unlimited conflict are clearly much larger than those of a century ago. But the now catastrophic risks of conflict are partly offset by the "statistically" greater chances of conflict, owing to the diffusion of nuclear weapons. The most recent international system managed *inter alia* to avoid the dissemination of the instruments of violence into many hands; the major Powers maintained an oligopoly of nuclear weapons. If there is a radical breakthrough in fusion technology in the future, however, it may even be possible to speak of "cheap" or "free" neutrons. If such developments occur, legitimate governments may have much greater access and semi-official or unofficial groups considerable access to nuclear bombs.[16] Major Powers, in such an eventuality, would certainly increase both the number and capacity of communications links among them so as to forestall conflict by miscalculation or misapprehension. At the same time, mischief-

---

[16] Herman Kahn writes: "Free neutrons would mean that many kinds of nuclear fuels would be very cheap. With these nuclear fuels and with the kind of technology that is likely to be available in 1969, it may literally turn out that a trained and technically minded person, even one who is a member of a relatively primitive society, would be able to make or obtain bombs. This would raise forcefully the question of the illegal or uncontrolled dissemination of bombs. (One can today buy machine guns, artillery, tanks, and fighter aircraft on the gray market.) Thus the 1969 equivalent of the Malayan guerillas or the Algerian rebels or the Puerto Rican nationalists, or even less official groups such as gangsters and wealthy dilettantes, might be able to obtain such bombs." "The Arms Race and Its Hazards," in Brennan, *op. cit.*, p. 118.

making by either great or small states, acting separately or in conjunction, will grow enormously. Nuclear wars among lesser nations, anonymous nuclear attacks — all these will hold the possibility of involving the Great Powers.

Nuclear capacity widely disseminated, moreover, may partly bridge the gap between great and lesser states. The smaller nations of the past have hesitated to propel themselves into war with the major Powers because of the overwhelming military superiority of the latter. The number of states which had to be taken into account in the making of a given diplomatic decision was not large in previous epochs. Smaller nations could be treated as dependent variables, bending to the will of the Great Powers. The diffusion of nuclear weapons may possibly further and perpetuate this pattern; it may also increase the number of independent national variables.

The Nth Country Problem gives rise to other complexities. As nuclear information and delivery systems are made more generally available, some highly dissatisfied states will eventually acquire them. In the past Great Power status was conferred on nations with great resources, adaptable technology, and a certain diplomatic *savoir-faire*. Accomplishment was the precondition for recognition as a major Power. A nation could not master the military arts without first having made substantial achievements in science, economy, and political culture. In other words, Great Powers of the past had made important gains, and could look on the national and international scenes with no little satisfaction. It did not follow from this that Great Powers would be "satisfied" Powers; disruption was as much the rule as the exception. But with certain notable exceptions Great Powers were usually ready to limit their objectives. The Nth Country phenomenon, however, may permit the transmission of weapons to wholly dissatisfied nations. Reckless or radical groups, bent on a wholesale adjustment of the national or international *status quo* may have access to weapons and means of delivery. In the Nth Country instance, Great Power status is not conferred through a heritage of past achievement, it is obtained temporarily by gift, grant, or purchase from "freely competitive" suppliers.

Fear of the consequences of war has been a deterrent to its initiation in the past. After the near-disastrous Napoleonic Wars, nations and statesmen were temporarily moved to exorcize military devils in the creation of the Concert of Europe. Before long, however, the recollection of war dimmed, and the effort expended to prevent recurrence dwindled. The "objective" impact of war changed not a whit, but the appreciation of its consequences diminished. After World War II and the dropping of the atomic bomb, the dangers of war were for a time held uppermost in the minds of statesmen and peoples. The publicly acknowledged development of even more virulent means of destruction contributed to the conviction that war must be avoided. With the passage of time, however, it could be anticipated that the fear of large-scale war would decline. In the past the more remote catastrophic war, the less the effort devoted to preventing it. The fear of war declined as peace and time healed its scars. At some point, in the future there is likely to be a reduction of efforts to prevent future all-out war. Present discussion of the nature of central war tends to undermine the conviction, once universal, that such war is "unthinkable." In some measure, the opprobrium heaped upon such discussion is a tribute to the persistence of the notion that nuclear war is too horrible to be rationally contemplated. At the same time, the very existence of such rational contemplation is indication that what was once "unthinkable" can now be thought about. One may expect this speculation to be broadened, not restricted, in the future.

Mobilization speeds attained a new peak in 1962. Reaction time was drastically cut, though future developments suggested a "relatively invulnerable" deterrent with no little "hold" capacity. During the early 1960's, however, an adequate deterrent force possibly entailed a telescoping of war or peace decision-making. As Albert Wohlstetter pointed out: ". . . the problem of forestalling deliberate attack is inseparable from that of preventing war by miscalculation. The solution of one can be made comparatively easy only at the expense of the other." [17] A lack of time to explore all the available political and military solutions for a crisis itself constituted a factor for war. Much more than was the case in 1914, reaction-time of the early 'sixties was likely to force hasty decisions on military grounds, and thereby to truncate the process of political decision.

[17] "Nuclear Sharing: NATO and the N plus 1 Country," *Foreign Affairs* (April, 1961), p. 363. A truly stable and relatively invulnerable deterrent might alleviate this problem.

*Capacity* patterns do not seem to hold the key to future stability and peace. Regulative agencies, such as the United Nations and ancillary bodies, had some success in disposing of problems within the underdeveloped nationalist regions of the world. In the Great Power confrontations in Europe, on the question of disarmament and control of weapons, however, they found little success. The crucial questions for the future were whether the mature nationalist countries of Asia, Africa, and the Middle East would be able to act as constraints upon big Power policy in the first instance and whether they would be able to afford sufficient environmental variety to contain expansion by the great nations in the second. In the generation after World War II the uncommitted were not notably successful on the first count, but they made considerable achievements on the second. Environmental variety was adequate to neutralize potential conflict in the uncommitted areas. As the 'sixties unrolled, however, the uncommitted nations might not be able to contain disruptive policies. The notion of neutrality appeared to envision a mid-point on a continuum linking the actions of the bipolar Powers. The Soviet Union and the Communist bloc were able to alter the position of the neutrals by adopting ever more extremist positions, in effect, pushing farther out on the policy-continuum. The neutralists, perhaps perforce, then had to move further away from the Western nations in order to retain "neutrality" as between the two blocs. The problem posed was that the Western group might not fully readjust their own position on the continuum; this would involve the regulation of neutralist policy by the Soviet bloc. It would constitute an important reversal of the position in which the neutrals were able to contain and to channel the policies of the Soviets. If the neutrals were to gain the capacity to affect or even to control the international system, they had to make sure that the policies of the bipolar antagonists were responsive to a fixed center position, firmly adhered to by the uncommitted. If, on the other hand, neutrality was to be defined merely as a function of Soviet extremism, the neutrals would lose influence in the system. As unilateral American action in Cuba proved, the Western bloc was not likely to accept as regulatory intermediaries a group of nations whose policies could easily be shifted and altered by Soviet decision-making. Thus, neutral adaptation to a new mid-position permitted the great states to drift further apart than ever before. The greater the distance between the two protagonist blocs, the less likelihood their contradictory policies could be accommodated short of war.

It is, of course, impossible to predict future happenings on the basis of a limited number of variables. Direction, control, resources and capacity may not be crucial variables of future international systems. But they have apparently been important determinants of international systems in the past. Moreover, insofar as their operation can be understood, prognosis for the future cannot be optimistic. Directional factors may see new ideological conflicts. Control patterns may well replicate the uncertainties and instabilities of nineteenth century internal politics; and there is no indication that problems of control will be any less acute in the future than they have been in the past. They may well be more acute. Resource patterns will be unlikely to simulate past situations, but they contain destabilizing portents, nonetheless. After every major period of cataclysm and war, the will to prevent recurrence has eventually declined; even wars believed in advance to be disastrous have occurred when control has become an overriding preoccupation of national leaders. The telescoping of political policy-making in the event of a military crisis is also not a salutary phenomenon. Finally, the controls and capacities of regulative and environmental forces seem not to be increasing, and relative to the nature of the probable disturbance, may actually be decreasing. It may no longer be possible to count on the mature uncommitted Powers as constraining influences. Direction, control, resources and capacity do not themselves make either a necessary or a sufficient case for instability and war. But if the precedents of the past have any value, mankind will do well indeed to avert a further period of international instability and conflict.

## CONCLUSION

If any major conclusion emerges from the preceding pages it is that there tends to be a correlation between international instability and the domestic insecurity of elites.[18] This correlation does not

[18] Professor David C. Rapoport concludes that highly unstable Praetorian states do not risk war. Even successful campaigns risk political overturn at home. While this author would be somewhat less convinced of the pacific nature of Praetor-

hold in all instances. War may occur in the absence of internal instability; internal friction may occur in the absence of war. In many of the chaotic international patterns of modern times, however, the two factors were associated. This tentative finding is averse to both doctrines and modes of analysis of certain previous theories.[19] The most venerable, and at the same time currently respectable contrary view is that the international system itself holds the keys to the cause of war and peace. Individual state policies are the product of international mandates and requirements. It is the system of international equilibrium, the balance of power system, or the mode of organizing international relationships which is decisive for peace and tranquillity. If the formal organization of the system were changed, war might be exorcized. World government, a reformulated United Nations — these would successfully regulate international politics. At the extreme, drastic changes at the international level undoubtedly would work such a transformation; the difficulty with this prescription is that it is difficult to administer. Neither the League nor the United Nations was adequate to the task, and a more powerful world political organization is beyond our efforts. As Kenneth Waltz writes: "The remedy, though it may be unassailable in logic, is unattainable in practice."[20] The institutionalist theories of Leonard Woolf did not transform the system, and they blinded us to more important realities. World government will not be achieved without fundamental changes in the actors themselves.

The reaction against such internationalist views became overpowering after World War II. The institutional fallacies of the League, the abject reliance upon formal organizations as a substi-

---

ianism, there is an essential difference between the two notions of internal instability. Professor Rapoport's discohesion refers not only and not primarily to the relations between regime and people, but to the tenuousness of the social bond itself. Social discipline does not exist in a Praetorian state. The internal instability cited in this book refers to the connection between people and regime, and it assumes a measure of social cohesion. In the first case war *might* merely alienate the Praetorian guard without contributing dependable popular support; in the second case war could produce great popular support and also make for social accord. See D. C. Rapoport, "A Comparative Theory of Military and Political Types" in Samuel P. Huntington (ed.), *Changing Patterns of Military Politics* (Glencoe, Ill., 1962).

[19] See particularly Kenneth N. Waltz, *Man, the State, and War* (New York, 1959).

[20] Waltz, *op. cit.*, p. 238.

tute for policy, and the patent disharmonies of interest were stressed unendingly after the war. Institutions were not the remedies for conflict, for conflict was endemic in the nature of man and states. Motivational determinants, both individual and national, were pronounced the final bases of international action. According to a majority of scholars, power was the energizing motivation of individual and nation, and international relations was perforce "a struggle for power." In time, other motivational characteristics were adduced and the struggle for power had to make way for "purpose," "ideals," and competing ideologies. All seemed agreed, however, on the explanation of international politics in terms of fundamental human and social motivations. The problem of this line of theory, of course, was that it awaited a change in the nature of man. No policy scientist could alter the struggle for power or banish conflict from the international scene. Again, remedies could not be applied.

The present analysis calls attention to the internal organization of the state itself. In so doing it harks back to a tradition linking liberals and socialists, Kant, Wilson, and Mazzini. But unlike all of the above, it does not prescribe any particular political form or constitution. It does not favor republicanism over despotism or liberalism over socialism, and certainly it does not prefer nationalism over dynasticism. It prescribes domestic stability and internal peace as the vehicle of international stability and external peace. This prescription is not easily filled. Domestic change is almost as chaotic as international change, and the arenas of action are almost numberless. Yet domestic governments exist; there are agencies to administer palliatives; there are bureaucracies to install reforms. Internal institutions are already formed. At the same time, the international supports for domestic stability can be mobilized, and international resources are available for the task.

In the final reckoning, however, one cannot be optimistic. Economic development may be an unsettling phenomenon in the net;[21] nationalist furor is scarcely stabilizing. And even stable domestic regimes are sometimes involved in war. Internal pacification and renovation may be both more vital and more simple than wholesale reorganization of the international environment, but that is little assurance that either will be accomplished in time.

[21] See S. M. Lipset, *Political Man* (London, 1959), pp. 68-70.

# INDEX